DISCOVERING YOUR SELF

Breaking Walls – Building Bridges

Discovering Your Self is a remarkable and original personal account which examines the psychological walls we build around us. In it, Reinhard Kowalski, a consultant clinical psychologist and psychotherapist, develops his model of psychotherapy and psychosynthesis in a personal, psychological, clinical and political way. The result is a psychological guide-book through an increasingly complex, changing and confusing inner and outer world.

His exploration draws on re-formulated cognitive behaviour therapy, stress management, and psychosynthesis psychotherapy, as well as Leontyev's activity theory, and the works of Grof, Wilber and Masterson. In addition, Douthwaite's economic considerations and the process of German unification, with its symbolism of the 'Wall coming down', are discussed in a psychotherapeutic way. The discovery of 'Self' is seen as a process that needs constantly to deal with 'breaking walls and building bridges' between the different aspects and levels of our being.

Throughout the book there are experiential exercises and meditations, based in psychosynthesis, that are relevant for therapists and for individuals who are on their own journey of personal growth. The book aims at sharing with the reader ways and means of becoming conscious of our own inner 'greenhouse', the closed system within, and of breaking through the walls that we have built within us, around us, and between each other.

The result is a fascinating book that challenges our widely accepted views of ourselves in a practical and experiential way.

Reinhard Kowalski is a psychotherapist in private practice and a member of staff at the Institute of Psychosynthesis in London.

DISCOVERING YOUR SELF

Breaking Walls – Building Bridges

Reinhard Kowalski

London and New York

First published 1993
by Routledge
11 New Fetter Lane, London EC4P 4EE

Simultaneously published in the USA and Canada
by Routledge
29 West 35th Street, New York, NY 10001

Extracts from *No Boundary: Eastern and Western Approaches to Personal Growth* by Ken Wilber, © 1979 Ken Wilber, reprinted by arrangement with Shambhala Publications, Inc., 300 Massachusetts Avenue, Boston, MA 02115. Extracts from *The Growth Illusion* by Richard Douthwaite, published 1992 in the UK by Green Books Ltd, Dartington, Totnes, Devon, also reprinted with permission.

Typeset in Times by Witwell Ltd, Southport

Printed and bound in Great Britain by
Mackays of Chatham PLC, Chatham, Kent

British Library Cataloguing in Publication Data

A catalogue record for this book is available from the British Library.

Library of Congress Cataloging in Publication Data

Kowalski, Reinhard, 1948–
Discovering your self : breaking walls, building bridges / Reinhard Kowalski.
p.   cm.
Includes bibliographical references and index.
1. Psychosynthesis. 2. Self-actualization—Problems, exercises, etc. 3. Kowalski, Reinhard, 1948- —Mental health. 4. Europe—Politics and government—1945- —Psychological aspects. I. Title.
RC489.P76K68   1993
158′.1—dc20   92–45835
CIP

ISBN 0–415–07649–8   0–415–07650–1 (pbk)

I dedicate this book to my father, Josef

CONTENTS

List of illustrations   viii
List of exercises   ix
About the exercises   xi
Foreword   xii
Introduction   1

1 SETTING THE SCENE   5
2 PSYCHOTHERAPY AND PERSONAL CONFLICT   19
3 COGNITIVE AND BEHAVIOUR THERAPY   25
4 BEYOND COGNITIVE-BEHAVIOUR THERAPY   58
5 BOUNDARIES   67
6 ACTIVITY THEORY   83
7 THE GROWTH ILLUSION   97
8 PSYCHOSYNTHESIS – THE HIGHER PERSPECTIVE   106
9 STRESS   124
10 DOMINATION AND PARTNERSHIP   144
11 UNIFICATION PROCESS – GERMAN EXAMPLE   156
12 STEPPING OUT   177

Notes   182
Bibliography   184
Index   186

ILLUSTRATIONS

FIGURES

3.1	Flow chart: anxiety and panic attacks.	42
3.2	Vicious circles.	43
3.3	Circles and spirals.	57
4.1	Cognitive-behaviour therapy and acceptance.	59
4.2	Cognitive-behaviour therapy and boundaries.	59
4.3	Emotional synthesis.	62
5.1	Basic perinatal matrices.	72
5.2	Levels of consciousness.	81
6.1	Emotional and spiritual aspects of 'car'.	94
8.1	The psychosynthesis egg diagram.	109
8.2	Objects as protection.	111
8.3	Objects as distraction.	113
8.4	The psychological greenhouse.	115
11.1	Conformist and warrior.	169

TABLE

3.1	Problem analysis sheet (Elaine).	38

CARTOON

9.1	Fred and the banana skin.	131

EXERCISES

1.1   Reflection: Setting the Scene   8

1.2   Exercise: Inner Sanctuary   14

2.1   Reflection: My Circle   24

3.1   Reflection: The Stories   31

3.2   Exercise: Structured Analysis   45

3.3   Exercise: Relaxed Breathing   50

3.4   Exercise: Self-blame   53

3.5   Exercise: Affirmations   55

4.1   Meditation: Feelings   63

5.1   Exercise: Body Awareness   80

6.1   Reflection: The Objective World   96

7.1   Exercise: Objects and Activities   99

7.2   Exercise: The Growth Illusion   101

8.1   Reflection: Your Psychological Greenhouse   115

9.1   Reflection: Stress   124

9.2   Reflection: Life is a Struggle   127

9.3   Stress Management Exercises: 131

      1. Fred and the Banana Skin   131
      2. Analyse a Stressful Situation   133
      3. Body/Feelings/Thoughts   134
      4. The Tyranny of the 'Shoulds'   136
      5. Meditating with a Tree   137

10.1   Reflection: Domination and Partnership   146

11.1   Reflection: Your National Identity   165

11.2   Reflection: Fighting and Conforming   171

ABOUT THE EXERCISES

This book contains many experiential exercises, which are listed on page ix. In most cases the exercises are meant to help you go more deeply into the material that is presented in the preceding text. It is entirely up to you, the reader, how you want to deal with them.

The exercises are not meant to impose a 'workbook' on to you. Please feel free to use them in a way that feels 'right' for you. You may just want to ignore them now and come back to them later. Or you may want to read them at this stage, without 'doing' them. Or you may want to do them, amend them, and/or use them in your work with yourself and others. The choice is yours.

R.K.

FOREWORD

Wisdom

Wisdom is everywhere in the Universe,
we have learnt not to see it,
not to hear it, not to sense it.

Our senses have to be selective,
because there is so much,
so much to see, to hear, to sense.

So we search,
we select,
and the more we search out there – the less we find,
the more we select out there – the less we have.

Because what we are really searching for out there,
is in here.

In here is the wisdom,
that can see, can hear, can sense,
the wisdom everywhere.
Connection between here and there and everywhere,
becomes possible,
inevitable,
necessary.

How can we start searching in the right place?
How can we stop searching in the wrong one?
What does it take,
to let go of our selections,
our possessions?
What does it take to let go,
of searching as we know it,
in order to find and choose?

Reinhard Kowalski, August 1992

The greenhouse is used by gardeners to speed up growth. It amplifies the heat of the sun and creates a growth environment that is independent of outside temperature fluctuations. We get 'speedy growth'. We also know about the 'greenhouse effect', the 'greenhouse gases', the way our whole planet is turning into a gigantic greenhouse where things are 'heating up'. I see this heating-up process as not just climatic, but also psychological, interpersonal, social, political, technological, economical, and spiritual. The climatic greenhouse effect can be doubted, and argued about; the heating up in the other areas of our being is difficult to ignore; it is difficult not to feel some of it. Massive changes are taking place all around us: the disintegration of the Soviet Union and of Eastern Europe, the unification of Germany, the growing tension between the 'first' and 'third' worlds, the collapse of business empires, the ongoing recession in Europe and in the United States, the increasing speed of change all around us.

As I have been writing this book, it has become increasingly difficult to keep up with the speed of developments and changes. I have been trying to bring the 'greenhouse perspective' into psychotherapy, and at the same time, not surprisingly, the psychological greenhouse effect has increasingly been influencing my written words in a peculiar way. The external changes that I see reflected in what my clients bring to me are manifesting themselves at a frightening speed. All over Europe, all over the world, different crises are emerging and growing stronger. Contradictions, conflicts, panics are around me and within me and I think the same is true for the people I do therapy with. We all express it differently and I find it difficult to remain objective in all this.

When I started writing this book, the central theme was rather nebulous, but I knew it had something to do with the unification process in Germany. I also knew that I wanted to build bridges between behaviour therapy, cognitive therapy and psychosynthesis, including psychoanalysis; and I wanted to include my personal experience as a psychotherapist, as a person and as a German. I have now lived with my writing, or this writing has now been part of my life, for about one year. Many times I was stuck, many times the ideas were coming so fast that I did not manage to write them all down. All in all it has certainly been a journey of trying to put my experience into words and the words influencing my experience, etc. Consequently the book has not been written as you will read it. The part on German unification was written first, other parts followed, new developments occurred, new experiences happened for me, other bits were written, the part on German unification was restructured, rewritten, amended and so on. The word processor has made it all possible. Then I started going through the process of 'knitting': scrolling through all my writings, and again rewriting, changing, adding new ideas, new experiences, but aiming at making it 'hang together' – somehow.

Then I had to decide when and where to stop. But, as I am writing this, I have not quite stopped yet, and the greenhouse seems to be hotting up even further. Today, interest rates in the UK were increased from 10 to 15 per cent. I read about all those money speculators making vast profits in currency speculations, thus creating the interest rate rises and devaluations they had been predicting. I am aware that all this does not relate any more to the way people want to be on their lives' journeys, but that it strongly influences those journeys, and that that influence is growing stronger by the minute. The heating-up is really happening! But I cannot rejoice any more in being 'right'.

Today I was thinking about the money in my savings account, and I was thinking about what I wanted to use it for. It is earmarked for 'stepping out', living in Ireland for six months and looking at the 'greenhouse' from over there. I do feel I have deserved it. Then I started thinking about the crisis and about the currency speculators who are 'making' so much money out of this; and I went to my bank in the afternoon to try to convert my savings into German marks in order to buy sterling again once it is devalued. The clerk was not able to do the transfer because the bank's foreign branch was flooded with requests from people who wanted to do just the same. I wanted to make an extra grand out of this utterly ridiculous and alienated 'crisis'. I wanted to join the leagues of the currency speculators in order to make a 'profit'. 'But wasn't it all for a good, non-capitalist cause? After all, I have worked hard for my savings and I am not going to use the money to exploit anyone.' Does that reasoning still work? How opportunistic can I allow myself to be? Do I really need to ask myself how much I am prepared to stand up for what I believe? Is writing this book just another attempt to find a way of getting some profit out of the collapsing system?

I think I can say 'no' to the last question, because I have lived too much with my writing; I am creating something and I think I deserve payment for it so that I can live in this world. After all, the royalties on a book are minute anyway. But I am still concerned about the speed of the heating-up process that I sense outside and inside. Will what I am writing now still be relevant when this is published in probably nine months' time, in terms of my experience and yours? Will we still be publishing books in nine months' time? Or am I panicking too much, and it all has to do with my make-up, my childhood, my unresolved conflicts?

I don't know, other than that there is some truth in all the above questions. But I don't know the answers, and I wish I could give you the answers in this book. All I can do is invite you to share some of my searching, hoping that it may guide you on your search. I am standing here, on the edge, just as you may be, suffering the same contradictions and conflicts, just as you may be. Most of all I should like to invite you to join hands with me and all the other searchers on the edge. Maybe jointly we can better explore that unknown space ahead of us.

I am grateful to many people who have knowingly and unknowingly helped me with this book. First and foremost I should like to say thank you to the many clients or patients that I have had the privilege to work with and to learn from, and who have allowed me to accompany them on part of their journey. Thank you also to all my colleagues at the Institute of Psychosynthesis in London – they have all been a source of inspiration. I should also like to thank all those colleagues in my work with whom relationships have not been easy. They have helped me understand how difficult and necessary partnership has become. In this context I should also like to express my gratefulness for all that I have learnt in my fourteen years in the National Health Service, even through the increasingly adverse conditions of the last few years, which ultimately contributed to me leaving the state service. Special thanks are due to my partner, companion and counterpart, Aine. She has been my teacher in harmony and love, as well as in adversity; and she has taught me how difficult and wonderful and necessary partnership is.

INTRODUCTION

One of the foremost writers on Psychosynthesis, Pierro Ferrucci, states one of the most essential truths in therapy, and probably in life in general:

> One of the most harmful illusions that can beguile us is probably the belief that we are an indivisible, immutable, totally consistent being. And finding out that the contrary is true is among the first tasks – and possibly surprises – that confront us in the adventure of our psychosynthesis.
>
> (Ferrucci 1982: 47)

John Rowan calls subpersonalities 'the people inside us' (Rowan 1990). This book is written by several people, by several different parts of myself. These different parts, or 'subpersonalities', speak with different voices and describe different experiences, and they address different parts of you, the reader, differently. However, this is not quite as confusing as it seems, because it also contains three elements of consistency:

1 The medium of the book, the written word in the English language, remains consistent throughout.
2 There is something like a centre, the 'real self', the 'organising principle', the 'soul', in all of us. It is the 'producer, who stages the whole show with expertise, good timing, and tactful handling of the actors' (Ferrucci 1982: 64). In psychosynthesis the therapeutic aim is to guide the client to a clear experience of the 'self', which can then exercise choice over identification with or disidentification from a particular subpersonality. Such a central, co-ordinating principle runs, I hope, throughout the book.
3 This 'essence' of the book is trying to speak to *your* 'essence'. Even though I, the writer, might sometimes be less aware of it, the purpose of the book is there. It is your task, as the reader, to allow your 'soul' to hear, so that the communication can be from 'purpose' to 'purpose'.

I should like to introduce to you the different parts of me that are writing:

1

1 **The psychotherapist**: the subpersonality that has been developing over the past sixteen years. I shall introduce him to you in more detail later.

2 **The writer**: he has been there since my adolescence, when I started to write poetry. Since then he has developed in different directions, writing stories, scientific articles, and more recently science fiction. His most important characteristic is that when I allow him to be dominant, he expresses things that only he can express. I think he is the most artistic part of me, and often the other parts don't know where his written words come from, like a painter or composer does not know where his inspiration comes from.

3 **The foreigner**: as the 'outsider' he has been there for a long time – not wanting to be German in the 1950s and 1960s, moving away from my parents' coal-mining working-class environment, moving away from Germany altogether. I know that the tendency for this subpersonality has been brought about by my being an only child. The foreigner/outsider has helped me to be an outside observer, an important aspect to being a psychotherapist, but he has also made close relationships difficult at times.

4 **The rebel**: he is very closely related to the foreigner/outsider. He does not easily accept established views and institutions, and he is deeply suspicious of them. He grew up in the 1960s and was a Socialist. He serves by questioning established beliefs; he sometimes makes life difficult by his stubborn rejection of anything that smells of establishment.

5 **The conformist**: he is the opposite of the rebel. He trusts and he desperately wants to belong. He often gets hurt, especially when he rejects the critical faculties of the foreigner and the rebel.

I think that these are the five main subpersonalities that are writing this book. I hope that the other four will co-operate with the writer by putting their positive qualities into service. However, there will undoubtedly be times when conflicts between them will arise and become obvious.

WORKING WITH SUBPERSONALITIES

In therapy, the work with subpersonalities can be very effective. For a detailed theoretical and practical discussion of this area I should like to refer to Rowan's (1990) excellent book on the subject. In my own therapeutic practice I only work with a client's subpersonalities when I feel that they are actually in the room, when I can see, feel or hear different parts of the client. I might then say: 'A part of you seems to be saying this, and another part that. I wonder who those different parts are, where they come from and what they want to say to each other'. It can then be very revealing to ask the client to be the different parts on different chairs, including taking on the body posture, facial expression and voice of each part. The aim would be to get the two (or more) parts to talk to each other, because they are usually in some kind of battle. An example would be a situation where the 'strong part' of a person has the attitude 'I must always be strong and cope with everything that comes my way; others must see me as strong and coping'. The attitude towards the 'weak and vulnerable part' would be something like 'Leave me alone; I don't want you; you are pathetic; Shut up'. It can be very difficult for the client to allow those two parts to interact, because the strong part will always try to suppress the weak part, whereas the weak part can then develop the tendency to 'act out' by having temper tantrums in the form of panic attacks, depression, etc.

The weak part may well be the 'inner child', and I often use that analogy with clients: 'How does a child react when it does not feel heard? It becomes rebellious and throws temper tantrums'. At that stage clients often remember how they were not heard as a child, and they can realise how they are now doing just the same to their own inner child. The task in therapy then is to bring the two parts into relationship – the strong part needs to be able to hear and to protect the weak part, and the weak part needs to feel heard, accepted and even appreciated, because it usually does have something very valuable to say. The process of connecting with the vulnerable, hurt inner child can be emotionally very powerful. It is as if suddenly a previously blocked connection is being made into the past, and all the emotions of anger, fear and abandonment can break through. It is then important that the therapist can model appropriate 'holding' for the client's strong part, because the strong part will not be accustomed to handling such a direct outburst from the weak part. The therapist needs to give enough time (it is no use starting a subpersonality exercise in the last ten minutes of a session), needs to focus on the strength and power of the emotions, and finally needs, with the client, to make sense of the whole experience.

Sometimes it can be useful to use the 'third position' in the work with subpersonalities. This could be a set-up where there are three chairs in the room, one for each subpersonality (or polarity) and one for an independent observer. The client takes on all three positions. The observer comments on the often difficult interaction between the two parts. In psychosynthesis terms this 'observer' would be the 'higher position' that can synthesise the opposing forces of the lower level.

A 'safer' way of working with subpersonalities would be to use drawing and writing. A subpersonality map could consist of each subpersonality being represented by circles, where size and colour reflect the strength, importance and character of the subpersonality. Distances between circles can symbolise the distances between the different parts, and lines between circles can symbolise strength of connection or disconnection. Such maps can be visually very revealing, and in groups another person can be invited to comment on the visual impression and on the details. In one-to-one therapy the therapist can take on that role.

The following questions, in the form of a daily review, can help identify and explore subpersonalities:

1 Which different subpersonalities were predominant at different times today? What circumstances (inner or outer) made them emerge or withdraw? Were there any conflicts between them?
2 What were the valuable qualities and what were the limitations outstanding in each subpersonality? How did each help me or get in my way?
3 What did each want? What would it like my life to be if it could have fully its own way?
4 Were my subpersonalities in harmony with what 'I' wanted to do, or did I have to go along with them? What part did I take in harmonising and directing them?

The principles and practicalities of working with subpersonalities apply to the work with relationships in general, whether they are between individuals, groups and nations, or between conflicting emotions, thoughts and behaviours. In all those areas, the expression of emotions, open and honest dialogue, and the honouring of the other side are the tools for negotiating the 'space-in-between' in order to come into the relationship. Throughout this book we will come back to these principles, because 'psychotherapy in the greenhouse' has to be about changing our relationships – between parts of ourselves, between each other, and between groups and nations.

1

SETTING THE SCENE

INTRODUCTION

What is the purpose of this book, of me writing this book?

Yes, I do enjoy seeing my name in print. Otherwise I would probably not have gone through the trouble, and trouble it is, of writing articles, a book, and editing a series of books. However, such flattering of the ego is usually very short-lived, and often the downfall after a brief period of 'fame' can be a hard fall indeed. Satisfying the narcissistic part of my personality cannot be all there is to it, although it is probably one motivator.

I have been making notes, writing stories, encouraging my clients to write, for a number of years now. My therapy work has reached a stage, and my life has reached an age, where I feel that integration and 'bridgebuilding' have become important. We are living in a world where fragmentation and integration co-exist all around us. Life itself is the interplay between fragmentation and integration. For example, Germany has reunited, while the Soviet Union and Yugoslavia have been disintegrating.

I should like to explore the purpose of this book by describing a few scenes, telling a few stories. They are scenes that have touched and motivated me. Please read the stories with an open mind and open heart. Observe how you respond to the stories and what the stories trigger off in you, in terms of thoughts, feelings, memories, physical sensations. After the stories there will be an exercise for you to explore your response.

Scene One

I am looking down into the valley. The mountains on the other side are invisible, because the clouds have come down so far; they even cover the green fields and the scattered trees in gentle mist. Beams of light from the invisible sun are trying to break through the cloud and mist, turning the grey into bright white. Then thicker layers of cloud appear again; raindrops form and begin to fall. The white mist on the land comes down and lifts in a silent rhythm. I am in the mist; raindrops are falling on me. The mist blanket is now lifting; houses, fields, and trees in the valley are becoming clearly visible. The blanket from the heavens is gliding across the valley, gently and wetly stroking the earth. A sheep is calling from somewhere in the valley, there is the brief sound of human hammering, and birds sing on their flight from one tree-top to another.

Scene Two

I am sitting in my car, stuck in a huge traffic jam on the M25 (a circular motorway around the periphery of London). It is one of those very hot and humid summer days that we have been getting lately. I am sweating. I'd love to open the car window, but I know that I would then breathe in even more directly the fumes of all those other cars around me. Even though there aren't any clouds around the air looks misty, with a yellow-reddish glow. Aeroplanes are flying low over my head, carrying vast numbers of fellow humans to their destinations. The weather-forecast man on the radio says the air quality in London will be very poor today. My eyes feel sore and my nose is running; my head is wondering how to make up for my delay in getting to my destination: I'll be running late, again. I feel imprisoned: in my car, in between appointments, in the air around me that I *have to* breathe, in the heat, the deadlines, the destinations, the cars and people around me and above me. Even the car radio, producing the most human sounds around me, feels inhuman, an intrusion.

Scene Three

Ozone depletion – last act? Will skiing in the sunshine be dangerous? Will beach-fun on the North and Baltic sea coasts become a thing of the past? Scientists have found chlorinemonoxide levels over the northern hemisphere which are 50 per cent higher than over Antarctica. The result: When the spring-sun comes the ozone layer over Europe may break.

(*Der Spiegel* 10 February 1992: 202)

Scene Four

After having spent nine days in Germany over the Christmas period, I flew back to England on Boxing Day, picked up my car and drove to Ireland on the following day. Germany over Christmas was full: full of shopping, eating, drinking, consuming. Crowded shopping areas, masses of well-presented colourful and tempting goods everywhere – I wanted to buy; new needs were emerging all the time. Then suddenly I was sitting in my car, waiting to board the ferry at Fishguard. I was looking at the sea, the cliffs, the scattered houses on top of the cliffs. A feeling of emptiness and

6

loneliness arose. This feeling intensified over the following days in a cottage in beautiful natural surroundings in Ireland. The emptiness became a physical sensation, bringing up sadness and tears, and the desperate yearning for structure and security.

Scene Five

From Mondays to Fridays, most people assume that nature is simply a mechanistic inanimate system; the world is a storehouse of natural resources to be exploited by man as he sees fit for human profit. However, at weekends and especially on holidays, most people revert to a quite different attitude to nature. On Friday evenings, the roads leading out of the great cities of the Western world are clogged as millions of people try to get back to nature in a car. . . . A lot of people for example want to get rich, if necessary by exploiting the natural world, causing appalling damage to the environment so they can buy a beautiful place in the country surrounded by acres of unspoilt nature to get away from it all. . . . I think that we have to face up to the fact that the 9–5/Monday to Friday attitude is one of the principle causes of the ecological crisis at the present time.

(Sheldrake 1991: 16)

Scene Six

A man in his early forties sits opposite me. He has been referred to me by his doctor because of 'stress'. He says life just isn't the same. He can't switch off from work any more – worries, worries, worries. He gets sweats and palpitations whenever he has to attend a meeting with more than one other person. He, who used to love meetings, talking, performing. Where had his self-confidence gone? He wants it back; he wants life to be the way it used to be. He is also beginning to ask himself why he is doing what he is doing. He says he has just been drifting; drifting into his career, his marriage, his family, and suddenly it doesn't feel quite right any more. He is scared that he will be found out at work, because he no longer feels motivated to do his important job. Where will his career, his life, go? Everything seems a muddle, and the most dominant feeling is fear.

Scene Seven

Tony O'Malley, friend and artist, wrote this after a walk with his three-year-old son:

I went for a walk with Brian to survey a tree that might afford some artwork. It was situated down by a river that winds its way through an

7

almost level flood-plain. It is a small river but a jolly one. The flood-plain is dominated by giant oaks, some ash, elm, and lime. Many of these stand on the banks of the river.

The sun was shining and it was cool. Some cows watched with interest as Brian and I made our way to beneath the tree in question. In the distance it had appeared to be dead but from under its haughty limbs a lively countenance still remained. It had a few years left in it.

We turned back along the way we had come, stopping to linger by the gurgling water. I was surprised by an intensity of peace. A very quiet joy was in my heart. Brian was in unfamiliar territory and needed frequent touching to maintain a sense of security. And yet he resisted continual contact such as holding hands. He would let me carry him now and again.

We were stopped by a tree that stood on the bank with a gaping oval-shaped hole facing the river. I was immediately tempted to climb inside. As I did I felt threatened by the darkness inside. The hole was just large enough for me to squeeze through and inside my legs found the ground some distance away. I stopped and listened for bees as it wasn't the first time I had entered a house without an invitation. There was no sound other than the river's voice. I eased myself in and asked Brian if he wanted to come too. He nodded and I lifted him in and down.

It was completely dark at first except for the light that entered through the hole. I was standing in a room about four feet in diameter and about twelve feet high. Some light entered through another hole at the tree's top, and a bit of light came from one side. The walls were dry and flaky with decayed wood. There was a musty sweetness in the air in there but most of all there was a complete silence. Like Brian I was in unfamiliar territory, amazed.

1.1 Reflection: Setting the Scene

What were your thoughts and feelings while you were reading the seven scenes?

Consider that all your responses, thoughts, images and reading behaviour are relevant. You may find that in particular those responses that you would like to forget about, or that were only brief glimpses of something, are very relevant. They may point towards important areas in your inner world that you are not quite conscious of.

With an awareness of your rational, emotional and physical reaction to the scenes, close your eyes for a few minutes and be inside yourself.

Without forcing anything, and without trying too hard, allow an image or a symbol to emerge into your consciousness.

Make a drawing of the image or symbol here:

This drawing is your starting point for working with the material in this book. It has emerged out of an interaction between you and the stories. It symbolises a point of stability for you, arising out of stories that reflect conflict and contradictions. The image or symbol will probably say something about how you deal with conflicts and uncertainty. But do not try to make logical sense of your image at this stage. See this initial symbolic expression as a seed that you do not want to turn into a rigid monument by putting words to it. Rather, refer back to it later and reflect on your changing attitude towards it.

STABILITY AND FLEXIBILITY – THE INNER SANCTUARY

The search for meaning has always been part of our human journey through life. We want to know why we are here, what our life is all about. This means that we often find ourselves in circumstances where we try to make

9

sense of contradictory situations, experiences and feelings. At the same time we do not like uncertainty and we want to create 'facts', only to realise later that the facts that we have laboured so hard to establish lead us to new conflicts and crises. So there we are again, facing turmoil and crisis, while all we want is a 'quiet life' and peace of mind, the kind of life which has the happy ending that we admire in certain novels and films.

At the same time we are living in a world where the speed of change is accelerating. We are faced with new conflicts and contradictions all the time. The qualities that we need most are both 'stability' and 'flexibility'. Evans and Russell have formulated it well:

> This is one of the most pressing needs of our times: to develop the capacity to be more at peace with ourselves; to find a still centre of inner stability and calm from which we can think and act with greater clarity and creativity. . . . [At the same time] we must be prepared to question all our assumptions concerning who we are, where we are heading, what we really need, and what is most important. . . . Inner flexibility does not conflict with the need for greater stability; they each depend upon the other. If we cannot maintain an inner calm we may find ourselves clinging to set patterns of behaviour for a sense of security. On the other hand, when there is peace within we are much freer to respond to change – and to respond more appropriately. Thus flexibility does not mean being blown hither and thither by the winds of change; when we are flexible we are like a tree in the wind – anchored firmly by its roots, yet able to bend with the storm.
>
> (Evans and Russell 1989: 13–14)

One of the purposes of this book is to help you find your own inner centre of stability and, if you are a counsellor or psychotherapist, to help you help others to find it. This connectedness with our inner centre of calmness and stability is different from the artificial stability that many of the 'human achievements' offer us. It is something that belongs to you personally, while it also allows you to be deeply connected with others and with the world around you. It allows you to be flexible, while at the same time you do not feel that you are betraying yourself out of the pressure to adjust to constantly changing external demands.

The awareness of this centre, however, usually develops out of crisis and conflict rather than out of the avoidance of crisis and conflict. Emmanuel expresses it beautifully:

> Learn, in your solitude, the way to your inner sanctuary. You will eventually wear a path there. To get to the silence you must go through what might appear to be a mined field. There are so many denials, objections, what if's. The way to that sanctuary can indeed sound like the Fourth of July. How, then, does one get there? One first must be

willing to listen to the fireworks. It will be educational. You have no idea how filled with noise you are. The illusion that seems to demand your constant attention is insatiable. Only in your silence can the Greater Reality touch you. Only in your silence can it be received.

(Emmanuel 1989: 204)

The Psychotherapy Boom

The psychotherapy boom is an expression of a widespread desire for this inner sanctuary. Articles in newspapers and magazines, television and radio shows where you might even be able to talk to a therapist on the telephone are not unusual any more. The popularity of men's issues, women's issues, gays' issues, reflects a widespread psychological yearning. This longing for inner fulfilment seems to be related to how we have used to excess external junk to fill up that inner void that is ultimately our sanctuary.

There has been an enormous development in the psychotherapy scene over the past decade. In their guidebook *Holistic London* (1990) Kate Brady and Mike Considine try to bring some order into an increasingly disordered area. Their guidebook lists approximately 60 different psychotherapies and about the same number of 'body therapies'. Many of these different approaches have their own training institutes. Where does this leave the customer, the person who feels he or she needs some psychotherapy? How do people decide that they are in need of psychotherapy or counselling? How can people make an informed choice in the face of such a multitude? Do we as psychotherapists all need to do endless training in all sorts of different approaches in order to then have the 'right' one available for each client?

All the above issues are beginning to be addressed by developments within the 'UK Standing Conference for Psychotherapy', where the different schools of thought are trying to develop standards for the training and practice of psychotherapy. The process is not easy, and unfortunately is often dominated by battles between the different groups. How is it that not even 'aware' psychotherapists manage in their relationships with each other what they are supposed to be teaching their clients – to come into partnership with repressed parts, emotions, people? History also has some examples of how psychotherapy, here psychoanalysis, seems to have found it difficult to see itself as part of the wider system of society, and has therefore unconsciously acted out the external battles within the British Psycho-Analytical Society. Rayner (1991) quotes a 1940 letter by James Strachey to Edward Glover, who was then running the meetings of the British Psycho-Analytical Society, where he writes: 'Why should these wretched fascist and (bloody foreigners) communists invade our peaceful compromising island?' (Rayner 1991: 18). This was written in 1940 while

11

there was a war raging in Europe, and the war in the Psycho-Analytical Society was the one between Kleinians and Freudians. Rayner wonders:

> It is puzzling that there should be such passion on matters of theory in the midst of a world war. The situation was that London was being bombed nearly every night, and many did not know whether they would survive, let alone what would happen to analysis – to which they had given their lives. They felt they were the protectors of precious ideas which were threatened not only by bombs but from within their colleagues and themselves. Also, it was hardly possible to go on practising analysis, which is vital to keep coherent analytical ideas alive. Ideological venom and character assassination were released under these circumstances. Where many people found a new communality under the threats of war, the opposite happened to psychoanalysts in London.
>
> (Rayner 1991: 18–19)

One of the main themes of this book, and one of my main concerns, is how closely psychotherapy is linked with the societal and organisational systems around us. This connection is becoming stronger in the 'heating up' process of the psychological greenhouse, in terms of what our clients bring to us, how we respond to it and how we as therapists deal with our own inner greenhouse. The issue of the 'professionalisation' of psychotherapists, the aim of the UK Standing Conference, can serve as an example. Regarding professionalisation, there are two positions:

1 In the argument for professionalisation it is usually claimed that it is necessary, in order to protect the client, to adhere to standards of training and professional conduct, to have adequate status as a therapist, and to have clear guidelines and ethical standards for the practice of psychotherapy. At first sight no one would argue the usefulness of this.
2 However, taking into account the 'other side' reveals the complexity of the issue. In the magazine *I to I* Nick Totton argues that the standardisation of the psychotherapeutic profession will deform psychotherapy without protecting the consumer in whose name it is pursued (Totton 1992). It is aimed to form a 'National Council for Psychotherapy' out of the present 'UK Standing Conference for Psychotherapists', with a register likely to be established in 1993. Totton sees great dangers and a lot of bureaucratic uselessness in this. He argues that the main driving forces are 'bureaucracy's eternal quest for something new to make rules about' (Totton 1992: 26), the fact that 'in the rest of Europe every activity is controlled – it's illegal to do anything not specifically permitted', and 'careerism'.

As a psychotherapist, wouldn't it be nice to share the same status as a doctor? Wouldn't it be handy if newcomers went through a long and expensive training which offered lots of teaching and supervision work? Within psychotherapy people have begun jockeying for position, putting their training courses and accreditation procedures in place, inventing hurdles for the next generation – hurdles they themselves will never have to jump! The new rules have a little thing attached called a 'grandfather clause', which basically exempts anyone already practising.

(1992: 26–7)

Totton emphasises the advantages of the present status of psychotherapy and the creativity that is possible, based in English Common Law, where anything not explicitly forbidden is legal. He also argues that present consumer protection is sufficient, because 'bad' or unpopular therapists will just not receive any more referrals, while an organised system could lead to the 'closing ranks' phenomenon that the medical profession often exhibits in the face of public criticism. Totton's most important point, however, is that he describes psychotherapy as a meeting between two individuals, where honesty and open-heartedness are the main ingredients for healing and growth. This 'authenticity', he argues, throws into question many of the ways in which society is currently organised, and therapy therefore often becomes a process of moving people away from social norms and conformity.

Why then should we apply the norms and rules of our patriarchal and dominator society to a process that is essentially based on partnership and non-conformity? I can sympathise with this view.

A second argument against the manner in which psychotherapy is professionalised recently appeared in *Clinical Psychology Forum*. The main thrust of the argument here is that the basis for any such process should lie in the questions of what is psychotherapy all about, who needs it, and how can we as therapists serve those people in need?

Indeed, there is a tightrope being walked. How can we act in this world without being part of systems that create the neuroses that we want to heal? How much do we need to conform in order to be 'acceptable' without becoming opportunistic? How can we synthesise the polarities while having a foot on each side?

Psychosynthesis has always been on the fringes of the 'official' therapy world. It has explicitly aligned itself with the 'new science' movement (Kapra, Sheldrake, Wilber, etc.), and mysticism and spirituality have been important elements in its development. Its teaching and therapy methods have been based on concepts like 'inside-out learning', 'inner wisdom' and 'the superconscious'. It is only recently that the concepts and methods of psychoanalysis and group analysis have been introduced into the training and practice of psychosynthesis psychotherapy.

It seems important to be recognised by the 'official world' of psychotherapy, and in itself the implementation of rules and regulations, the laying down of criteria and competencies for training, supervision and practice are not a bad thing. However, it is vital to be aware of the purpose and values in all this.

Even within psychotherapy there seems to be the need for sanctuary. However, such sanctuary cannot be reached by trying not to be part of the 'system'. We are part of it, whether we like it or not. I should like to refer back to Emmanuel's quote earlier, and I should like to invite you to carry out an exercise to begin to develop a sense of your own inner sanctuary.

1.2 Exercise: Inner Sanctuary

This exercise aims at giving you a first sense of your inner sanctuary. Again, as with all the exercises and reflections, do not try too hard and accept whatever happens to you as a result of the exercise.

Read through the instructions first and then sit down comfortably with your eyes closed. Give yourself up to ten minutes uninterrupted time, and keep your body relaxed during the exercise.

Go back to an important time in your life. It may be a time in your childhood or adolescence when you strongly believed in something or when you felt you were searching for something that was very important to you. Remember the thoughts and feelings you had at the time. Imagine yourself at that time. What did you look like? What were your attitudes at the time?

And now be yourself back then. Be inside your body at that time and look out into the world. What does the world outside look like? What important images and people do you see? What feelings do you experience?

Then connect back to yourself in the present time. Can you get a sense of how similar it was then to how it is now? Can you experience the same YOU looking out of those eyes now as it was then? Try and get a sense of that part of you that has remained the same throughout your life.

And now scan your whole life, and realise that it has always been YOU leading it. Lots of things have changed, but it has always been YOU who has been there.

At the end of this exercise, make some notes or a drawing about your experience.

MY PERSONAL JOURNEY IN PSYCHOLOGY AND PSYCHOTHERAPY

Scientific Versus Personal

I have now been working, thinking and feeling as a psychologist and psychotherapist for sixteen years. This book includes me and those sixteen years of my life, and it probably goes back even further if we ask why I am doing what I am doing in this life. Fritjof Capra emphasises that even in nuclear physics, the concept of the neutral, scientific observer is becoming an illusion. 'New' scientists like Capra and Sheldrake emphasise the interconnectedness of all things, and the concept of Gaia, the idea that the earth is one living organism, is gaining in popularity. Jung's concept of the collective unconscious points in the same direction. In pagan beliefs the 'Web of Wyrd' symbolises this connection between all things, and any movement anywhere within the web passes through the whole web.

Hence I am not trying to create the illusion that I can distance myself from the words that I am writing. This book is a reflection of my story; it has to be. 'Scientific' textbook writers often try to hide themselves (and from themselves) behind numbers, theories, concepts and statistics, and are thus replicating one of the greatest ills of our time – covering up, hiding the personal behind the rational, hiding the heart behind the mind. It is becoming increasingly obvious that, as a species, we have reached the limitations of this approach. However, this does not mean that we need to, or should, neglect the 'rational approach' or the 'rational mind'.[1] 'Inclusion' seems to be the key here. The psychiatrist Ronald D. Laing described the heartlessness of scientific psychiatry by reviewing the textbook descriptions of schizophrenia:

> [In schizophrenia] the head [cognitive function] is divorced from the heart. Textbooks describe inability to feel, lack of sight, imperviousness, robotization, mechanization, the loss of sense of feeling for quality, often self-confessed feelings of futility and meaninglessness. 'Schizoid' individuals maybe have 'insight', but it is without feeling, it's heartless; thinking may be precise, but it's without heart. When, as a medical student I came across these descriptions in medical textbooks for the first time, I thought they were a very good description of medicine itself, including psychiatry. The heartlessness, the divorce, the split between head and heart. The fragmentation indeed disintegration, behind all that, and its disavowal and projection. The unavailing cognitive efforts to put pieces together. The 'institutionally reinforced' imperviousness of the cognitive scheme, the self-perpetuating, self-confirming nature of the process, which can never prove itself wrong by itself. What is being described is not what it appears to be:

15

the description is largely a reflection, as in a mirror, unrecognized as such by those looking into the mirror and seeing themselves.

(Laing 1976: 107–8)

Jung expresses his views on rationality and religion:

Our rationality [*Vernunft*] is a wonderful gift and an achievement that should not be dismissed, but it covers only one aspect of reality, which also consists of irrational aspects. Natural laws are not axiomatic, they are only statistical probabilities. Reality mainly consists of irrational aspects, including our psyche. That is why a mechanisation of our psychological life is impossible. We are, like the primitives, at the mercy of a dark world with its unpredictable possibilities. That is why we need religion, namely for the careful examination of the existing, and less rationalisation, the overestimation of the rational intellect.

(Jung 1989: 101, my translation)

Like so often in our history, what used to be 'progress', namely the scientific approach to our world and ourselves, seems now to be holding us back. Psychotherapy in particular is an area where 'heartlessness' should be impossible. Unfortunately this is not strictly the case, and I often find it extremely confusing and painful to read mainly psychoanalytic descriptions of 'psychopathology'. People are labelled patients; their suffering is called 'the material'; their desperate attempts to control their world is called 'manipulation'; they are seen as 'sick patients'. I am usually left with the experience of coldness and mental strain.

What needs to happen is the inclusion of the personal, moving away from the notion of the psychotherapist as the 'impartial' observer. But we also need to 'include' the scientific approach, just as much as we need to include our personal and collective past in the process of self-discovery.

This book tries to be integrative and inclusive in a variety of ways. Throughout, my personal experience will be part of the exploration. This does not, however, mean that I am writing an autobiography. I am trying to overcome the outdated division between the personal and the non-personal for the following reasons:

1 My story is one part of the full story that makes up 'psychotherapy'. I am part of it and 'it' is part of me. Fritjof Capra refers to David Bohm's theory, which states the notion of unbroken wholeness in the cosmic web, and is described with 'the analogy of a hologram, in which each part, in some sense, contains the whole. If any part of the hologram is illuminated, the entire image will be reconstructed, although it will show less detail than the image obtained from the complete hologram' (Capra 1982: 87–8).

2 My thoughts and feelings about, and skills in psychotherapy have grown out of my activities as a psychotherapist. Activity theory (Leontyev,

Vygotsky, Galperin) sees the thought processes of an individual human being as a reflection of the results of his activities with his environment. Each activity changes the environment as well as the human being carrying out the activity. Hence I am partly a reflection and a crystallisation of what is going on 'out there'. This takes place and comes into form in my work with clients, but also in my other experiences.

3 And last but not least, how can we continue to write about something as personal as psychotherapy without including ourselves as a person?

I shall therefore write about my personal experience throughout this book, including my personal experience of writing. This is as important as the theoretical and practical issues that I am writing about. The 'dance' between the personal and the impersonal in itself has to serve as a model for psychotherapy. I should like to start by giving a brief summary of my story. More personal experience will be found throughout.

Personal and Scientific

I did my psychology degree (M.Sc.) in 1976 at Freie Universität Berlin, followed by one year of behaviour therapy training with Vic Meyer at the Middlesex Hospital, followed by a year of work in youth counselling in Berlin. My clinical psychology training from 1978 to 1981 ended with the BPS Diploma in clinical psychology. From then I pursued a health service career in adult mental health.

In 1981, during my training, I was introduced to a range of humanistic and transpersonal therapy approaches, gestalt therapy, psychodrama, John Heron and psychosynthesis. The last approach 'made sense' to me. I forgot about it and came back to it (or did it come back to me?) in 1985. At the time I was seeing too many clients in four different settings, doing 'good work' and rapidly approaching burn-out levels. I then started training in psychosynthesis and I am now a psychosynthesis trainer and supervisor.

Since 1985 my clinical work and my personal work on myself have become increasingly interwoven and connected. I now feel that one cannot happen without the other if we want to avoid getting stuck in the black hole called 'burn-out'.

In Miller Mair's (1989) terms I have probably been on the journey from psychology to psychotherapy and I might now be starting the journey back, and 'bridgebuilding' has become an important model in my thinking and in my therapy work. Central concepts in psychosynthesis are 'acceptance' and 'inclusion' (see Ferrucci 1982). For me this means that I do not reject my behavioural and cognitive/behavioural background, but try to include it in my work. This is very similar to the process in therapy where we try to help clients accept and include painful past experiences rather than cutting them off and rejecting them.

In my therapy work I include behavioural and cognitive methods and the psychotherapeutic concepts of psychosynthesis. A first attempt at putting it in writing was my book *Over the Top* (Kowalski 1987). Since then I have been talking and thinking about it, and, most importantly, I have applied what I call 'bridgebuilding' in my therapy work. To state it briefly, I am very excited about how behavioural and cognitive approaches in therapy can create for the client a rational, common-sense and safe context, through which deeper emotional issues can then be addressed. For me, behaviour therapy is not superficial, even though some behaviour therapists may still apply their model superficially.

2

PSYCHOTHERAPY AND PERSONAL CONFLICT

> The greater the contrast,
> the greater the potential.
> Great energy
> only comes
> from a correspondingly
> great tension
> between opposites.
>
> (C.G. Jung, quoted in Hayward 1987)

Psychotherapy is about helping people to deal with contradictory or opposing forces within themselves, between themselves and others, or between themselves and the outside world, or all of these together. The therapeutic process aims at bringing this mostly unconscious tension between polarities into consciousness, thus changing the experience of being victim to mysterious spells into one of becoming the conductor of the orchestra of our inner and outer forces. This also means learning to live with the tension that is created by conflict, and discovering and using the creativity that is in that tension.

However, a lot of the time these conflicts operate at an unconscious level, and we are not even aware of the different parts that are in conflict. What we then do experience consciously, or what comes through into our awareness, is the resulting tension, either physically (anxiety, panic attacks, fear), emotionally (fear, depression, anger), or behaviourally (behavioural disorders like obsessive compulsive behaviour, violence, addictions, etc.). The 'neurosis' is then the overt expression of covert processes.

Ken Wilber writes about 'the symptom':

As the first step in therapy on this level, we need to make room for our symptoms, give them space, actually begin to befriend the uncomfortable feelings, called symptoms, that we have heretofore despised. We must touch our symptoms with awareness and as much open acceptance as we can command. And this means to allow oneself to feel depressed, anxious, rejected, bored, hurt, or embarrassed. It means that where formerly we resisted these feelings in all sorts of ways, we now simply allow these feelings to display themselves. Indeed, we actively encourage them. We invite the symptom right into our home, and we let it move and breathe freely, while we simply try to remain aware of it in its own form. That, very simply, is the first step in therapy, and in many cases it is all that is required, for the moment we truly accept a symptom we also accept a large part of the shadow concealed in that symptom. The problem then tends to disappear.

If the symptom is persistent, we proceed to the second step of therapy at the persona level. . . . All we do is begin to consciously translate any symptom back to its original form. . . . The essence of this second step is to realize that any symptom is simply a signal (or symbol) of some unconscious shadow tendency.

(Wilber 1979: 97–8)

Wilber then proceeds to give a 'dictionary for translating symptoms back to their original shadow forms':

SYMPTOM	ITS ORIGINAL SHADOW FORM
Pressure	Drive.
Rejection (Nobody likes me)	I wouldn't give them the time of day!
Guilt (You make me feel guilty)	I resent your demands.
Anxiety	Excitement.
Self-consciousness (Everybody's looking at me)	I'm more interested in people than I know.
Impotence/Frigidity	I wouldn't give him/her the satisfaction.
Fear (They want to hurt me)	Hostility (I'm angry and attacking without knowing it).
Sad	Mad!
Withdrawn	I'll push you all away!
I can't	I won't, damnit!
Obligation (I have to)	Desire (I want to).
Hatred (I despise you for X)	Autobiographical gossip (I dislike X in myself).
Envy (You're sooo great)	I'm a bit better than I know.

(Wilber 1979: 98–9)

Wilber describes here the psychodynamics of defence mechanisms, especially projection. His view is that polarities only exist because we have created artificial boundaries between the two poles and sent the rejected pole 'underground', thus creating a battle between the two. Therapy needs to restore the unity of those polarities, because they cannot exist without each other. We cannot conceptualise light without dark, joy without suffering, like without dislike. This unification is also what the work with subpersonalities, as described earlier on pp. 2–4, tries to achieve.

Psychotherapy is essentially a process of 'sense-making'. The therapist supplies the client with models and maps for the journey through the world of the psyche. The therapeutic relationship is:

1 The space where the journey is planned and evaluated;
2 part of the journey itself; and
3 the space in which and into which elements of the client's and the therapist's experience are reflected and projected and where they can be made conscious; the relationship in the consulting room serves as a model and a mirror of the outside world.

These three dimensions of the therapeutic relationship relate to different therapy approaches, although often the difference is in the emphasis rather than in an exclusive focus on one dimension. The most important task of the therapist is to be aware of and to 'hold' all these aspects of the therapeutic space and to use their potential for the benefit of the client. 'But what is "to the benefit of the client"?' I hear you ask. Answer: to create awareness, to free the Will so that conscious choices can be made.

INTRODUCTION TO PSYCHOSYNTHESIS (PERSONAL)

At this point I would like to introduce psychosynthesis, the psychotherapy approach upon which all this is based.[1] There are many different ways of doing this, and I should like to remain within our tradition and start in a personal way. Towards the end of my training I wrote the following evaluation of myself in relation to psychosynthesis:

A few months ago I watched a programme about Marilyn Monroe on television. The Elton John song *Candle in the Wind* was played and I was touched to tears: she had lived her life like a candle in the wind, never knowing who she should cling to when the rain was setting in. I have played the song a lot since then, always being deeply touched by it. No, I did not see it in any way related to me. My image was that of a blonde, fragile girl – misunderstood and famed to death.

And then – now, I am feeling very lonely and fragile and the need to cling to something or someone is very strong again. In my therapy I am working on my lack of boundaries, my fear of women, my desperate need for closeness and my fear of commitment. The 'candle in the wind' has arrived and I can let go of the song.

This is the kind of learning psychosynthesis has been for me, allowing sense to develop out of the senseless, allowing meaning to emerge, because it will.

In my foundation year in 1985 the Friday evening seminar was called 'Journey of the Soul'. That sounded much too religious for me. I made sure that I was much too busy, workwise, on Friday evenings, to be able to attend. Nobody forced me to attend either. My journey, yes, my particular, special journey was accepted, even though I wasn't aware that I was on a journey, apart from the trip from Clapham Junction to Polegate; and that was with British Rail. Perhaps I am not doing myself justice here, because, looking back, there had always been a knocking, a calling: poems, pains and palpitation. In summary, this, for me, is what initially attracted me to psychosynthesis: inside-out learning; experience first and then the willingness to use models to make sense of the experience and then integrating the models into new experience as an ongoing process, a journey along sense and non-sense. Circles and spirals are the images rather than a line between A and B. And this applies to me and my world, my clients and their worlds, and the space where all our worlds and journeys interact and life and meaning are created.

Sometimes I did not know whether I was integrating the training material or whether the training material was integrating me. Different models, analytical, synthetical, confrontational, pathological, were all presented by very convincing and charismatic people. So I found myself applying this or that new technique to this or that client who happened to be the next one. And that was OK. I learned from it and in the end I always ended up trusting (or mis-trusting) me and my intuition, and in that I was able to integrate the training material.

I see my development as a therapist throughout the training as a spiral, the ongoing process of dialectics and synthesis. Initially I was the behaviourist who worked with intuition. Then I was beginning to use psychosynthesis models in a rather mechanistic way – to the meadow, up the mountain, down the mountain, etc. At the same time my trust in my intuition was growing, and some of the models were making sense of my intuitive style. Then the analytical models created confusion, but led to me including myself in the process in a different way (transference and counter-transference). And now I am back with my intuition at a different level: sensing and sense-making have become a dance of creativity and I am discovering beauty in the unknown.

I often struggle with wanting to take on too much responsibility for my clients; yet at the same time I know that sometimes exactly that is needed in order to create the sanctuary with them. I also struggle with giving them structure and waiting for their structure to emerge, but that struggle can be very creative.

INTRODUCTION TO PSYCHOSYNTHESIS (STORY)

Ferrucci tells a story to explain the vision of psychosynthesis:

After years of searching the seeker was told to go to a cave, in which he would find a well. 'Ask the well what is Truth', he was advised, 'and the well will reveal it to you'.

Having found the well, the seeker asked that most fundamental question. And from the depths came the answer, 'Go to the village crossroad: there you shall find what you are seeking'.

Full of hope and anticipation, the man ran to the crossroad, to find only three rather uninteresting shops. One shop was selling pieces of metal, another sold wood, and thin wires were for sale in the third. Nothing and no one there seemed to have much to do with the revelation of Truth.

Disappointed, the seeker returned to the well to demand an explanation, but he was told only, 'You will understand in the future'. When the man protested, all he got in return were echoes of his own shouts. Indignant for having been made a fool of – or so he thought at the time – the seeker continued his wanderings in search of Truth. As years went by, the memory of his experience at the well gradually faded until one night, while he was walking in the moonlight, the sound of sitar music caught his attention. It was a wonderful music, and it was played with great mastery and inspiration.

Profoundly moved, the truthseeker felt drawn toward the player. He looked at the fingers dancing over the strings. He became aware of the sitar itself. And then suddenly he exploded in a cry of joyous recognition: the sitar was made out of wires and pieces of metal and wood just like those he had once seen in the three stores and had thought to be without any particular significance.

At last he understood the message of the well: we have already been given everything we need; our task is to assemble and use it in the appropriate way. Nothing is meaningful as long as we perceive only separate fragments. But as soon as the fragments come together into a synthesis, a new entity emerges, whose nature we could not have foreseen by considering the fragments alone.

(Ferrucci 1982: 21–2)

The following exercise invites you to look at all the different 'bits' that make up your life. Can you develop a sense of what is trying to emerge?

2.1 Reflection: My Circle

Look at yourself going about your daily business. See yourself doing all the different things you do. See the activities, objects, and people that fill up your space and time.

Be aware of and acknowledge your feelings as you imagine this.

And then ask yourself:

Am I the director of my daily activities?
Am I choosing to do what I am doing?
How do all the different parts of my life hang together?

And then imagine yourself drawing a circle around you. Inside the circle is your space. There is only you inside the circle. All the people, objects and activities of your life are outside the circle. Look at them and be aware of your space inside the circle.

Now remember the story of the truthseeker and the well, and with that story in mind look at all the different parts and fragments of your life from inside your circle.

Can you sense what is trying to emerge, or what wants to be built out of all those bits and pieces?

Don't worry if you do not get a clear answer like a sitar. Just allow yourself to begin to look at your life in this way.

After this reflection, take a large sheet of paper and draw a circle in the middle of the sheet. Then draw (or write) all the people, objects and activities that you saw in the reflection. Be aware of their distances from the circle and from each other. Also be aware of their sizes and what colours you use.

If possible, work with your drawing using a friend or therapist in the following way. First you spend at least five minutes describing your drawing. Your friend is not to interrupt you. Your friend can then ask you questions. But don't get into a discussion.

Finally, your friend gives you feedback about his/her experience of your drawing and of your presentation. Your friend may also see patterns and structures in your drawing that are important.

3

COGNITIVE AND BEHAVIOUR THERAPY

As I mentioned earlier in my brief biography, my initial therapeutic training and experience was in behaviour therapy and cognitive therapy. One important aim of this book is to include these approaches and to build a bridge between them and psychosynthesis. In order to do so, I should like to bring in a historical perspective.

HISTORY

When I started training and working as a clinical psychologist, my main interest was in working with patients with anxiety problems. At the time, in the late 1970s and early 1980s it was quite a challenge to deal with phobias, agoraphobia, so-called 'free floating anxiety'. Enthusiastically we developed what came to be known as 'anxiety and stress management' (AMT). Cognitive therapy came from across the Atlantic, initially being mainly applied and researched in the treatment of depression. We began to use it with our anxiety patients, trying to come to grips with the relationship between people's thoughts and their physical sensations of anxiety and panic. Relaxation techniques were developed and it did work – we were able to teach people to control their anxiety and panic attacks. The 'behaviour analytic' approach (more about this later) helped patients to make 'common sense' out of their problems; they learned to think differently, and they were able to use techniques to control the actual physical panic when it occurred. In my book *Over the Top* (Kowalski 1987) I tried to develop a cognitive self-help approach for patients.

Historically, the development and practice of behaviour therapy and cognitive therapy in the 1970s were important for a variety of reasons. Nowadays these approaches are often dismissed as being mechanistic, non-psychological, superficial, etc. At the time, however, behaviour therapy opened up a whole new world of psychotherapy. As a critique of the exclusiveness of analytical psychotherapy, it boldly reformulated many of the neurotic disorders in a 'scientific' way. Observable behaviour became the focus, rather than mysterious unconscious processes. Patients and their accounts of themselves were taken at face value, and 'learning principles' were applied to the aetiology of their problems and to the therapeutic programmes.

Behavioural approaches were adopted enthusiastically by clinical psychologists within the British National Health Service (NHS). It allowed this young profession to move on from being 'test-bashers' to becoming therapists. Behaviour therapy fitted the bill, because it seemed to be open to scientific validation, thus fitting well into scientific clinical psychology. An endless stream of journal articles appeared, mainly in Britain and the US, painstakingly investigating the minutest details of maladaptive behaviours and of the therapeutic programmes used for 're-learning'. It was the time of 'therapeutic optimism' – change was seen as possible, predictable and manageable. New formulations and the testing and discussion of new hypotheses stimulated new ideas.

The result of all this creativity was particularly obvious in British NHS psychiatry. Suddenly clinical psychologists were offering adjuncts and alternatives to the traditional medical treatments. Patients who were not suitable for analytical psychotherapy were seen by psychologists and a psychological approach to their problems was tried out. This included the wide range of phobias, but also obsessive compulsive disorders and even ward programmes with more severely disturbed patients.

Gradually the medical establishment, mainly psychiatrists and general practitioners, accepted behavioural and cognitive therapy for their patients and the referrals to clinical psychologists were peaking. Over a decade later it is common practice now for medical practitioners to refer patients for cognitive therapy. Clinical psychologists have paved the way for psychological treatment approaches to be integrated into general practices, hospitals and psychiatric units.[1]

Another area where clinical psychology and cognitive behaviour therapy and the associated therapeutic optimism and enthusiasm have created new ways is in teaching and training. The 'workshop' movement took off in the 1970s. One-day, two-day, and three-day training workshops on topics like anxiety and stress management, cognitive therapy of depression, assertion training, social skills training and so on were organised and run mainly by clinical psychologists (including myself). New teaching methods like role-plays, large group and small group exercises changed the rather boring university style lectures into something much more experiential. The 'doing aspect' of behaviour therapy found its way into skills acquisition as well as into therapy.

Thus the structured approach of behaviour therapy led to a wealth of new therapeutic and teaching methods that were widely applied in the different fields of health care and clinical psychology: psychiatry, primary health care, mental handicap, psychosomatic medicine, behavioural medicine, family and couple therapy and group therapy. It would go beyond the scope of this book to give an overview of all those areas. In psychiatry, or adult mental health as it is now called, the main areas of application were, and still are, the treatment of anxiety and panic disorders, depression, and obsessive compulsive disorders. I am not going to attempt to give a comprehensive review of the application of cognitive and behaviour therapy with those three diagnostic categories. However, I shall use the area of anxiety and panic attacks to present the value of the structured approach in a practical and experiential way. The overall context for appreciating cognitive-behavioural practice will be psychosynthesis. This means that both disorders and therapeutic approaches will be looked at and evaluated from the psychotherapeutic perspective of psychosynthesis, hence incorporating cognitive-behavioural approaches within a wider (deeper, higher) context. Consequently, a historical, emotional and spiritual reformulation of cognitive behaviour therapy will be attempted.

The area of anxiety and panic disorders will be used to present the individualised behaviour-analytic approach, which was developed by Vic Meyer and his associates at the Middlesex Hospital, London, in the 1970s and 1980s. The value of the approach lies in its 'sense-making' potential. Therapist and patient develop a model of the patient's problem that is acceptable to both of them and which forms the basis for their joint venture, i.e. the therapy programme. Vic used to use a blackboard as an external representation of the patient's problems. In addition he also used a lot of charisma – though he would not have liked to see it that way. The main focus of the sense-making applied has always been the relationship between thinking, physical sensations and behaviour.

Depression is probably the most commonly diagnosed psychiatric disorder, and, with the scandals around benzodiazepine tranquillisers, it has become the new battleground for psychological versus medical model. Cognitive therapy approached depression in the 1970s with the premiss that it is the patient's depressive thinking patterns that cause the depressed mood. This is contrary to the medical model which states that it is the depressed mood, i.e. depressive illness, that causes the depressive thinking. Ultimately it is probably a bit of both. However, cognitive therapy has created diagnostic and therapeutic approaches that emphasise the relationship between a person's thinking and his emotions. Therapeutic methods try to change attitudes and thinking patterns in order to indirectly change the emotions. Recent models that have developed out of cognitive therapy are again trying to include a more psychoanalytic perspective, like the 'emotional synthesis' model which will be presented in detail later. Rather than seeing emotions as a mere product of (ir)rational thinking, these models try to appreciate the complexity and the interrelatedness of thinking and feeling processes, not least through the inclusion of unconscious processes.

In order to look at the diagnostic categories and at the cognitive-behavioural therapy approaches within a psychosynthesis context, the following aspects of psychosynthesis will in particular be applied:

- imagery/symbols;
- inner wisdom – inside/out learning;
- reflections;
- acceptance, inclusion;
- the interaction between rational and emotional.

ANXIETY AND PANIC ATTACKS

Looking back at it all now, I ask myself why I used to be so interested in anxiety disorders and panic attacks. Perhaps it had to do with my own unacknowledged fear. Perhaps it had to do with the growing fear that I was sensing in the world around me. Whatever the reasons were, today fear seems to be the main complaint that clients bring to me – fear of each other, fear of emotions, fear of annihilation, fear of not being good enough, fear of not surviving.

I should like to use agoraphobia and panic attacks as an example for this process of 'sense-making' that cognitive and behaviour therapy can offer. Overtly there is the fear of going out, the fear of people, the anxiety and panic attacks. However, if we look at the process of what is happening in more detail, we discover the complexity.

Here are a few stories that people have written about their agoraphobia and panic attacks. The stories and some of the material that follows are taken from my book *Over the Top* (Kowalski 1987).

1. Richard, Aged 36 Years

It was the last working day before Christmas, during the morning in my London office. I experienced a progressive build-up of strange and unpleasant physical sensations. I left the office to drive home about midday. I felt the urgent need to get home quickly – a sort of panic and loneliness. As I drove out of the centre the physical sensations became progressively worse. It seemed difficult to catch my breath and I had the feeling that something I couldn't control would happen. By the time I reached a town outside London I had to stop the car in a lay-by and found myself walking up and down the grass verge. I kept thinking I was going to collapse. A driver stopped and asked if I was feeling OK. I told him I was not and he drove me to his local general practitioner in the nearby town. The doctor was in and within seconds I had broken down in front of him. I cried for a good few minutes. The doctor checked my blood pressure and did an ECG. No problems with either. He asked what I thought was wrong. I think I replied that everything seemed wrong and I felt feelings of uselessness and loneliness. Whichever way my mind worked it was always blaming myself for everything, a complete lack of confidence and secureness. The general practitioner gave me 10 mg of Valium. I drove home and went to bed early. Most of the symptoms had gone. I did feel very drained mentally.

2. The Same Richard

Months later something very similar happened. While working in my London office one morning a progressive feeling of losing control of the mind and of concentration developed. I felt helpless and totally insecure. I left the office mid-afternoon and took the underground to Notting Hill Gate to collect my car. On the tube the build-up of tension and feeling of difficulty in catching breath became so bad that I had to get off one stop early at Queensway. I felt the need to get away from people and I walked the rest of the way, trying to pull myself together before driving home. I ended up walking to St Mary's Hospital where I told them I felt unwell. The doctor saw me and basically went through the same procedure as before. I did not find myself in such an emotional state as before; I was just relieved that someone had convinced me that I would be OK. A further 10 mg of Valium and off I went in the car, back to my home.

3. Gillian, Aged 42 Years

My eldest daughter was to appear in a dance sequence at her school. My husband and I were invited to the event. I felt quite calm about going. However, I am always apprehensive about going out. We walked into the school, my husband just ahead of me with my youngest daughter. I looked around; the middle of the hall was empty, ready for the dancing. There were chairs all around the edge for the audience. My legs wouldn't move, I couldn't seem to walk. I tried to call my husband but my voice didn't have any volume. I froze. Fortunately, at this point my husband turned and realised I was in trouble. He came to me. I told him that I couldn't move and that I couldn't face going down those steps to the chairs. He persuaded me to hold on to him and we walked slowly towards our seats. As I walked down the stairs everything seemed to close in on me. I also couldn't seem to focus properly. I became very hot and there was a thumping in my ears. Every pulse in my body seemed to be jumping out of my skin; my legs were like jelly; I was shaking; my heart seemed to be vibrating; my hands were tingling. I felt sheer panic. I would have left then but for my little girl. Fortunately, at that moment the dancing began and as I watched I started to relax and forget about my body and the symptoms gradually disappeared. This happened about a year ago. There have been many school events since and I always feel very apprehensive about attending. I try to face up to each one by relaxing as much as possible and telling myself that there is nothing to fear.

4. Ian, Aged 29 Years

In June last year I was staying with friends in Hastings. My wife and I decided to go to the horse races at Brighton. On the drive to Brighton I could feel myself becoming very tense. I felt sick, my head was swimming and I remember it being very difficult to concentrate on driving. When we arrived in Brighton we had to park on the seafront and I settled back in the car, trying to relax. I had already taken two-and-a-half mg of Valium that day. Although I felt quite bad I forced myself to drive up to the racecourse. After we parked I got out of the car and found that my legs did not want to work properly. I had to sit down on the wing of my car for a while. When we finally went to the track we sat down away from the crowds and I remember telling myself how ridiculous this all was. As the race meeting progressed, especially when I was immersed in the events, I found I began to feel better. On the drive back I felt much better apart from being tired.

5. The Same Ian

In early March I was at work and at about 10.30 a.m. I was told that a select few were to be taken for a drink by senior management and I, for some reason, was one of those chosen. Immediately I felt an urgent need to visit the lavatory. When I returned I just sat at my desk, the thought of going out being ever present in my mind so that I could not concentrate on anything else. I began to feel sick, became very hot and had to visit the lavatory again. I am not sure, but I think I took more than two-and-a-half mg of Valium that day. Once it was time to go, we got together and then had to wait for somebody who was late. As I had to go, I just wanted to get it over with. Once we were on our way I actually felt slightly better. After a stiff double Scotch I began to feel better although I felt somewhat outranked by most people present. I was relieved when it was all over, although I felt somewhat light-headed.

6. Claire, Aged 28 Years

The worst occasion involving my various symptoms was on the day of my first appointment with a psychiatrist. I had suffered a lot of physical symptoms, and had not been outside the house for three months. Eventually I had decided I was 'cracking up', and so on the morning of the appointment I had a huge head wobbly, and a panic attack. The symptoms were: chest pains, diarrhoea, violent pains down my legs, nausea, migraine, shallow breathing, etc. It occurred to me that I had a burst appendix, cardiac arrest, blood poisoning, food poisoning, or had picked up a tropical disease while on a trip abroad. I couldn't move, felt faint, and was not convinced that this was all due to anxiety, apprehension about the appointment, or a deviant method of not going outside. Eventually my brother dragged me off to the GP who examined me, and consequently claimed I wasn't dying. When I heard this, the symptoms decreased until one hour before I was due to see the psychiatrist, whereupon they started again, particularly in the car where I thought the whole world was going to crash in on me, or that we would drive into the reservoir, into the back of a bus, blow up, or be struck by a huge earthquake in the middle of the high street. During the appointment I used three boxes of Kleenex, and made extraordinary statements, such as 'I'm dying', or 'I think I'm going to vomit', or 'The ceiling is moving', 'I'm schizophrenic', 'I'm going mad', or 'I'm mad'.

How do these stories affect you, the reader? In psychotherapy the emotions that the therapist experiences often say a lot about the patient. They can be pointers that guide us through the maze of the patient's experiences. Usually, the patient is a victim of his/her experiences; and those experiences are often so powerful that he/she cannot see any structure or sense in them. Our task then is to help the client develop the ability to become an 'observer' of his/her difficulties, rather than being stuck in the position of the victim.

In order to illustrate the process of 'including' the therapist's feelings in the process, I should like to invite you, the reader, to include your thoughts and feelings in the process. The following reflection uses the stories and the people in the stories, and you who has read the stories. Our thoughts, feelings, and experience about things usually are a reflection of ourself and of the things, and of our relationship (past and present) with 'the things'.[2]

3.1 Reflection: The Stories

1. *Remember what you experienced when you read the clients' stories:*

What were your feelings towards and about the person?

What thoughts were going through your mind?

What was your reading behaviour? Did you skip through the stories? Did you reread parts?

And then ask yourself how your experience could be related to the client's experience. If you are reacting to the client's story in a certain way, chances are that other people in the client's environment will react to their story in a similar way. You might also be experiencing something from 'between the lines' of the stories, something that the client cannot or does not want to experience.[3]

2. What structure do you see in the stories?

Clients, from their victim perspective, are usually not able to see any structure in their experience. It is all chaos, something that just hits them over the head from behind. Hence it can be a valuable starting point to apply some logical structure to the experience.

Behaviour therapy and behavioural analysis are extremely useful tools to analyse people's stories in a logical and 'common-sense' way.[3] The following questions would be asked in order to identify a stimulus–response pattern in the available information:

a) What are the antecedents, the triggers (internal and external) of the panics?
b) How is the panic experienced (physically, cognitively, behaviourally)?
c) What thoughts, attitudes, mind-sets are connected with the panics?
d) What is the outcome of the experience?

See if you can apply these questions to the stories you have read. Also be aware if you experience resistance to the application of such a structure to people's experience. What is the resistance about? What are you learning about yourself and about the people who have written the stories by asking those questions?

(Note that the emphasis here is on the asking of the questions, rather than on the answers, which differs considerably from a purely behavioural approach.)

Behaviour Therapy as Sense-making

Rereading these stories that were written by some of my clients a few years ago, the first feeling that obviously hits me is fear. According to Ken Wilber's dictionary, anxiety is repressed excitement, and fear is repressed hostility or anger. There certainly does not seem to be much excitement in the story-writers' lives, and I can also sense their anger with the roles they have to play.

But in addition I feel desperation and loneliness, and I see little children facing a world that is too big for them. The world in the stories is a cold, demanding world, where the story-writers 'have to' function. I sense a lot of internal and external pressure and also an inner emptiness. I am wondering what kind of life those people are leading. They seem stuck and lonely. What are their goals and aims in life? What are their beliefs and values? They seem to be longing for an outer authority that tells them where to go and what to do; and they find that outer authority in doctors, hospitals

(Richard, Claire and Mary), or in Valium or alcohol (Ian). Their focus is very much on their physical symptoms: they see themselves as physically ill. It is as if the physical symptoms of panic serve to fill up the inner void by putting adventure and drama into lives that would otherwise be boring and meaningless. Between the lines we can sense something of the emotional conflicts that the physical symptoms are expressing. Richard in particular uses emotional words like 'loneliness, breaking down, uselessness, blaming, lack of confidence' in his story. However, all the story-writers are initially looking for solutions to their unpleasant physical symptoms and not for ways of exploring the underlying emotional conflicts.

This is the point where a structured behavioural analysis can be the first step on the path to exploration:

1 Identifying the triggers of the physical symptoms can help suggest that there are specific situations, whether external or internal or both, that bring about the symptoms. It also indicates that there are a multitude of other situations that do not cause the symptoms.
2 Analysing the connection between physical sensations and thoughts, self-statements, mind-sets, attitudes, and realising how panic thoughts can cause or exacerbate physical panic sensations, can be the patient's first step towards a more psychological approach.
3 In general, this behavioural way of 'sense-making' can create an important attitude change. The problem changes to something that can be observed, analysed and understood. The patient begins to shift from being a victim to someone who can begin to exert some control over the problem.

In essence it is the following model that behavioural analysis applies to patients' problems:

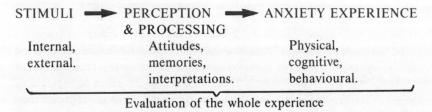

STIMULI ➡ PERCEPTION ➡ ANXIETY EXPERIENCE
& PROCESSING

Internal,	Attitudes,	Physical,
external.	memories,	cognitive,
	interpretations.	behavioural.

Evaluation of the whole experience

This evaluation of the whole experience then creates the expectations for facing similar situations in future. The problem is that the whole process consists of conscious as well as unconscious components. And this is also the point where the battle between behaviourism and Freudianism began. The polarisation between the two schools of thought has filled volumes. Having taken part in those battles, it feels almost blasphemous now to argue for integration and assimilation. The following section gives a brief glimpse into the polarised past.

Behaviour Therapy Versus Psychotherapy

Behavioural definitions of 'fear' started with Watson, the father of behaviourism, who proposed that the innate stimuli for the fear reaction were limited to loud noise, sudden loss of support, and pain. All other stimuli which can obviously create fear in the individual, were seen as the result of the classical conditioning process. Hence, the fear reaction was seen as being a 'learned response', which, given the right therapy, could be unlearned (Watson and Rayner 1920: 1–14).

Gray gives the following case example of a woman with obsessive compulsive hand-washing rituals:

> The first thing we did was to ask Mrs S exactly what conditions would prompt her to carry out this ritual. The most illuminating thing about her reply was that no one had ever asked her this question before. Apparently, all her therapists, over a period of eleven years, had been so convinced that the 'true cause' of Mrs S's obsessions lay deep in her childhood that none of them had thought it necessary to enquire what it was that precipitated them now. It turned out that the stimuli for Mrs S's obsessions could be classified quite easily into three kinds: those connected with splintered glass or similar material; those connected with dirt; and those connected with the possibility of pregnancy. (Never having been asked, Mrs S had never thought about her illness in this way before, and she had no idea before our enquiry that her behaviour conformed to this relatively simple pattern.) Being psychologists, and therefore rather simple minded, we did not stop to consider what occult symbolism might be hidden behind these fears (of splinters, dirt and pregnancy), but resolved instead to do our best to remove them.
>
> (Gray 1971: 239–40)

It is both refreshing and sad to look back at the optimism and arrogance of behaviourists in the early 1970s, peaking in the statement that 'there is no evidence that psycho-therapy ('talking' therapy) of the psycho-analytic or any other kind leads to any greater or more rapid improvement than being left on a waiting list' (Gray 1971: 241). Unfortunately, the evidence at the time was very much based on findings with 'mono-symptomatic phobias', and on the assumption that wider and more general fears were just a quantitative extension of the phobias of dogs, spiders, snakes, thunder, etc. However, this began to change once behaviourists started to deal with increasingly complex cases, and with the emergence of 'cognitive therapy'. The behaviour-analytic approach, mentioned earlier, helped the development of behaviour therapy from the application of well-defined techniques in the treatment of equally well-defined symptoms into a more comprehensive approach to the individual client as a whole including his/her problems.

Behaviour Therapy Case Study

In order to illustrate the sense-making properties of behaviour therapy I should like to present a case study. The therapy procedure used in this case is based on Vic Meyer's 'behaviour-analytic approach', which was probably the most advanced and creative use of learning principles in the late 1970s and early 1980s. The case is presented here to remind us of the practical value of behaviourism in providing an easily understandable and usable cause–effect model to structure the complex information that clients often present.

Referral Letter

Elaine, a 29-year-old married woman with two young sons, was referred to the psychology clinic in a health centre by her GP. The following referral letter was sent:

Dear Psychologist,

This patient, who is an ex-policewoman, is married to a charming, but to her own confession, less intelligent chef/waiter from a Greek island. She has two young sons, the eldest of whom she finds very difficult to manage. To my mind she has never been adequately able to stop being her parents' little girl.

I thought you might like sight of the attached letter. I am at the moment concentrating on what I feel is an underlying depression by treating her with 50 mg of Lentizol at night and Ativan 1 mg tds. However, I feel you might well be able to help her deal with her anxiety.

Yours sincerely,

General Practitioner

Enclosed with this referral was a letter written by the patient to her doctor. This letter was as follows:

Dear Doctor,

Before I had children I was strong, healthy and happy. My thyroid problems created the start of my inability to cope with myself. It was you who told me to go home and pull myself together. I took your advice very seriously and won through. I had another baby and from the day I had him old anxiety troubles progressed. Eventually it was discovered my thyroxine tablets needed re-adjusting several times beween March and July last year. I battled along although many days

I didn't cope and I felt unwell. Then last October I suffered severe stomach pains at night, my stomach turned over and over. The doctor diagnosed an ulcer and the treatment and diet caused further dreadful pains. They made me so ill I phoned the emergency doctor on several occasions. For this I was sternly told off. I nose-dived lower and lower under the strain of looking after my family, believing I had caused the pains myself through worry. Eventually I needed a month in hospital and an emergency operation to remove an inflamed gall-bladder and three enormous stones. I weighed 7 stone when I came home after Christmas. Since then once again I've desperately tried to be strong. But I haven't stopped worrying. My son is now four. He is extremely active, demands all my attention and patience. He is prone to tantrums and temper, is very noisy and gives me no peace. My husband works until 2 a.m. I am lonely in the evenings and miss adult companionship – someone to discuss my problems. My problems were mainly in the late evening and night, until recently. I can't sleep or I just drift off when I awake (involuntarily) in a panic-state. I suffer palpitation, hot face, and deep fear. This would repeat itself three or four times during the night. I am frightened I will suffer a heart attack. I am frightened because I can't control it and hate the feeling. Each morning I would wake tired and drained. I went to my doctor. He gave me Tranxene to help me sleep. These tablets worked. But I began to feel anxious and panicky in the earlier part of the evening. I'd feel faint, miserable. I'd cry and feel morbid. I'd have days where my son just became unbearable and I'd shout, scream and smack – then I was caught in a vicious circle. Back I went to the doctor. He prescribed Bolvidon. I took one. It was so strong I fainted on the stairs (something I've never done in my life) the next morning. This caused more problems, more fuss, more misery. I slept off the tablet all the following day and then returned to the doctor. He gave me Ativan 2.5 mg to be taken at night. They helped me sleep and stopped my stomach churning. But gradually my anxiety over particularly the last month has spread into the day. My stomach turns non-stop. Then I'll have a quiet day and without even thinking, it'll start again. Two weeks ago I stayed in hospital with my son whilst he underwent the removal of his tonsils and adenoids and the fitting of grommets. I desperately wanted to be unselfish and cope – I went to pieces. I didn't show it to him I know but I didn't sleep, I had panic attacks, I cried non-stop when I wasn't with him, I had pins and needles in my elbows and fingers. I felt a wreck and what's more I just could not pull myself out of it – and I tried so hard. We came home and I felt myself frighteningly out of control. So down to the doctor I went, never fully able to explain myself. He gave me Surmontil 25 mg, three times a day. I had one in the morning and night and then the following day another. I somehow drove to mum's. I felt like a walking zombie, nauseated, lifeless and despairing. Here at last I could talk to the people that understood how much I want to be fit and mentally normal. Sometimes I am completely unable to cope with the children or with life. I shake, I get myself in an utter state, I am thin and can't put on weight. Sometimes I can't eat all my food. Although for the past week I've eaten well. I feel like I shall end up in a mental hospital (or going like my nan). I desperately want help. Even now I know I haven't managed to describe the depth and state I've got myself in. Probably because writing this letter tonight, I feel peaceful, secure maybe and I've had a break from my son as mum and dad took him out for the day. I don't want to be alone right now. I am frightened I may batter my son – I feel violently aggressive with his naughty ways. I do love him dearly. I am frightened I am still ill with some other diseased organ, i.e. pituitary gland, adrenal gland. I worry I've got multiple sclerosis because of pins and needles in my hands, and my knees are stiff. I can't control my feelings and have no warning when I shall go down again. Usually my son is the person to blame – but I don't know – I'm not sure. I wanted to see you because I am not afraid of what you think of me. I want to hear your opinions and I trust you. Please help me. I have been taking 1 mg of Ativan three times a day today. I don't want to be on drugs forever – that worries me too. But I must get some medical advice and help. I want reassurance and perhaps a check up to make sure I'm not sick. If I need to see a psychiatrist to help me I'm willing to listen. I'm muddled, guilty and unhappy. Please help me.

Yours sincerely,

Elaine

P.S. I am happily married although my poor husband has had a lot to put up with.

Assessment Session

The patient was then seen for an assessment interview and a behavioural analysis was carried out. For this, a 'problem analysis sheet' was used, derived from Meyer's 'behaviour-analytic approach' (see Table 3.1). This approach aims at developing a problem formulation which '(1) relates all the client's complaints to one another, (2) explains why the individual developed these difficulties, and (3) provides predictions concerning the client's behaviour given any stimulus condition' (Meyer and Turkat 1979: 261).

Table 3.1 Problem analysis sheet (Elaine)

Personal history		*Self image*	
		+	–
Always nervous; diarrhoea before dances, problems with boyfriends.		intelligent	can't control symptoms
1975–1977	Policewoman in London – enjoyed it.	logical	worries about health
1978	Thyroid problems after first child; with child and husband at his home in Crete. Palpitations triggered by petrol pump noise. OP thyroids – but still problems.	good company	feels a burden on others
		kind	no faith in self
March 1980	Thyroid problems controlled with medication.		
March 1981	Second child, difficult birth; panics at night pre-birth; return home – stress, noise, can't cope, panics.		
May 1981	Thyroids wrong again.		
July 1981	Thyroids stabilised.		
October 1981	Stomach problems started.		
November 1981	Gall-bladder problems started.		
December 1981	Gall-bladder removed; still stomach problems – prescribed Valium.		

Stimulus-response pattern at present

S $\longrightarrow$ R $\longrightarrow$ C

S	R	C
Drifting off to sleep	A: hot in mouth, body shaking, stomach, knees, palpitations	Husband: concerned, kind, but does not understand; she doesn't accept his help.
Concentrating on self		
Conversations	C: 'must get help'	
In hospitals	B: deep breathing, turning over, tries very hard to control	
Emotional music on TV		
Petrol pump noise	A = autonomic	
Children's noise	C = cognitive	
	B = behavioural	Parents: supportive and understanding.
Own bad temper with kids		

Source: Kowalski 1986

The Behaviour-analytic Approach

The behaviour-analytic approach was developed at the Middlesex Hospital. It is particularly relevant to show how this approach goes beyond traditional behaviour therapy. Meyer and Turkat summarise as follows:

> We begin typically by generating a list of all the behavioral difficulties the client is currently experiencing. Each problem is listed in general terms with the aim of generating an exhaustive list. The list of behavioral difficulties serves a variety of purposes such as structuring the clinical interview, specifying the range of problems the individual is experiencing, and, most importantly, providing the therapist with information for generating hypotheses. Preferably, the list of problems and subsequent information is recorded on a blackboard or some other medium which the client and therapist can visually refer to. . . . Visual inspection of the behavior problem list often provides clues as to how the presenting complaints may be related and account for one another.
>
> (Meyer and Turkat 1979: 262)

Of particular importance seems to be the visual representation of the client's problem. Clinical experience suggests that this process can facilitate the 'externalisation' of a previously internalised problem, thus allowing the client to step back and to look with the therapist at the problem in a different way. This process of 'unlearning' is very similar to the process of learning described by Galperin (1969) and other Russian psychology researchers.

Meyer and Turkat describe further benefits of their 'analytical approach':

> One example is the individual who is complaining of panic attacks in automobiles driven by someone else and about panic around the individual's boss at work. Immediately the technology-oriented behavior therapist would begin desensitization to such situations. On the other hand, the behavior-analytically oriented clinician might examine the relationship between these complaints and conceptualise the common antecedent in this situation as 'being out of control'. Thus the therapist may check for further evidence of this hypothesis and notice that the individual feels uncomfortable travelling on buses, trains and planes, experiences anxiety during unplanned events, and over inexplicable heart rate increases etc. . . . Treatment based on exposure to being out of control then would appear to be more appropriate than treatment aimed at modifying the two original complaints.
>
> (Meyer and Turkat 1979: 267)

This search for underlying themes was quite unique to the behaviour-analytic approach, and in a way formed the bridge between cognitive therapy and behaviour therapy.

The following points of the behaviour-analytic approach need to be kept in mind for the present case:

1 The behaviour-analytic assessment provides a 'common-sense' causal psychological model which clients usually find comfortable to accept.
2 The model appears scientific enough to enable clients to move from one system (the primary health care medical one) to another.
3 The externalisation on blackboard or paper allows for a co-operative therapeutic relationship, where both client and therapist can look at an external representation of the client's internal problems.
4 The model makes use of 'here-and-now' as well as biographical information in a focused and structured way.

Formulation

On the basis of the problem analysis sheet and all the other information available the following formulation was then developed with the client:

Elaine has always been a nervous person and she seems to have been easily conditionable (e.g. petrol pump noise still triggers panic). As a policewoman she was able to control herself and her symptoms under a regime of discipline coupled with a sense of achievement. At present she is rather dissatisfied with her role as housewife and mother, which has resulted in a feeling of helplessness and uncontrollability regarding herself and her symptoms. A variety of illnesses following the birth of her first child have made her hypersensitive to physical sensations. Elaine is now convinced that all her symptoms (and her autonomic arousal) are due to physical illness. At the same time she has a strong need to be in control of herself and her life. This discrepancy has resulted in a low self-image, and she can only turn to her parents for help.

Therapy Outcome

Elaine was also asked to carry out 'self-monitoring of her symptoms', using a 'self-observation chart', on which the client records in writing each occurrence of symptoms in a systematic and sequential way, thus becoming aware of the stimulus–response–consequence pattern. Three weeks later, she came for her second appointment and in that time she had experienced her symptoms on only two occasions. Using the structure of her self-observation chart she had been able to explain the occurrence of the symptoms, and this had greatly reduced their impact. Elaine had also begun to discuss relationship problems with her husband and she had made the decision to work on the marriage.

In this case, the process of carrying out a thorough behavioural analysis fell on fertile ground. It provided Elaine with a logical explanation of her complaints. In addition she was asked to tape-record some 'emotional' music, which she claimed would usually trigger panic attacks (see 'problem analysis'). In the session she listened to the music while her heart rate was monitored with a bio-feedback machine. As a result of listening to the music her heart rate did increase. However, during the following discussion, Elaine reported that she had actually enjoyed listening to the music. The experiment proved to us that she had developed a hypersensitivity to all autonomic arousal and that she was likely to interpret even pleasant arousal as 'panic'. (The body speaks a rather simple language, and its messages are therefore open to all sorts of interpretations by the mind.) In Wilber's terms the experiment proved that her anxiety was related to repressed excitement. Thus, self-monitoring and a bio-feedback experiment both served to confirm the initial formulation. As a result of the 'logical' explanation (sense-making), backed up with some reality-testing (bio-feedback) , Elaine became able to regain a sense of control over herself and her life, and her panic attacks soon disappeared completely.

Conclusions

Elaine was a typical patient who would be referred to a clinical psychologist by their doctor. An important part of therapy for clients like Elaine consists of de-medicalising them, i.e. offering them a model that allows them to change the way in which they attribute the symptoms that they have previously taken to the surgery. A structured model like the behaviour-analytic approach seems to have the potential to facilitate such re-attribution. If this proves to be so, i.e. that re-attribution can replace for the client one belief-system with another, we shall at the end be left to judge how much more appropriate the new system is, and whether this new system will allow us and the clients to 'really' identify and solve the presenting problems.

In psychosynthesis terms, Elaine's will was caught in her worries about physical symptoms, and with this she went into a system, the medical one, which requires and reinforces passivity (yielding, unresisting, submissive = will-lessness). The behavioural approach enabled Elaine to retake responsibility for herself. Her will was freed through the redefinition of her problems into something that could be observed, dealt with, changed through her own efforts. The benefit of behavioural techniques seems to lie in their ability to demonstrate to the patient that there is hope that he/she could achieve some mastery over life's difficulties.

FEAR AND ANXIETY – A STRUCTURED MODEL

In my book *Over the Top* I developed a flow-chart model of anxiety and panic attacks. The complexity and/or complicatedness of this model of interdependent vicious (or 'maintaining') cycles is obvious. The niggling

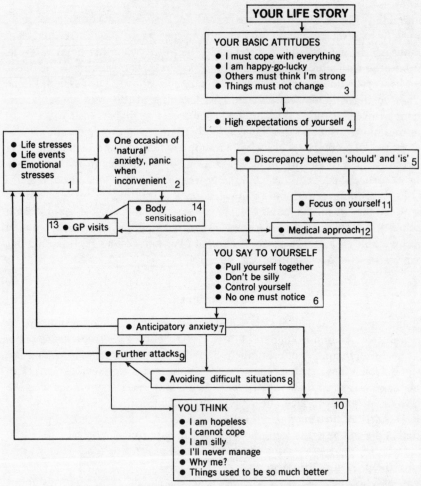

Figure 3.1 Flow chart: anxiety and panic attacks.
Source: Kowalski 1987

doubtful question becomes whether complicated models like this remove us from the context of 'holistic experience' of life and human problems. Again, perhaps what is needed here is the inclusion of thoughts and feelings *about* the model in the appreciation of the model.

Figure 3.1 represents a cognitive model of anxiety and panic attacks. The story of anxiety, panic and stress usually starts with certain life stresses or with the accumulation of those stresses over time (1). At such a time of physical and mental vulnerability the physical experience of spontaneous anxiety or panic is more likely and it can happen when it is particularly inconvenient and when the person least expects it, like while driving the car, while shopping or at a social gathering (2). When such a spontaneous panic attack happens to someone who is particularly sensitive and who has the

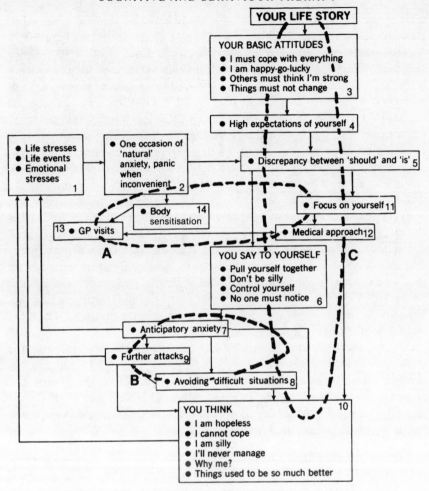

Figure 3.2 Vicious circles.

attitude 'I must cope with everything' (3), resulting in high expectations of him or herself (4), then the panic attack is likely to create a discrepancy between what is and what the person thinks should be (5). Non-acceptance of the experience can then lead to the 'pull-yourself-together' attitude (6), which in turn creates more anticipatory anxiety (7). All this is bound to make life more stressful (1), and it can lead to the avoidance of all potentially frightening situations (8), which in itself can lead to further attacks (9). The end result of the vicious circles and the non-accepting attitude can then become depressive self-blame (10), which, again, causes more stress and makes future attacks more likely (1).

Apart from illustrating the importance of thoughts and attitudes, the chart also addresses other issues. The whole process from (1) to (1) can be seen as one big vicious circle, which is made up of two smaller ones, while they are held up by the 'backbone' of attitudes (cognitions) (see Figure 3.2). Vicious circle **A** is the medical/physical one. It starts off with people's tendency to focus on themselves and their bodies (11) when they experience a real self–ideal self discrepancy (5). The frightening physical sensations of panic and anxiety are then readily interpreted in a medical way as a 'physical illness' (12). Such a medical approach can then get further reinforced by visits to the doctor, medical investigations, and possibly medication (13). Furthermore, this medical vicious circle is strengthened through the physical sensitisation that takes place as a result of the panic experience(s) (14).

Vicious circle **B** is the avoidance one. It starts off with anticipatory anxiety (7), which causes people to avoid doing certain things or being in certain situations. A 'fear of fear' develops. If we then start to avoid driving the car, going into the supermarket or being at social gatherings, the fear of fear tends to grow, because we never put it to the test. And when we finally are, for whatever reason, facing the feared object or situation, chances are that we do so with a considerable amount of tension and autonomic arousal, consisting of our anticipatory anxiety and of the normal startle reaction that happens whenever we face new (or almost new) situations. Thus the conditions for further attacks are ideal (9).

The backbone **C** that energises and maintains the medical and the avoidance vicious circles is the person's attitudes (3,4,6,10). It ranges from perfectionism (3) to defeatism and depression (10). Behaviour therapy and cognitive therapy address the interaction between **A**, **B** and **C**. Different techniques and approaches focus on either **A**, **B** or **C**. These are examples of the different techniques and methods:

A. Seeing a psychologist/psychotherapist instead of a doctor; applying a psychological model to the problem rather than a medical one; self observation; behavioural analysis (see Elaine, pp. 37–40).
B. Facing the feared situations/objects; breaking through the avoidance pattern; systematic desensitisation; flooding; *in-vivo* exposure; relaxation techniques to deal with anticipatory anxiety.
C. Modifying self-statements; developing a more realistic, positive attitude; acceptance of what is, rather than wishing it away.

COGNITIVE-BEHAVIOURAL TECHNIQUES

In this section I am inviting you to apply structured cognitive-behavioural techniques in the form of reflections and explorations to yourself. There will be one or two exercises for each of the categories **A**, **B**, and **C**. However, the exercises are not 'purely' cognitive-behavioural, but rather they are based in cognitive-behavioural principles, while going beyond it.

The Sequence of Events (A)

The techniques and methods that fit into this area are described in Elaine's case study on pp. 35–41. This includes the application of a non-medical, psychological, yet structured model to the problem, thus helping the patient to retake responsibility for herself by including the problem, overcoming a split, an artificial boundary. Behavioural analysis, self-observation charts, all serve this purpose. The exercise below is the application of a structured, sequential behavioural analysis to an emotion. The sequence is 'stimulus (part one)–response (part two)–consequence (part three)'. The 'three systems analysis' is included by focusing on behaviour, thoughts and physical sensations. The exercise can be useful in the uncovering of 'forgotten' or 'blocked off' experiences. It goes beyond behaviourism mainly in the manner in which the information is pulled together. The way in which this is done corresponds with the 'inner learning' principles of psychosynthesis.

3.2 Exercise: Structured Analysis

This exercise is in three parts. Read each part first, then sit down comfortably, close your eyes and follow the instructions. Keep your body and your breathing relaxed throughout. It will help you remember. Before making notes after each part of this exercise check the instructions to see which bits you may have forgotten. This may give you clues about where your blocks are. The answers may well be behind the blocks.

PART ONE

Remember a recent occasion when you felt anxious, depressed, stressed, upset. Identify as much as possible the day, time, and location of the start of the feeling(s) by scanning back through time.

Once you have identified the situation when and where the feeling started, imagine yourself vividly in that situation just before the feeling started. Picture yourself, the surroundings, other people, the sounds and smells, the temperature.

Then try and be yourself in that situation.
What was it like to be in that particular situation?
What did you experience?
What were you doing or saying?
What were others doing and saying?
What were your feelings?
What physical sensations did you experience?
What thoughts were going through your mind?
Did you remember something from the past?
Did you anticipate something in the future?

You may find it a bit unpleasant to remember everything in so much detail. Or you may find that there are blocks to remembering. Your mind may drift into thinking about other things. Keep your body and especially your breathing calm and relaxed, and gently guide your mind back to the situation.

Once you have explored the context of the beginning of the feelings, see if you can get a sense of what may have been the trigger(s). This may not be very clearcut, and perhaps it seems like there was no trigger, like it all happened 'out of the blue'. If that's the case, focus especially on the things that you did not want to remember, or the things that you had forgotten and only just remembered. Also look at the situation as a whole: Was the constellation similar to ones that you have found difficult in the past? Is there a pattern that goes back a long way?

Now make some notes about what you have found out about the trigger(s) of those feelings.

PART TWO

Now go back to remembering the situation. But this time focus on your experience of the anxiety, depression or other feeling that you have chosen.

Then try and be yourself in that situation. What was it like to be in that particular situation? What did you experience?

See if you can get a sense of what your feelings were trying to tell you. Was it a message from the past? How relevant is that message now? Again, make some notes about your exploration.

PART THREE

Now go to the point in time when the anxiety, depression, or other feeling stopped or changed (if it did). What were the circumstances under which it changed? Did it have anything to do with anything you did, said, thought or felt? Did it have anything to do with other people's actions?

Make notes.

Look at the three sets of notes you have made during this exercise and apply the following criteria to them:

1 What is the rational learning? How could you summarise the information?
2 What is your 'gut reaction' to the notes and the reflection in general?

3 Is there an image or symbol for you as a result of this exercise? Draw it if you want to.

Hidden Triggers

The 'behavioural analysis' exercise above is particularly suited to uncover 'hidden triggers'. These triggers are usually semi-conscious, which means that they can come into conscious awareness with exercises like the one above.

Example One

Ian (who wrote stories 4 and 5 on p. 30) told us about one of his panic attacks at work. On the day of the Derby he was having lunch at his desk. He then went over to one of his colleagues, who had a portable television set under his desk, intending to watch the race. Suddenly Ian experienced pressure behind his eyes and a general feeling of shakiness. A dose of Ativan made him feel better. But as soon as the drug had worn off in the afternoon the panics returned, and stayed with him until he got home.

We went through his experience in great detail, trying to find a trigger. We could not find anything. Then we talked about Ian's holiday which was due to start the following week. He was feeling quite apprehensive about it, because not only was he taking his wife and baby daughter, but also his parents and his mother-in-law. As he was to be the only car driver he was concerned about the long journey to Cornwall, and in general he felt extremely responsible for his family having a good holiday.

Then Ian mentioned quite accidentally that he had telephoned his mother from work on the day of the Derby. It emerged that he had telephoned her just before he went over to his colleague's desk. Ian then remembered that he had started feeling quite tense when the phone was ringing at his mother's end. She then told him about all the new dresses she had bought for the holiday, etc. The telephone conversation probably reinforced Ian's rather ambivalent feelings about the holiday.

After the telephone conversation, Ian pushed it all out of his mind, and went over to his colleague's desk. Then the panics started.

What does this tell us about hidden triggers?

1 Ian's telephone conversation with his mother connected him with feelings of responsibility for his family, and also with his inability to put others second. He probably experienced powerful unpleasant emotions, which he tried to push out of his awareness as quickly as possible.
2 Things that trigger panics may be thoughts or feelings that do not fit into the normal course of events. In Ian's case, being reminded of his holiday did not fit into his work routine and his excitement about watching the

Derby. The telephone conversation with his mother was therefore not recalled later on, because it did not fit into the logical chain of events at work.

3 Having a panic attack usually means that logical thinking gets impaired. Once it is over we want to forget about it altogether. Our memory of what happened in detail is therefore very limited.

4 In Ian's case the trigger was being reminded of a situation where he desperately wanted to cope, i.e. providing a good holiday for his family. He did not want to have any negative feelings about the holiday, so he had to deny all negative feelings that were there. This denial of negative feelings can then take attention away from 'feelings', leaving more energy available for attention on 'body', and unpleasant physical sensations as a direct result of repressed (non-accepted) negative feelings. The vicious circle of unpleasant physical sensations and more attention being available for those sensations can thus be started.

Example Two

Bill, an airline pilot who had recently temporarily given up flying because of his panic attacks, described a recent panic experience. It happened while he was standing in the doorway of his home, watching his wife, an airline hostess, dressed in her uniform getting ready to go to work. No trigger was obvious.

Bill was then asked to remember vividly everything that had happened at the time, using the above exercise. He then recalled that just before seeing his wife in her uniform, he had watched on the television a news item about an airline crash.

Bill's story seems quite similar to Ian's. He also 'forgot' about an event that probably connected him to rather negative emotions. In this case it may have been his worries about both him and his wife being in the airline business. In addition to those real fears it probably also connected him to the fact that he was not able to do his job at the time.

The above two examples illustrate how a sequential behavioural analysis, with its focus on detail and its inclusion of action, thoughts, feelings and physical sensations, can uncover repressed or 'forgotten' material. The inclusion of that material can contribute to the sense-making process, and it can open the door to looking at deeper emotional issues.

Facing the Dragon (B)

The cognitive-behavioural techniques that aim at interrupting vicious circle B are the ones that help people face unpleasant emotions and/or the situations that are associated with those emotions. The fight/flight response is a natural reaction to the experience of fear. However, the consequences of prolonged avoidance are numerous.

Certainly one of the most spontaneous and natural reactions to the experience of a panic attack is the thought 'I've got to get out of here'. This is especially true when the person experiencing the panic is in a shop, a cinema, on public transport or in any other enclosed space. Often this is connected with the overpowering wish to go home or to another place of safety. Leaving the office, getting off the underground, going out of the room for a few minutes, visiting the lavatory, all aim to remove oneself from a frightening stressful situation. So what's wrong with that, you may ask? Well, in the long run the following paradoxical effects tend to occur as a result of repeatedly leaving the situation:

1 Once the problematic situation – shop, office, car, underground, etc. – is left, there is usually fairly instant relief from the panics. The experience that 'leaving was worth it' has been made; the action of leaving is reinforced by the subsequent relief from a panic attack. Thus the action of leaving is strengthened as a powerful coping strategy for future panic occurrences.

2 Leaving the situation can therefore easily develop into a bad habit, and in future the slightest experience of panic symptoms can cause the person to run away from any situation where the slightest feeling of anxiety or panic occurs. The result is less and less tolerance of panics because the action of leaving has become an automatic habit.

3 After using this coping strategy for a while the person 'just knows' that certain situations are not for him/her. And what is the point in going to the supermarket yet again if you have left it after two minutes the last ten times you went? Out of anticipatory anxiety and a sense of hopelessness, avoidance begins to develop. Certain situations and activities are avoided and more or less good excuses are found.

4 You may by now, quite rightly, feel that the consequences of 'leaving the situation' are rather numerous and far-reaching. The following point adds to the complexity. After a long period of avoiding situations that have in the past been connected with panics, e.g. supermarkets, trains, being away from home, the avoiding person becomes less and less accustomed to being in those situations. They become strange environments for him or her. If this person is then, for whatever reason, forced to go into one of those situations, he or she reacts to the experience like anyone entering a strange situation – with apprehension and alertness. These sensations in themselves can then be the triggers for a full-blown panic attack. And the sad end-result of the vicious circle may then be the attitude, 'This proves it; I should have known better; I shouldn't have gone into the situation in the first place; I am hopeless'.

Flooding, desensitisation, *in-vivo* exposure, are all ways of helping the patient face the unpleasant situation. In systematic desensitisation this is done in small steps, using relaxation methods to keep the physical fear as low as possible throughout, while in flooding the aim is exposure to the feared situation over prolonged periods of time. The rationale behind flooding is that, physiologically, once the fear peaks it does automatically go down. Avoidance prevents this 'post peak' experience, and flooding tries to re-create it.

The most commonly used exercises in cognitive-behavioural work are relaxation exercises. The following exercise uses relaxed breathing as a way of letting go of physical tension, and of preventing hyperventilation.

3.3 Exercise: Relaxed Breathing

This relaxation exercise works best when you listen to it from a tape.[5] The focus of the exercise is to breathe correctly with the diaphragm, thus correcting the tendency to hyperventilate in stressful situations. The exercise also suggests images, and it can help you get in touch with, and through, physical blocks. It can also help you develop a more favourable 'relationship' with certain parts of your body. With regular practice you will learn to relax rapidly wherever you are.

The numbers in brackets indicate the pauses in seconds that you should leave if you want to make up your own tape.

This exercise is designed to help you relax using your breathing and your imagination.

Now concentrate on your breathing. Put your right hand on your stomach, just above your waistline. Now take a few deep breaths – in and out – in and out. Make sure your stomach comes out when you breathe in and that it goes in when you breathe out. Continue breathing regularly and calmly. Push your stomach out a little bit when you breathe in, and pull your stomach in a little bit when you breathe out. Your diaphragm expands when you breathe in to fill your lungs, and it contracts when you exhale. And with your right hand on your stomach, just above your waistline, you can monitor that you are breathing properly – filling and emptying your lungs. Try this for a few moments – your stomach comes out when you breathe in and it pulls in when you breathe out. (20)

Also make sure that you don't hold your breath in between breathing in and out. Breathe in continuously and smoothly and then breathe out continuously and smoothly, without holding your breath. Keep your breathing regular and shallow, in and out through your nose. Your stomach expands when you breathe in and it contracts when you breathe out. At the same time keep your chest as still and relaxed as possible. (20)

You are now breathing calmly and regularly, and I want you to concentrate your mind on the word RELAX. Say RE to yourself when you breathe in and LAX when you breathe out, still making sure that your diaphragm does most of the breathing work, monitored by your right hand. Say RE when you breathe in and LAX when you breathe out, RE – LAX. And your stomach expands as you breathe in and it contracts as you breathe out. (10)

Keep saying RE to yourself when you breathe in and LAX when you breathe out. Keep doing this and make sure that you don't move your tongue or your mouth when you say RE – LAX to yourself. RE when you breathe in and LAX as you breathe out. (10)

If you are now satisfied that you are breathing correctly, your stomach expanding when you breathe in and contracting when you breathe out, remove your right hand from your stomach area. Remember to put your right hand on your stomach whenever you want to remind yourself to breathe properly. (10)

You may find it helpful to imagine the word RELAX written in huge letters in front of your eyes. Imagine the letters are made from huge blocks of concrete and you are exploring the letters of the word RELAX. (5)

Explore the letter R. (10) Explore the letter E. (10) Explore the letter L. (10) Explore the letter A. (10) Explore the letter X. (10) RELAX. (5) And now choose one letter from the word RELAX which could be your favourite letter at the moment. Make up your mind quickly and choose one letter. Imagine that letter in front of your eyes for a few moments. (10)

Remember this letter and the word RELAX whenever you want to remind yourself to relax by controlling your breathing. (10)

With your mind you are now telling your body to relax, allowing tension to flow out with each breath out. And as your body is becoming more relaxed, your mind will also be able to relax more and more. You are using your mind and your breathing to relax your body. This in turn will also relax your mind. (10)

Concentrate again on your breathing and on the word RELAX. Say RE to yourself when you breathe in and LAX when you breathe out. Make sure that your stomach still expands when you breathe in and contracts when you breathe out. (10)

Now concentrate on different parts of your body, breathing into them and letting tension flow out from them with each breath out. Saying RE when you breathe in and LAX when you breathe out. (5)

Concentrate on your hands and on your arms. Breathe into your hands and arms, saying RE when you breathe in and LAX when you breathe out. Let tension flow out from your arms and your hands with each breath out. Your hands and your arms are becoming heavy and relaxed. (10)

Now concentrate on your neck. Tell your neck to relax and let all the tension flow out, saying RE when you breathe in and LAX when you breathe out. (10)

Now concentrate on your face and let all the tension flow out from your face. Your face is becoming smooth and relaxed. (10)

Now focus your attention on your stomach. Let go of all the tension in your stomach area. (10)

Now tell your back to relax more and more. You are still saying RE when you breathe in and LAX when you breathe out – no effort at all. Let all the tension flow out from your back. (10)

Now concentrate on your legs. Let go of all the tension from your buttocks down to your toes. (10)

By concentrating on your breathing and on the word RELAX you have allowed tension to flow out of your body. (5)

Now choose one particular part of your body for more relaxation. It may even be an organ or an area inside your body. Perhaps choose a part of your body that you are concerned about at the moment. (10)

Imagine that your relationship with that particular part of your body is rather tense, creating a block or a wall between you and that part. (10)

Try to break through the wall by breathing into that part of your body and letting tension flow out from it. Imagine that the power of your breathing is gradually breaking through the wall, creating a hole through which tension can flow out when you exhale. Continue doing this for a few moments. (20)

And now, slowly and in your own time, open your eyes again and be fully alert and awake.

I do find that often with this exercise, strong emotional experiences can occur. Cognitive-behavioural techniques could probably not explain such occurrences, but later on I shall be discussing Ken Wilber's model, and presenting one of his exercises that deals even more directly with physical/emotional blocks. 'Bioenergetics' would probably also have a lot to say about this. However, the above exercise seems to have a good mix of releasing physical tension and beginning to focus on inner blocks without going too deep too quickly.

Self-talk (C)

In our daily lives we are constantly evaluating situations and ourselves. This process takes place at different levels of consciousness and awareness. In cognitive therapy the aim is to make this process conscious, i.e. to put words to it. 'What was going through your mind at the time? What did you say to yourself? What was your attitude then?' are questions that aim at putting words to it again. 'Again', because that is how the mental process of evaluation and self-evaluation developed in the first place, before it became unconscious and automatic. The process of 'internalisation' in children has the following stages:

1 Performing an external activity, trial and error, feedback through result of activity.
2 Self-talk (aloud) while carrying out activity.
3 Self-talk (silent) while carrying out activity.
4 Wordless inner mental activity while carrying out activity.
5 Wordless inner mental activity regardless of external activity.

The aim in cognitive therapy then, is 'go back' to stages two and three where the process of evaluation and self-evaluation can be externalised and modified. In a way the whole of psychotherapy aims at this, because it tries to make unconscious and emotional processes conscious by experiencing them and talking about them. Let's try a few exercises which are relevant for therapy and which illustrate the points that cognitive therapy is making.

3.4 Exercise: Self-blame

What's wrong with that, you might ask. Isn't it better for me to blame myself rather than others? Well, it would probably be best if you could develop an 'objective' attitude towards your problems. But we often hear the following from clients: 'Isn't it silly that I have this problem. I feel so stupid. Everybody tells me there is nothing wrong with me. I really shouldn't go and see my doctor all the time, when he has to deal with all those people who have "real" illnesses'. Does this sound familiar to you?

A similar attitude often develops towards anxiety and panic attacks. Statements such as the following are very common: 'I hope no one has noticed. Will I make a fool of myself? Everybody else is so strong, and I am so weak.'

It is quite obvious that all the above statements reflect a negative attitude towards yourself. We sometimes call these statements or thoughts 'negative self-talk'. With this negative self-talk we usually run ourselves down, thus making us feel weak and pathetic. And when we feel weak and pathetic about ourselves, we are not exactly in the best position to face anxiety-provoking or stressful situations. Again this makes it all rather complicated, and the following vicious cycle can emerge:

You blame yourself for the weakness of having panics. As a result you feel less strong and generally more anxious. Hence you are more likely to experience further anxiety and panic attacks.

Sit down quietly for a few minutes with paper and pen ready.
Now assess how you usually talk about yourself and how you present yourself to people you are close to (family, friends).
What kind of remarks do you make about yourself?
Think back to the last time you talked about yourself to somebody.
Write down anything negative and self-blaming you can remember on the left-hand side of the paper.
Now try to remember how you usually think about yourself and your problems.
What do you say to yourself about yourself? Just think about some of the statements described at the beginning of this section, and see if they feel familiar.
Again, write down any negative and self-blaming statements that you can identify on the left-hand side of your paper.

Now look at the left-hand side of your sheet of paper. One by one, go through all the negative, self-blaming things that you say to yourself and to others about yourself. And change each statement a little bit so that it becomes more positive. For example, 'I am just completely hopeless' could turn into 'I am hopeless some of the time, but sometimes I am quite competent'; or 'These symptoms I have mean that I am totally incapable of leading a normal life' could turn into 'These symptoms are a nuisance, but I am now doing something about them'. Write down these slightly more positive statements on the right-hand side of your sheet of paper opposite the negative ones. Write down slightly more positive statements even if you don't quite believe in them. Doing this regularly will gradually help you to retrain your thinking, and to develop a more constructive attitude towards yourself.

This exercise involves a 'two column' technique, and is used in one way or another in most forms of cognitive therapy. The important elements are: the

54

verbalisation and externalisation of normally internal and often semi-conscious self-evaluations, and the rational dealing with those usually irrational self-evaluations through trying to find modified and more balanced alternatives. It is then hoped that these alternatives are gradually internalised as new 'mind-sets'. In cognitive therapy situations, questions like 'How convinced are you of the way you are seeing this? Can you imagine that someone else would interpret this situation differently?' aim at facilitating this process.

3.5 Exercise: Affirmations

The work with 'affirmations' is not strictly based on cognitive therapy theory, but their usefulness can easily be seen in cognitive therapy terms. Affirmations aim at changing attitudes by verbalising the ideal as if it were present reality. They can be a very powerful tool if used correctly, because they aim to directly change core beliefs. The work with 'affirmations' is based on the theory that they put out an energy that can create or manifest their content. A cognitive therapy explanation would see them as a means of changing someone's attitude towards themselves. The following exercise aims at you finding an affirmation for yourself.

Sit down with your body and mind relaxed and close your eyes. Imagine yourself operating in the world at that moment: at work, at home, with colleagues, friends and family. Then ask yourself: What core beliefs about myself are operating in my life? Make a written list of the core beliefs that you can identify.

Look at the list of core beliefs and identify the most powerful negative one. It may be beliefs like 'I cannot make decisions', 'No one can possibly like, love, or accept me', 'I don't trust myself'.

Now close your eyes again and reflect upon that one core belief.
Imagine that belief speaking to you. What energy do you feel coming from it?
What is the voice like that is expressing the belief?
What feelings and physical sensations does the belief create in you?
Are there any images or symbols that are connected with it?

Now imagine a voice from deep inside you talking back.
Connect with the qualities of clarity and strength and with your breathing. And formulate the words that could talk back at the belief.

What would that other voice say? Allow that other voice to express the opposite of the core belief.
What energy do you feel coming from that voice?
What feelings and physical sensations does this create in you?

Are there any images or symbols connected with it?

Make notes about your experience with the two voices, and then write your affirmation. Observe the following rules:

1 Use the present tense – 'I am . . .' rather than 'I will/could be . . .'.
2 Be positive; state the attitude you wish to create as if it were already achieved.
3 Be personal, use 'I' or 'me'.
4 The affirmation should establish the image of something already achieved, 'I am . . .' rather than 'I will be . . .'.
5 Use action statements, 'I do . . .' rather than 'I can . . .' or 'I have the ability . . .'.
6 Include your name in the affirmation.

Work with your affirmation every day. The best times are just before going to sleep and before you start the day. Write the affirmation on cards and pieces of paper and put them somewhere where you will 'run into' them during the day, e.g. in your wallet, in the car. Visualise the end result as you say, write or read your affirmation. The affirmation will bring up negative emotions. Just acknowledge the emotions without getting pulled into them. Continue working with the affirmation until it has become integrated in your consciousness. You will know that this has happened when your mind responds positively and when you begin to experience the intended results.

Cognitive and behavioural therapies are mainly dealing with thinking and doing, with the relationships of rational human beings and their relatively predictable environments. Well, that's it then, isn't it? Looks like a good enough model, nice chart, makes sense. Have we got it sussed? The answer, as it is so many times, has to be YES and NO. Critics of the cognitive-behavioural model say that it doesn't include emotions, the unconscious, spirituality, the transpersonal (and perhaps the weather forecast?). Behaviourists respond and say, 'But we are scientific, we concentrate on observable behaviours, testing hypotheses, while you are only speculating about things that cannot be scientifically investigated'. The 'tit-for-tat', the 'I'm right, you're wrong' is in full flow: Behaviourism is too superficial; psychoanalysis is too wishy-washy; humanistic therapies are too lovey-dovey; psychosynthesis is too mystical.

But maybe there is no ONE right approach. Maybe different approaches look at different bits of reality. And even though thinking and doing are the intervention points for cognitive and behaviour therapy, this does not mean that they do not indirectly have an effect on emotions, the unconscious, the sense of higher purpose. Earlier on I used the term 'backbone' for the attitudes and cognitions in Figure 3.2 on p. 43 (C). When we look up at the

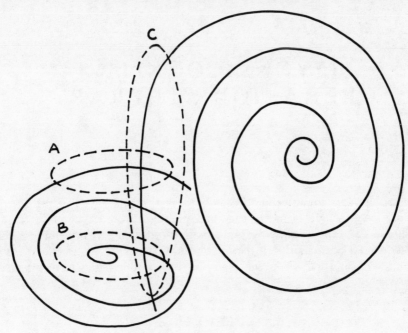

Figure 3.3 Circles and spirals.

sky we can see the Milky Way as 'the backbone of the night', but we know that what we are seeing is part of the spiral of our galaxy. We also know that our (Earth's) position in that galaxy determines what we see. Even our sense that we are looking *up* at the sky is only determined by Earth's gravity – on a larger scale we are just looking *out*. Let us then assume that the vicious circles and the connections within and between them are only parts of larger realities. If we take up that position, what we see might look something like Figure 3.3.

4

BEYOND COGNITIVE-
BEHAVIOUR THERAPY

In recent years cognitive and behavioural researchers have expanded their models to include elements that had previously been ignored, like the emotions and the unconscious. Information-processing theory and research has focused particularly on the relationship between cognitions and emotions. I should like to present some of these models that have practical relevance.

ACCEPTANCE

This is the way in which I see the wider context of behavioural and cognitive approaches to therapy (see Figure 4.1). The concept of acceptance, helping our clients to accept where they are at the moment, carries the cognitive-behavioural model into the realms of the emotions and the unconscious. The process of acceptance is the bridge between rational cognitive and behavioural therapy and a deeper form of guiding our patients to discover their inner world. This relates very much to what Ken Wilber writes about 'acceptance' of the symptom (see pp. 19–20).

Cognitive and behavioural methods (1) usually aim at change, achieving control over unpleasant sensations and situations, and at helping clients to restructure their lives (2). These are the traditionally masculine qualities and skills on which most of our industrialised society is based. The 'official' aims of such therapy seem to reinforce and strengthen the boundaries that we have created in our consciousness between good and bad, happy and unhappy, anxious and calm. At this level it is not so different from the 'quick fix', the 'happy pills', the systems (e.g. medical) and industries that are based on the illusion that happiness and calmness can exist without their so-called opposites. Fortunately, cognitive and behavioural methods have a 'side-effect' as well (unfortunately, traditional behaviourists would pay little attention to this as yet). They interrupt the vicious circles of avoidance (fear of fear) and medicalisation and thus enable people to face their fear. This usually leads to more awareness and to some degree of acceptance of the fear. It requires courage and fearlessness to face the fear; and where there

58

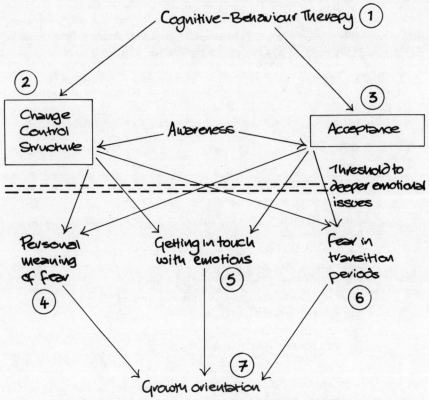

Figure 4.1 Cognitive-behaviour therapy and acceptance.

was only panic and fear of fear, both fear and fearlessness can develop. It is as if through facing the fear, becoming more aware of it, and accepting it more, an original condition (boundary) has been re-created (see Figure 4.2).

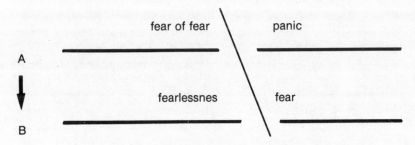

Figure 4.2 Cognitive-behaviour therapy and boundaries.

Condition A: The vicious circles have created a 'higher level', artificial contrast (boundary) between 'fear of fear' and actual panic. Fear can

59

dominate a person's life to such an extent that even when (s)he does not have a panic attack, there is still the fear of having one soon (anticipatory anxiety). Real fearlessness happens only 'by accident' and is hardly noticed, because it is always overshadowed by the fear of fear.

Condition B: Cognitive and behavioural methods can help restore a more original condition where fear and fearlessness live side by side. This condition will still have an artificial boundary by assuming that there can be one without the other, and thus create 'setbacks' to condition A.

Fear

Listen to your fear with a wise ear.
What are you afraid of in life?
What are you afraid of in yourself?
You must challenge fear and ask it what it means to
say.
As you go into the fear, with eyes open, heart open,
and courage flowing freely,
you will see that fear is only an empty room.
Fear is only as strong as your avoidance of it.
The greater your reluctance to see the fear,
to accept it and embrace it,
the more power you allow it.

(Emmanuel 1987: 109)

Let us now return to Figure 4.1. The above quote indicates how far cognitive and behavioural therapies can go and how limited they are. However, both achieving control and accepting can lead on to accepting the fact that there are growth opportunities in adversity, that there is strength in the acceptance of weakness, and out of that can develop a willingness to learn from conflict and contradiction (7). Cognitive and behavioural therapies (CBT) can lead to the point of such awareness, but in order to go further into it psychotherapeutically, different models are needed. It needs to be emphasised that the client may not want to go into it any further and is quite happy with having achieved some level of control and acceptance. Yes, the client may be avoiding something, or may be setting the scene for a relapse, but it is nevertheless the client's choice at that point in time which needs to be respected. The 'deepening' or 'growth' process will happen in its own time and, as therapists, we need to trust our judgement and intuition to decide whether we actively encourage it or not. After all, we are only using models in order to communicate, understand, connect, and our client may be using a different model at the time.

Figure 4.1 mentions the following models that can be used beyond CBT in order to go deeper into the issues that may have been opened up would cover the following areas:

(4) **The personal meaning of fear**. After accepting and facing the fear, you may explore with the client: How has it served you? What did you need to protect? How has it made you strong?

(5) **Getting in touch with emotions**. Explore emotions other than fear by using fear as a 'link': What is your fear of joy, excitement? How have you learnt to suppress, deal with your sensitivity/vulnerability?

(6) **Fear in transition periods**. This relates to the specific fears that emerge in transitions between childhood and adolescence, adolescence and early adulthood, mid-life and old age. Often the fears in these transition periods have a very specific flavour. For example, the task in early adulthood is to become independent, to gradually move away from home and to face the world. This needs guidance and preparation. On the other hand, the 'mid-life crisis' is much more a 'crisis of meaning', which often requires the reorientation of attitudes, goals, and activities, while at the same time past attitudes, goals and activities need to be accepted and the learning that they have provided needs to be acknowledged.

Emotional Synthesis

In recent years there have been developments in CBT which are trying to introduce some notion of the 'unconscious' into the therapeutic models. One of those models was Greenberg and Safran's (1984) 'emotional synthesis'. Based on information processing theory, they tried to integrate affect and cognition in order to develop an overall framework of therapeutic change.

Greenberg and Safran say that an emotional experience is the product of a particular type of information-processing activity which takes place at an automatic, pre-attentive level. They emphasise that even though it may be useful to distinguish between emotions, cognitions, physiology and action, in reality all these systems are fused. This statement in itself is very important. In therapy we often try to get people to 'get in touch with their emotions', to 'be less in the head', to 'feel rather than think'. Although this method may be appropriate at times, we need to be aware that by practising it we are creating a boundary between feeling and thinking. Would it not be more appropriate to ask: 'What are you experiencing at the moment?'

I am thinking in particular of men in therapy groups. I am thinking how often I see these men in their suits and ties, expressing the rational and logical approach that they are so used to in their business world, being asked by therapists: 'But where are your feelings?' Fair enough, they are usually disconnected from their emotions and that's why they are getting panic attacks. But does that really entitle anyone to negate their experience, however 'heady' it may be? In my men's group we seem to be able to handle it differently. We can just talk in our 'heady' ways, and after a while we know that the emotions are there anyway. We know that, even when we cannot put words to them as well as our female 'partners', it is the whole experience that counts, and that includes thoughts, feelings, behaviour. I think that the exclusive focus on 'feelings' can lead to a certain reductionism.

So Greenberg and Safran are trying to put an end to this. They say that it is the *synthesis* between thoughts, emotions, actions and events that makes the total experience. Rather than strengthening the boundaries between, for example, feelings and thoughts by valuing one more than the other, can we look at the whole thing and ask what the blocks (boundaries) are that create disharmony and discrepancy?

Figure 4.3 shows the 'emotional synthesis' model, and as you can see it is basically an extended 'stimulus–response' model.

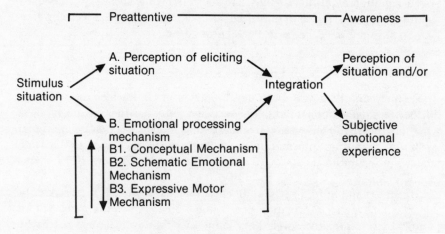

Figure 4.3 Emotional synthesis.

Greenberg and Safran say that particular stimulus situations trigger off (A) the perception of the eliciting situation, and, at the same time (B), an emotional processing mechanism. Even though I do not particularly like the term 'mechanism' here, I am very impressed with the way the authors define this mechanism. They see it as consisting of three parts, which are as follows:

B1. A conceptual system that has rules and beliefs about emotional experiences in general. This is a higher level system which contains abstractions from concrete experience but not 'feeling memories' themselves. It is a repository of memories and operations about feelings and the situational antecedents and consequences of feelings. It analyses concrete experience by drawing causal attributions, directing attention to specific experiences in memory, and by anticipating the future.

B2. This system contains emotion memories. It functions at an automatic level. These memories set up expectations as to what will occur in the emotional realm, they direct attention to specific features in the perceptual field, they activate or amplify perceptual-motor inputs, and they integrate information generated at the expressive motor level. These memories can also, as well as external stimuli, generate expressive motor responses.

B3. This system contains automatic motoric action tendencies, like facial expressions, body postures, etc. It is an in-wired system which is independent of learning. It is responsible for the experiential quality of emotion and for the distinctiveness of the experience of different feeling states.

The three systems are assumed to be hierarchical, and every level acts to synthesise the information derived from the level of processing directly below (upward arrow). In addition, changes at each level can activate changes at the level below (downward arrow). The whole process takes place pre-attentively and only the synthesised emotion comes into awareness.

Here is an example. Someone is being criticised and feels threatened. The facial/physiological perceptual motor responses (B3) trigger affectively laden emotion memories, which begin to direct attention (B2), and implicit rules about being hurt or criticised are activated and begin to govern the expression or inhibition of emotion (B1). At the same time the downward movement takes place: implicit meanings of the experience (B1) activate emotional schemata (B2) which direct attention and perceptual search activities, which then evoke expressive motor responses (B3). The synthesised emotion could then be: feeling threatened, slight perspiration, paralysis of attention, desperately trying to stay focused on what is happening in the stimulus situation.

The model has important implications for therapy. It could, for example, explain why cognitive therapy, which intervenes mainly at the B1 level, could modify the whole emotional experience. Failure to do so would probably mean that the influences from the lower levels are so strong that changes at the conceptual level are not sufficient. The same would be true for other therapeutic approaches, which mainly address one or the other mechanisms. An example of CBT also trying to address the B2 level was given earlier when we discussed the 'hidden triggers' (see pp. 47–8).

The following meditation tries to incorporate all the elements of the model, and it can lead to quite powerful experiences. It is best to speak the meditation on tape, leaving about twenty-second pauses between each paragraph.

4.1 Meditation: Feelings

Sit down comfortably, and in your own time close your eyes. Allow your body to relax, let your breathing be calm, and just be within yourself.

Be aware of the sounds you hear, the smells you smell, and be aware of the sensations from your body as well. But do not become involved with any of this. Just let it happen and don't react.

And now consider the word *feelings*. What does the word mean to you?

Do you remember something when you think about feelings?

Does anything in your body change when you think about feelings?

And now consider one particular feeling that is important to you. It might not have a name, but you know what it feels like, and it is important to you.

Focus your attention on the situations in which this feeling has occurred. Maybe you want to remember the last occasion when you experienced it.

How does this feeling connect you with other experiences in the past? Are there any memories coming into your mind? If there are, just acknowledge them.

What are you experiencing from your body now? Become aware of any bodily sensations that may have changed since you started this exercise.

Become aware of the muscles in your face. Be aware of the position of your head, your shoulders, your arms and hands. Also, be aware of your breathing and any other sensations from your body.

And now reconsider the feeling. What do you think about this feeling now?

Does it differ from what you usually think about this particular feeling?

What have been your rules about this feeling and how could you change them if necessary?

Leave this particular feeling behind now.

Check your breathing, and again focus your attention on relaxing your body. In your own time open your eyes again.

Greenberg and Safran state that many clinical problems can be conceptualised as a breakdown in the integration of emotion and cognition, i.e. in the synthesis of the emotional experience.

> Separation of 'feeling' and 'thinking' is, in fact, often a sign of dysfunction, and an important goal in therapy can be to correct this dysfunction. . . . It is more meaningful to speak about what level of the process of emotional synthesis we intervene at, rather than which

system – cognitive, affective, or behavioural – becomes the focus of our intervention.

(Greenberg and Safran 1984: 571)

The 'emotional synthesis' model seems to eliminate a boundary that has been created in CBT, namely the boundary between thinking and feeling. It seems to be the case that the deeper we go into the psyche, the more we are facing boundaries and the need to deal with them. CBT deals with the boundaries between behaviour, thinking and physical sensations by building bridges between them, thus helping the client to realise the connections in his process of 'sense-making'.

I feel that the issue of boundaries has become central in psychotherapy and in society. Boundaries define our relationships with parts of ourselves, with things and living beings, with other people, with groups, and between groups and nations. In psychotherapy, for example, subpersonality work is about the boundaries as battle lines between subpersonalities; in the therapeutic relationship the boundaries between therapist and client are used as a tool to help the client work on his own inner boundaries; all the therapeutic models that were presented earlier can be seen as aiming at making connections between parts, issues that have seemed disconnected; the word 'synthesis' as in 'psychosynthesis' means 'putting together'. The breaking of the Berlin Wall and the resulting problems with German unification is a boundary issue, as are the collapse of the Soviet Union, the disintegration of Yugoslavia, the problems in the EC. Boundaries limit us, protect us, and they define our relationships. We seem to have entered a world-wide process of rearranging our relationships. The 'old' boundaries do not seem to work so well any more; even the one between capitalism and socialism is rapidly changing.

I do believe that the diverse field of psychotherapy and psychotherapists has a lot to offer to all levels of boundary issues, be they intra- or interpsychic, political or economical, because it seems that the principles that operate at all the different levels of the erection or destruction of human boundaries are very similar. The problem is that most psychotherapists do not see themselves as political missionaries, but are quite happy to limit their activities to their consulting rooms. I feel that this narrow-mindedness is becoming outdated because our patients increasingly reflect wider problems in their individual and partnership struggles. The 'heating up' in the 'greenhouse' seems to be bringing everything closer together, thus amplifying our need for separateness. I feel that psychotherapists need to appreciate the boundary issues beyond the ones in the consulting room, so that we can really hear what our patients are saying to us, and because we have such a lot to say about all those relationship issues around us. Hence, my writing tries to be about boundaries by building bridges between different therapy approaches, by including economic and political theory, by including my personal journey in general and in writing this book, and hopefully by stimulating integration and a wider context for psychotherapy.

I referred earlier to Ken Wilber's model of boundaries. I should now like to discuss the issue of boundaries in detail.

5

BOUNDARIES

In his book *No Boundary* Ken Wilber develops a model of the different levels of consciousness and then slots all the main approaches to personal growth into the level of consciousness and the level of boundaries that they are dealing with. He says that right from the very beginning, human beings have named and categorised things.

> Adam was the first to delineate nature, to mentally divide it up, mark it off, diagram it. Adam was the first great mapmaker. Adam drew boundaries. So successful was his mapping of nature that, to this day our lives are largely spent in drawing boundaries. Every decision we make, our every action, our every word is based on the construction, conscious or unconscious, of boundaries. I am not now referring to just a self-identity boundary – important as that certainly is – but to all boundaries in the broadest sense. . . . The peculiar thing about a boundary is that, however complex and rarefied it may be, it actually marks off nothing but an inside vs. an outside. For example we can draw the very simplest form of a boundary line as a circle, and see that it discloses an inside versus an outside. But notice that the opposites of inside vs. outside didn't exist in themselves until we drew the boundary of the circle. . . . In short, to draw boundaries is to manufacture opposites. Thus we can start to see that the reason we live in a world of opposites is precisely because life as we know it is a process of drawing boundaries.
>
> (Wilber 1979: 17–18)

Wilber's insights are brilliant. But is he not missing one important point, a point that is exposed in the above quote? He seems to exclude from his considerations the 'self-identity boundary'. But isn't this where the need to draw boundaries originates? Is it not the recognition of each individual human being that there is 'I' and 'other' that presents the first boundary?

OBJECT RELATIONS THEORY AND BOUNDARIES

Psychoanalytic 'object relations theory' deals with the issues and psychological problems that can arise in the process of a human infant separating and individuating from mother which ultimately is the process of setting boundaries between 'self' and 'other'. The various forms of intrapsychic 'splittings' that can take place in the process are ultimately seen as the conditions that can lead to narcissistic and borderline personality disorders. Without going into the complexities of the theory, it is easy to comprehend that this first separation process sets the scene for all future ones. The disorders of the self are then seen as 'the failure to develop a stable, cohesive, separate, and individuated self' (Klein 1989: 31). Typical splitting attitudes would be: I am good, you are bad; I am bad, you are good. These patterns are seen as a result of the infant's 'separation-individuation process' having been arrested, usually between the ages of one and three. As a result, borderline and narcissistic personality disorders develop.

Masterson (1989) has developed a theoretical and treatment model that combines object relations theory, Mahler's separation-individuation model, and Kohut's self-psychology into a 'psychotherapy of the disorders of the self'. According to this model, in the borderline personality self and object (the internal representation of mother) are both split between 'good' and 'bad', and 'object constancy' is not developed. Object constancy refers to the ability of the child to 'hold' in his psyche a constant picture of mother in her conflicting aspects, which were up to then experienced as separate ones: good and bad, love and hate, present and absent. In the narcissistic personality the developmental arrest is also assumed to happen during the individuation-separation phase, and 'the failures in the self in achieving mature separation with the associated difficulties in sharing, empathy, and acknowledging the thoughts, feelings, and needs of others are most manifest; the failures in the self as individuated (self-activating and self-assertive) are often concealed and latent and become manifest only during periods of acute narcissistic disappointment or trauma or later in life when narcissistic supply lines and defenses dry up, wither, and fail' (Klein 1989: 35). As a result of these impairments a 'false defensive self' is assumed to develop,

> which relates to the real world through a pathological alliance with a maladaptive ego structure. The patient experiences this as a sense of discontinuity, fragility, or unstable self-identity; as distortions in the normal balance of investment in self and others; and as gross distortions between fantasies of what one contains and what people are like with the reality of what one contains and what people are really like.
>
> (Klein 1989: 34)

All these impairments are seen as a consequence of the underlying 'abandonment depression' against which the patient must defend.

Essentially, the model describes people's confused boundaries; people who, as a result of those confused boundaries cannot come into relationship with themselves or with others; they see themselves in others and others in themselves; they love others when they want to love themselves; they hate themselves when they want to hate their parents.

Therapy then aims at addressing and strengthening the patient's 'real self' through a range of therapeutic means. The most skilful therapeutic method is the 'art of confrontation' with the borderline patient. What is confronted in an empathic, introspective, and creative way is the borderline patient's (false self's) sole aim in therapy, which is primarily to 'feel better' at all cost. In order to achieve this, the patient either tries to turn the therapist into a 'primary caretaker', or into someone on to whom he/she can project his/her painful feelings. The therapist is made either 'all good' or 'all bad'. These strategies of the patient's false self are confronted in order to continuously address and strengthen the glimpses of 'real self' that might be there. This often leads to the patient having to face the underlying abandonment depression, which is the point in therapy when proper individuation and separation can take place, thus leading to the patient developing a mature and fused self.

As complex as the theory may look, I think in practice all therapists have been facing patients' projections, their 'acting out' behaviours, and have struggled to keep up some boundaries to contain the chaos. The assumption that there is a 'real self' somewhere which is being served by our struggles is not only a nice motivator, but this 'real self' actually becomes visible in the therapy room. The frustration in this phase of therapy is when I, as the therapist, can see the glimpses of 'real self' in the patient, but the patient cannot. Usually there is no point in just telling the patient what I see, because the 'false self' will fiercely defend against any such insights, as they entail the danger of having to face the abandonment depression.

The Masterson approach, based on object relations theory, deals with the psychological disorders that can be caused as a result of a wrong and defensive setting of the very first boundaries between self and others, and between good and bad. This development is fuelled by the fear of annihilation, the abandonment depression. The therapeutic relationship becomes the main healing factor in therapy and serves as a microcosm where the old boundaries are destroyed and more appropriate internal and external ones are built. In order to withstand the bombardment of projections, transference and counter-transference, the therapist himself needs to set clear boundaries for the therapeutic encounter.

How does this then fit with Ken Wilber's model of 'no boundary'? How can we invest a lot of time and energy into helping people to establish 'proper' boundaries if boundaries are ultimately a human-made illusion, and the oneness of all is the ultimate reality?

As with all models, the object relations approach covers one aspect of reality. We need a different model that includes both the setting and the elimination of boundaries. Otherwise the 'setting of boundaries', based on the object relations approach, can turn into the excessive and punitive 'boundary making' that is so prevalent in many of our traditional 'therapeutic' settings, and beyond that in the hierarchies and separations in our society and on our planet. On the other hand, the exclusive 'no boundary' approach can lead to a premature aim at symbiotic union, which may then be no more than a projection serving to defend against the abandonment depression, thus strengthening borderline and narcissistic pathologies.

BASIC PERINATAL MATRICES AND BOUNDARIES

Grof's (1979, 1992) model of 'basic perinatal matrices' (BPMs) has become one of the basic models in psychotherapy training and practice at the Institute of Psychosynthesis in London, and I think that it can help us to solve the boundary problem.

The BPMs define four different stages of the birth process. In his research, Grof found that these four stages recur as themes and key issues throughout people's lives. He sees these stages as setting up COEX (constellations of condensed experience) systems in people's unconscious, which act as dynamic governing systems that have a function at a specific level of the unconscious.

> Each COEX has a theme that characterizes it. For example, a single COEX constellation can contain all major memories of events that were humiliating, degrading, or shameful. The common denominator of another COEX might be the terror of experiences that involved claustrophobia, suffocation, and feelings associated with oppressing and confining circumstances. Rejection and emotional deprivation leading to our distrust of other people is another very common COEX motif. . . . Each COEX constellation seems to be superimposed over and anchored into a very particular aspect of the birth experience. . . . In addition to these perinatal components, typical COEX systems can have even deeper roots. They can reach farther into prenatal life and into the realm of transpersonal phenomena such as past life experiences, archetypes of the 'collective unconscious', and identification with other life forms and universal processes. My research experience with COEX systems has convinced me that they serve to organize not only the individual unconscious, as I originally believed, but the entire human psyche itself. . . .
>
> There is a constant interplay between the COEX systems of our

inner world and events in the external world. External events can activate corresponding COEX systems within us. Conversely, COEX systems help shape our perceptions of the world, and through these perceptions we act in ways that bring about situations in the external world that echo patterns in our COEX systems. Put another way, our inner perceptions can function like complex scripts through which we re-create core themes of our own COEX systems in the external world.

(Grof 1992: 24–26)

On the basis of his research with altered states of consciousness, Grof has defined the specific biological, psychological, archetypal and spiritual aspects of each of the four BPMs as a basis for identifying different COEX systems.

Perinatal phenomena occur in four distinct experiential patterns, which I call the Basic Perinatal Matrices (BPMs). Each of these four matrices is closely related to one of the four consecutive periods of biological delivery. At each of these stages, the baby undergoes experiences that are characterized by specific emotions and physical feelings; each of these stages also seems to be associated with specific symbolic images. These come to represent highly individualized psychospiritual blueprints that guide the way we experience our lives. They may be reflected in individual and social psychpathology, or in religion, art, philosophy, politics, and other areas of life. And, of course, we gain access to these psychospiritual blueprints through non-ordinary states of consciousness, which allow us to see the guiding forces of our lives much more clearly.

The first matrix, BPM I, which can be called the 'Amniotic Universe', refers to our experiences in the womb prior to the onset of delivery. The second matrix, BPM II, or 'Cosmic Engulfment and No Exit', pertains to our experiences when contractions begin but before the cervix opens. The third matrix, BPM III, the 'Death and Rebirth Struggle', reflects our experiences as we move through the birth canal. The fourth and final matrix, BPM IV, which we can refer to as 'Death and Rebirth', is related to our experiences when we actually leave the mother's body. Each perinatal matrix has its specific biological, psychological, archetypal, and spiritual aspects.

(Grof 1992: 29–30)

Understandably, Grof's way of connecting birth, biological, and spiritual elements in his model has made it attractive to psychosynthesis. Within psychosynthesis the model has been applied to key psychosynthesis concepts like 'subpersonalities', the qualities of 'Will' (= becoming) and 'love' (= being), and 'mind-sets'. I shall ponder the model here in its relevance to the question of boundaries. Obviously, the process of birth is the one in

71

which the newborn child is for the very first time faced with the need to establish its separateness from mother, i.e. its boundaries as an individual. This process of individuation and separation then continues over the years of growing up. In psychosynthesis the birth pattern summarised in the BPMs is seen as the 'archetypal journey of the "I" or "Will" through matter symbolised as the womb. (Also) the anchoring of the egg in the lining of the womb can be seen as the anchoring of spirit in matter' (IPLTM 1989: 10).

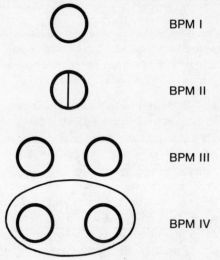

BPM I

BPM II

BPM III

BPM IV

Figure 5.1 Basic perinatal matrices.
Source: IPLTM 1989: 9

Figure 5.1 shows a symbolic representation of the four BPM stages. It also shows that the model is one of differentiation and separation (BPM I to BPM III), finally leading to a new stage of unity (BPM IV). The following COEX-elements are contained in the different BPMs (summarised from Grof and Institute of Psychosynthesis training materials).

BPM I: Selfishness

Primal union with the mother, intrauterine experience before the onset of delivery; experience of symbiotic union and 'oceanic oneness', timelessness, in touch with infinity; the 'good womb' experience; disturbances: 'bad womb' experiences, diseases and emotional upheavals of the mother, twin situations, attempted abortions.

In terms of other psychosynthesis concepts, the following characteristics of this matrix would apply:

1 Subpersonality identification: mystic subpersonality.
2 Regression ('No' to life): selfishness, conflict avoidance, authority issues.
3 Progression ('Yes' to life): surrender of separateness.

4 The Will (becoming): no Will – impotence.
5 Love (being): all is being, all is one.

BPM II: Dependence

Antagonism with the mother, contractions in a closed uterine system, spiritual experience of 'no exit' or 'hell', hopelessness, no escape, pain of separation, mistrust, loneliness; unbearable physical, psychological and metaphysical suffering that will never end.

In terms of other psychosynthesis concepts, the following characteristics of this matrix would apply:

1 Subpersonality identification: martyr subpersonality, victim subpersonality.
2 Regression: desire for unity, doubt in relation to worth, inclusion issues.
3 Progression: desire for individuality.
4 The Will: I have no choice, the environment is causal.
5 Love: acceptance of pain and separation, acceptance of dependence.

BPM III: Independence

Synergism with the mother, propulsion through the birth canal; light at the end of the tunnel; suffering and tension are intensified far beyond the level which is considered humanly possible – when it reaches the absolute experiential limit, the experience changes into a wild, ecstatic rapture of cosmic proportions, 'volcanic ecstasy', involving aggressive and destructive elements.

In terms of other psychosynthesis concepts, the following characteristics of this matrix would apply:

1 Subpersonality identification: rebel subpersonality, crusader subpersonality.
2 Regression: attachment to independence, blame and revenge, assertion issues.
3 Progression: co-operation.
4 The Will: experience of choice and ability to assert control.
5 Love: forgiveness and compassion.

BPM IV: Interdependence

Separation from the mother, termination of the symbiotic union and formation of a new type of relationship; death–rebirth experience; termination and resolution of the death–rebirth struggle, ego–death; similarity with BPM I, i.e. biological birth and spiritual rebirth; experience of cosmic unity.

In terms of other psychosynthesis concepts, the following characteristics of this matrix would apply:

1 Subpersonality identification: none.
2 Regression: attachment to experience.

3 Progression: selflessness, brotherhood, unconditional love.
4 The Will: atonement.
5 Love: redemption.

Obviously, from the point of view of boundaries, BPM IV is the most interesting phase because it implies the final separation from the mother. Grof calls it the 'death and rebirth experience':

> BPM IV also has a distinct symbolic and spiritual dimension. Psychologically, the reliving of the moment of birth takes the form of a death-rebirth experience. The suffering and agony faced in BPM II and BPM III now culminate with 'ego death', and an experience of total annihilation on all levels – physical, emotional, intellectual, and spiritual.
>
> (Grof 1992: 73)

But at the same time, the

> ego that dies in the fourth matrix is identified with a compulsion to be always strong and in control and to be constantly prepared for all possible dangers, even those we could never foresee and those that are purely imaginary. . . . The elimination of the false ego thus helps us to develop a more realistic image of the world and to build strategies of approaching it that are more appropriate and rewarding.
>
> (1992: 74)

According to Grof, this 'hitting rock bottom' experience can then lead on to higher spiritual realms.

> The experience of BPM IV can be accompanied by feelings of merging with the rest of the world, thus resembling the experience of unity that we discussed in the context of BPM I. . . . As we feel united with everything that is, the appreciation for natural beauty and simple, uncomplicated life takes precedence over most other concerns.
>
> (1992: 76)

Grof goes on to describe the transpersonal potential in the BPM IV matrix:

> Higher motivating forces, such as the pursuit of justice, the appreciation for harmony and beauty and the desire to create it, a new tolerance and respect for others, as well as feelings of love, become increasingly important in our lives. What is more, we perceive these as direct, natural, and logical expressions of our true nature and of the universal order.
>
> (1992: 77)

So, here we have a metaphor for the way in which separation and annihilation can lead to a new stage of interdependence and oneness. It sounds somewhat similar to the way in which, in 'personality disorders', the abandonment depression needs to be faced and worked through before the 'real self' can emerge. In terms of boundaries it means that the total establishment of boundaries is necessary before all boundaries can be eliminated.

I am now beginning to wonder how you, the reader, are coping with all those rather complicated models that I have tried to present. If you are a therapist, you may have found bits that relate to your experience with clients. If you are not a therapist, you may still be finding bits that you can relate to. However, the boundary issue is an important one, and please bear with me for a bit longer.

The BPM model, as a COEX, is assumed also to apply to other processes of human development, i.e. childhood (BPM I), adolescence (BPM II), adulthood (BPM III), mid-life crisis (BPM IV). We may even be able to see the development of humanity through the eyes of this model. It seems that humanity has reached BPM III, and is now facing the painful and exciting journey into BPM IV.

The object relations model of boundaries seems to address issues that arise in the development from BPM I to BPM III. The borderline personality disorder could be said to represent stuck-ness between BPM II and BPM III. The separation process never moves on to BPM IV, but oscillates between dependence and independence, antagonism and synergism, victim and rebel, self-doubt and blame. The narcissistic personality disorder represents a similar arrest, but it includes the energies of BPM I in its manifestation. We might even say that here BPM I and BPM IV get confused, and the turbulences of II and III are avoided by retreating back into BPM I, back into the positive womb. Nowadays we find a lot of 'mystics' who seem to have reached BPM IV, but are actually retreating back to BPM I.

In both, the borderline and the narcissistic patterns, it is the terror of the abandonment depression that leads to the failure of the development of appropriate boundaries, and thus to the failure of achieving the synthesis state of BPM IV, where the boundaries can be dissolved within a higher context.

The 'ego death' sounds very similar to what I see in clients when they let go of their defences and face the underlying abandonment depression. But it needs to be faced in order to get through to the light. Beforehand, sufficiently strong boundaries, or ego-strength, need to be established (BPM III) in order to utilise the 'progressive' and 'will' qualities in this matrix, which are 'co-operation' and 'the experience of choice and the ability to exert control'. Then the 'rebel subpersonality' can, through the qualities of 'forgiveness and compassion' be transformed into the 'transcendent mystic subpersonality'. I think that a positive BPM III identification would be 'the

75

warrior'. Only then can we face letting go of the ego in the death-rebirth struggle, which ultimately leads to Ken Wilber's 'no boundary' state.

The implications and questions for therapy are enormous. Psychoanalytic approaches probably guide people out of the stuck-ness of the first three BPMs by helping the establishment of proper boundaries, thus leading to independence. However, they are unlikely to facilitate the further step into BPM IV, which is the step towards interdependence, towards the elimination of boundaries. The political events around us can be seen in similar terms. For example, German unification has involved the sudden elimination of boundaries, not in order to move towards BPM IV-interdependence, but rather to move back to some kind of 'primal union' (BPM I). The step in the other direction would have involved the letting go of the 'ego' (the two Germanys) and facing the underlying 'abandonment depression', in this case the still unresolved and repressed reasons that have led to the division in the first place.

NO BOUNDARY

We can now return to Ken Wilber's 'no boundary' model. The BPM model shows that the move towards no boundaries has to go through the stages of individuation and separation with the establishment of proper boundaries. Both object relations and BPM models show how we can get stuck in this development, and how an illusionary move towards no boundaries can be nothing more than a regressive move back into the 'positive womb'. In order to get to interdependence, to partnership with ourselves, and between ourselves and others and our environment, we need to go through the 'mined field'; we need to go through the fears and the separations, the depressions and the loneliness.

Bearing in mind that Ken Wilber writes about moving towards BPM IV, we can now appreciate his passionate pleas for the elimination of the boundaries that we have created in our consciousness. The following quote seems to describe the development of rigid boundaries, characteristic of BPM III:

> The simple fact is that we live in a world of conflict and opposites because we live in a world of boundaries. Since every boundary line is also a battle line, here is the human predicament: the firmer one's boundaries, the more entrenched are one's battles. The more I hold on to pleasure, the more I necessarily fear pain. The more I pursue goodness, the more I am obsessed with evil. The more I seek success, the more I must dread failure. The harder I cling to life, the more terrifying death becomes. The more I value anything, the more obsessed I become with its loss. Most of our problems, in other words, are problems of boundaries and the opposites they create.

Now our habitual way of trying to solve these problems is to attempt to eradicate one of the opposites. We handle the problem of good vs. evil by trying to exterminate evil. We handle the problem of life vs. death by trying to hide death under symbolic immortalities. In philosophy we handle conceptual opposites by dismissing one of the poles or trying to reduce it to the other. The materialist tries to reduce mind to matter, while the idealist tries to reduce matter to mind. The monists try to reduce plurality to unity, the pluralists try to explain unity as plurality.

(Wilber 1979: 19–20)

It seems that the striving for unity is a deep craving that we have. But we have struggled so hard to establish our ego boundaries (BPM I to BPM III) that we have come to regard all boundaries as real, and unification is only imaginable as the elimination of one side in favour of the other. Rather than fighting for the elimination of boundaries, we fight for the elimination of the other side. It is a 'winning over' rather than a 'winning with'. The boundary is experienced as a battle line rather than a meeting point, because we had to battle so hard to establish our own first boundaries. As a result, the 'winning over' strategy dominates our society.

This goal of separating the opposites and then clinging to or pursuing the positive halves seems to be a distinguishing characteristic of progressive Western civilisation – its religion, science, medicine, industry. Progress, after all, is simply progress toward the positive and away from the negative. Yet, despite the obvious comforts of medicine and agriculture, there is not the least bit of evidence to suggest that, after centuries of accentuating positives and trying to eliminate negatives, humanity is any happier, more content, or more at peace with itself. In fact, the available evidence suggests just the contrary: today is the 'age of anxiety', of 'future shock', of epidemic frustration and alienation, of boredom in the midst of wealth, and meaningless- ness in the midst of plenty.

It seems that 'progress' and unhappiness might well be flip sides of the same restless coin. For the very urge to 'progress' implies a discontent with the 'present' state of affairs, so that the more I seek progress the more acutely I feel discontent. In blindly pursuing progress, our civilisation has, in effect, institutionalised frustration. For in seeking to accentuate the positive and eliminate the negative, we have forgotten entirely that the positive is defined only in terms of the negative.

(Wilber 1979: 20–1)

Could it then really be that the survival struggle for boundaries in the birth process has shaped the scientific and philosophical approaches of our culture? The process does not seem to be inevitable, as Riane Eisler (1988) shows in her analysis of ancient 'partnership' societies. A different approach to boundaries is also evident in many Eastern and pagan religions. As we shall see later, our culture seems to have developed the boundary model to such an extent that it has created 'boundary realities' beyond the birth experience in language, politics, societal structures, production and consumption, economics, science, and philosophy. All those realities have their own separating dynamics and make up the world into which we are born. They form the context which we enter through our birth struggle. We enter a 'BPM III–world', full of rigid boundaries. Is it surprising then that we get stuck at the same level and thus contribute to the stuck-ness of our culture? It is this realisation of the connectedness between inner and outer conditions that leads us to understand that inner (psychological) and outer (societal) changes cannot be separated, and that work on one level requires work on the other as well. The danger of having yet another boundary, namely the one between 'inner' and 'outer', is a particular pitfall for psychotherapy.

However, Wilber also investigates the creation of boundaries at basic levels of our experience.

Rather when we speak of 'loss of self' we mean this: The sensation of being a separate self is a sensation that has been misunderstood and misinterpreted, and it is the dispelling of this misinterpretation that concerns us. We all have that sensation, that core feeling, of being an isolated self split from our stream of experience and split from the world around us. We all have the feeling of 'self' on the one hand and the feeling of the external world on the other. But if we carefully look at the sensation of 'self-in-here' and the sensation of 'world-out-there', we will find that these two are actually one and the same feeling. In other words, what I now feel to be the objective world out there is the same thing I feel to be the subjective self in here. The split between the experiencer and the world of experiences does not exist, and therefore cannot be found. . . .

Initially this sounds very strange, because we are so used to believing in boundaries. It seems so obvious that I am the hearer who hears sounds, that I am the feeler who feels feelings, that I am the seer who sees sights. But, on the other hand, isn't it odd that I should describe myself as the 'seer' who 'sees' the things 'seen'? Or the 'hearer' who 'hears' the sounds 'heard'? Is perception really that complicated? Does it really involve three separate entities – a seer, seeing, and the seen?

Surely, there aren't three separate entities here. Is there ever such a thing as a seer without seeing or without something seen? Is there ever seeing without a seer or without something seen? The fact is, the seer, seeing, and the seen are all aspects of one process – never at any time is one of them found without the others.

Our problem is that we have three words – the 'seer', 'sees', and the 'seen' – for one single activity, the experience of seeing. We might as well describe a single water stream as 'the streamer streams the streamed'. It is utterly redundant, and introduces three factors where there is in fact but one. Yet, hypnotized as we are by Adam's word magic, we assume there must be a separate entity, the seer, and that through some process called 'seeing', the seer gains knowledge of yet another thing called the 'seen'. We then naturally assume that we are just the seer which is totally divorced from the seen. Our world, which is only given once, is thereby split right down the middle, with the 'seer in here' confronting, across a gaping abyss, the things 'seen out there'.

(Wilber 1979: 48–9)

Sometimes we all experience our experience as a unity, without boundaries. This can be as a 'peak experience', as sexual orgasm, or when we need to be right here 'in the moment' with our whole being, like when we play tennis or squash, when we ride a bicycle up a strenuous hill, etc. It is at times when the artificial boundary between body and mind is overcome that the greater unity can be experienced. Ken Wilber calls this the 'centaur level' of boundaries, where it

seems, in fact, that 'I' am almost sitting on my body as if I were a horseman riding on a horse. I beat it or praise it, I feed and clean and nurse it when necessary. I urge it on without consulting it and I hold it back against its will. When my body-horse is well behaved I generally ignore it, but when it gets unruly – which is all too often – I pull out the whip to beat it back into reasonable submission.

(Wilber 1979: 106)

Wilber then explores the 'emotional blocks in the body'. I should like to present here the exercise he suggests to remove these blocks for two reasons:

1 Ken Wilber firstly states that 'the important question is not, "How can I stop or relax these blocks?" but rather, "How can I see that I am actively producing them?" ' (p.114). He then suggests that it is a case of actively and consciously attempting to increase the particular tension, because as 'you deliberately begin to contract the muscles involved, you tend to remember what it is you are contracting your muscles against' (p.116). This approach is quite different from traditional relaxation exercises, which teach you to get rid of the tension. However, I do wonder whether in the 'tense your muscles and then relax them' exercise the tensing might be more important than the relaxing. Wilber's approach could also throw some light on the emotional cathartic release that can occur during relaxation exercises.

2 Might this technique also be relevant for the other levels of boundaries? Is one way of 'breaking walls and building bridges' to first of all strengthen the wall so that we remember why we built it in the first place? I think this could be one way of doing it. It would be fascinating to fantasise about the breaking of the Berlin Wall in that way. What if the complete populations of East and West Germany had been asked, as an experiential exercise towards the breaking of the Wall, to first of all consciously work on strengthening the Wall from their respective sides. In groups with facilitators they would have had ample opportunity to share their feelings about the process and their fearful projections on to the other side. Perhaps the breaking of the Wall would then have been easier, a relief rather than a threat. But this is just a dream.

5.1 Exercise: Body Awareness

After locating a specific block – let's say a tenseness in the jaw, throat, and temples – you give it your full awareness, feeling out just where the tension is and what muscles seem to be involved.

Then, slowly but deliberately begin to increase that tension and pressure; in this case by tightening your throat muscles and clamping your teeth together.

While you are experimenting with increasing the muscular pressure, remind yourself that you are not just clamping muscles, you are actively trying to hold something in. You can even repeat to yourself (out loud if your jaws aren't involved), 'No! I won't! I'm resisting!' so that you truly feel that part of yourself that is doing the pinching, that is trying to in-hold some feeling.

Then you can slowly release the muscles – and at the same time open yourself totally to whatever feeling would like to surface.

In this case, it might be a desire to cry, or to bite, or to vomit, or to laugh, or to scream. Or it might only be a pleasurable glow where the block used to be.

To allow a genuine release of blocked emotions requires time, effort, openness, and some honest work. If you have a typically persistent block, daily workouts of fifteen minutes or so for upwards of a month will almost certainly be necessary for significant results. The block is released when feeling-attention can flow through that area in a full and perfectly unobstructed fashion on its way to infinity.

(Wilber 1979: 116)

I should like to share with you again something of my process of writing. I am writing these words during the final stages of the 'knitting' process, and I have been really worried about connecting this bit to the next bit. How can I lead over from 'boundaries' to 'activity theory'? Is there any connection between these parts? 'There must be, otherwise it would not have been written', says one voice. 'You are just fooling yourself', says the other. And then, suddenly, I come back to an inconsistency that has always bothered me about Ken Wilber's book, an inconsistency that I have never been able to put into words. But suddenly it is there, loud and clear. Ken Wilber presents a chart of his model of the different levels of consciousness, and of the boundary that is typical for each level (see Figure 5.2).

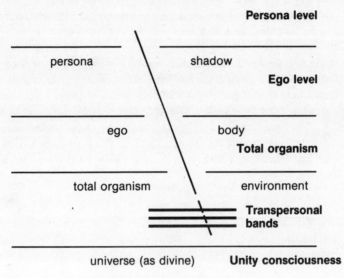

Figure 5.2 Levels of consciousness.
Source: Wilber 1979: 9

In his book Wilber discusses all the levels and the associated boundaries in great detail, apart from one. A discussion of the boundary between 'total organism' and 'environment' is missing. And here we have the connection with what is to follow in this book: activity theory and economic considerations leading to the 'psychological greenhouse model' are dealing with the relationship of the individual with his natural and human-made environment. I do not want to go as far as saying that Ken Wilber left it out so that I can write about it. I think it reflects a shortcoming in the psychotherapy field and in the growth movement in general. I hinted at this shortcoming earlier, and I feel it constitutes a boundary that psychotherapy and psychotherapists must overcome for the sake of our potential role in society. This level has traditionally been the action field of political movements, and psychotherapy has traditionally either reduced it to ego and persona issues, or expanded it to transpersonal and universal ones. Ken Wilber quite rightly writes:

81

For example, the ego misguidedly attempts to manufacture happiness, pleasure, or simple joy in living. We feel that pleasure is something intrinsically lacking in the present situation, and that we must manufacture it by surrounding ourselves with sophisticated toys and gadgets. This reinforces the illusion that happiness and pleasure can be piped in from the outside, an illusion which itself is responsible for blocking pleasure, so that we end up striving for that which prevents our own joy.

(Wilber 1979: 117–18)

Here he addresses the issue of consumerism, or what psychoanalysts may call the 'oral fixation'. However, he does not answer the questions of how it has come to be like this, and how it is that we are born into an economical and societal system where this is the 'done thing'. I feel that we need to address those questions if we do not want to continue to reduce environmental dynamics to either intrapsychic or spiritual ones, while at the same time politicians and economists are unaware of psyche and spirit.

Before moving on to including activity theory and economic considerations in our self-discovery, I suggest that you spend a few moments considering your own boundary issues. Look at the following list of issues and consider how each one operates in your life. Mark the ones that are real 'banana skins' for you.

Personal Boundary Issues

Being a perfectionist.
Can't be vulnerable.
Terrified of rejection.
Difficulties in forming or maintaining close relationships.
Can't stand physical closeness.
Putting others' needs first.
Feel guilty when criticised.
Need to be in control.
Terrified of responsibility.
Feeling of a 'black hole' inside.
Feeling anxious or panicky for no reason.
Can't identify my feelings.
Assuming responsibility for how others feel.

All the above issues point towards boundary problems as we have discussed them. We all have boundary problems, because we are living in a world with boundary problems. However, if you are aware that any one of the above issues really bother you, then working on them might be a good idea. Books on 'co-dependency' like Beattie (1987), or Weinhold and Weinhold (1989), offer a lot of sense and self-help advice.

6

ACTIVITY THEORY

All the models and approaches that we have shared so far contribute towards the exploration and elimination of boundaries at different levels of our consciousness. I have tried to build bridges between the models, because in my therapeutic practice they are bridged. Some of the bridges are a bit shaky and some remnants of walls are still there. A big wall in the psychotherapy world is the exclusion of important aspects of the outer world, the environment. In a recent article Ryle (1991) is investigating the link between 'object relations theory' and 'activity theory'. He summarises his exploration as follows:

> In developing the procedural sequence object relations model, the first aim was to find a way of integrating the ideas and practices of different approaches to psychotherapy and the second was to place psychotherapy in a broader theoretical setting. Neither cognitive-behavioural nor psychoanalytic theories are free from serious reductionism in their accounts of human experience, whereas activity theory, however patchily developed at present, proposes a view of individual development which places man in his full human and historical context.
>
> (Ryle 1991: 314–15)

What an exciting statement. I am aware that you, the reader, might not be able to join me in this excitement. As usual, the reasons for my excitement are emotional, theoretical, and practical. How can I possibly guide you to understanding what I mean; and how can this succession of words that I am writing do justice to the ideas, their effects, and their origins?

EXAMPLE

I am trying to contribute to the process of sense-making, a process that we are all engaged in. This book is an attempt at sense-making, including the structure and the way I am writing it. Both structure and process of writing are related to sense-making and to activity theory. You may find the following passages unusual. On the other hand you may find that I am really

83

trying to include my personal experience in my writing and that I am trying to teach from my experience, which includes me as a person and as a writer. I am trying to communicate with you, the reader, and at the same time I cannot be sure about your reactions. Consequently, I am writing to my 'fantasy reader' while you are increasingly getting to know me. Is this a weird situation? Perhaps it is not that 'weird' after all. I think it is what happens to us all the time when we are in, or when we try to be in, a relationship: we need to expose our 'self' more and more when we interact with objects or people; we need to make assumptions about the object's or the other person's reactions to our actions (projection), and then we may feel that we have exposed ourselves without really knowing enough about the other person or object. It is always a step into the unknown and that means that we have to take a risk, the risk of maybe getting it wrong, the risk of 'failing'. Suddenly we can feel very vulnerable. What we then need are courage and trust, based on some kind of a realistic estimate of our skills and knowledge. We need emotional and rational qualities in order to take risks, and to overcome our fear of doing so.

I could so easily hide behind being very rational and scientific. I could write from a position that exerts power, communicating 'I know and you don't'. Such an approach would protect me from the dreaded 'unknown'. Power would help me to create and control a reality that matches my assumptions. But it would also make me rigid and would render real relationship impossible. Well, I do not want to write like that any more, because I believe, deep down, that 'relationship' is more important than 'power'.

The above is, for me, an example of the application of activity theory. The relationship between the individual and the object is what changes both the individual and the object. Traces (material and psychological) of the individual enter the object, and traces of the object enter the individual. For this process of mutual reflectivity to take place, openness is an important quality. This is particularly true for the relationships between people. 'Power over' and 'control' reduce the potential in this process, because they try to imprint the assumptions of one side on to the other.[1]

LEONTYEV'S ACTIVITY THEORY

The Russian researcher and psychologist A.N. Leontyev (1981) applied the principles and methodology of Marx and Engels' historical materialism to the analysis of human consciousness. His book *Problems of the Development of the Mind* was published in the Soviet Union in 1959, and it received the Lenin prize in 1963. The first German edition came out in 1971, and it formed the theoretical basis for my psychology studies at West Berlin University in the 1970s. An entirely new branch of psychology, hardly known in this country and based on Leontyev, was developed in Berlin at the time and it became known as 'critical psychology'. However, even though supporters of 'kritische Psychologie' tried to develop a psychology of the class society, it became extremely intellectual and without concrete practical implications. It was a typical result of the academic revolution happening at German universities in the 1970s. For me, and others trained in this approach, the move to activity-orientated behaviour therapy seemed logical, even though it was ridiculed at the time by some of the theoretical purists. Many of those former purists are by now well-established psychoanalysts!

After this brief personal/historical introduction I should like to summarise some of the main points of Leontyev's theory, because I have the feeling that it could form an important bridge between behaviour therapy and psychosynthesis, thus expanding both into a new quality which can integrate/include psychoanalysis. It will also move us on to defining and exploring the 'psychological greenhouse'. This is a strange thought indeed: using a Marxist theory to bridge the 'bourgeois' theories of cause–effect behaviourism and spiritual psychosynthesis?

In Marxist tradition, Leontyev's analysis is both historical and scientific. He painstakingly analyses the relationships between subject and object in the organic and non-organic world. He then focuses on the process of interaction between living beings and their objects, ultimately the interaction of human beings with their environment. The development of human consciousness is then seen as an evolutionary and historical process, leading to the splits, contradictions and alienations of class society. In Wilber's terms Leontyev analyses the historical and societal development of boundaries by seeing their cause in our concrete dealings with our environment.

Any appreciation of the theory will need to take into account the fact that it was developed in the 1950s, a time when 'real socialism' was still thriving as a viable alternative to capitalism, and when the damage that overpopulation and massive exploitation of planetary resources are causing was not yet obvious. It was this unawareness of planetary ecological issues that allowed both capitalism and socialism to be based on the assumption of continuous growth of resources and productivity to satisfy the ever increasing needs of increasing numbers of people.[2] However, we now know differently, and we know that both systems have contributed equally to global warming, pollution and ozone holes. While it is not surprising that capitalism with its in-built value of profit and greed has reached this point, it will require more careful analysis to figure out why socialism got stuck in the same rut. Suffice it to suggest here that Marxist and socialist theories are still products (and would see themselves as such) of capitalist society and consciousness, and only in their vision of communism do they claim to be able to finally overcome the splits in consciousness and classes that are still operating in socialism, though in a more controlled manner, i.e. controlled through the dictatorship of the proletariat and scientific rationality.

The above considerations will be important to keep in mind in our exploration of Leontyev's activity theory, because they will allow us to go beyond the very grounded and practical notion of the 'collective' that the theory contains, into the realms of what is called 'the collective' by Jung and in psychosynthesis.

Activity as the Basic Unit of Life

The basis of activity theory is that the psyche and consciousness are a result of, a reflection between, the individual and his environment. The inner world can only be understood in its historical, phylogenetically and ontogenetically, relationship with the outer world. The mediator between inner and outer worlds is activity; activity changes the object of the action as well as the subject. The properties of the objective outer world become crystallised in the psyche as reflections gained through active dealings with the objects. As reflections mediated through activity they contain elements of both object and subject, and are therefore never purely objective nor purely subjective. Hence, whatever we think, feel, or do connects us with our own history and with the history of the world around us. Separateness and isolation become an illusion. The French philosopher Lucien Sève said that the concept of 'individuaiity' is only possible when it is a collectively agreed one.

Leontyev postulates that activity is the main charateristic of life in its universal form. This applies to all living organisms including plants:

> For the sun a green plant is an object in which it manifests its life-giving power, but the plant does not assert or in fact determine the sun's being, nor does the sun seek out the plant. For the plant the sun is not only an object that reveals its (the plant's) capacity to assimilate carbon dioxide through solar energy, but is also the primary condition of its life, an object that it actively strives for. The plant bends its stem towards the sun, stretches out its branches and turns the surface of its leaves towards it. These movements of the plant are not the direct result of sunlight alone; they are determined as well by its general state in regard to other vital processes; with certain internal conditions the branches of the same plant will wilt under the sun and its leaves shrivel; quite a different picture arises – the plant is 'averse' to the sun. . . .

> Thus the principal 'unit' of a vital process is an organism's activity; the different activities that realise its diverse vital relations with the surrounding reality are essentially determined by their object; we shall

therefore differentiate between different types of activity according to the difference in their objects.

(Leontyev 1981: 35–7)

Leontyev's latter statement seems to assign primary importance to the objects. This is somewhat different to the Jungian notion of the internal world as something quite different and separate from the outer world. Even though this may well be related to the central concept of an 'objective reality' in materialistic philosophy, it needs to be stated that he defines 'object' in the narrow sense as the 'object of the activity'. However, the important point is how activity is seen as 'the principal unit of a vital process'.

Consciousness – Objective Meaning and Personal Sense

Leontyev analyses the development of human consciousness historically. He basically says that there is no 'pure consciousness', nor anything like 'abstract man', which traditional psychological research and theory try to postulate. Consciousness and psyche are qualitatively different in primitive society (*Urgesellschaft*) and in industrialised capitalist society. The historical development of the function of language is vital in this process.

I should like to use a passage from a recently published book to explain the kind of situation that Leontyev is able to describe as the result of the historical development of human activity and consciousness. The story is taken from Ben Elton's book *Gridlock* (1992). In his 'Off-Planet Introduction' he describes a spaceship hovering above Earth, and the observations that the occupants of the vessel are making about our world.

Cars and Transport

This spaceship contained a group of television researchers from the Planet Brain in the process of analysing humanity, in order to compile a three-minute comedy item for their top-rated television show, That's Amazing, Brainians, which followed the early evening news.

The researchers were pleased, they had noted much which was amusingly amazing, and they assured each other that Earth had provided the easiest bit of researching they had done in aeons. Brain is populated by beings of immense intelligence and so far it had taken them only a quarter, of a quarter, of a single second to assimilate and comprehend humanity.

But then they were stumped. They had encountered one aspect of human activity which astonished and mystified even those hardened researchers. Researchers who thought they had seen every illogicality and lunacy that the universe had to offer. On this very planet they had

87

seen pointless wars and pointless destruction. But this one had thrown them. This one had them scratching their multiple thought podules in a perplexed manner and saying 'akjafgidkersh lejhslh hei!', which translates as 'Bugger me, that's weird!' The problem was one of transport. The Brainians could see the long, thin arteries along which the humans travelled. They noted that after sunrise the humans all travelled one way and at sunset they all travelled the other. They could see that progress was slow and congested along these arteries, that there were endless blockages, queues, bottle-necks and delays causing untold frustration and inefficiency. All this they could see quite clearly. What was not clear to them, was why. They knew that humanity was stupid, they had only to look at the week's top ten grossing movies to work that out, but this was beyond reason. If, as was obvious, space was so restricted, why was it that each single member of this strange life-form insisted on occupying perhaps fifty times its own ground surface area for the entire time it was in motion – or not in motion, as was normally the case?

(Elton 1992: 2–4)

Cars and our modes of transport serve as an example here. Other examples could be pollution and other destructive and self-destructive activities that we engage in. Can it make sense? What is the meaning of it? The simple answer to the car situation would be 'Well, we all want cars, big ones, small ones, fast ones, shiny ones, bigger than . . . ones'. But why do we all want cars? Status symbol, toys, mode of transport, comfort, needing to get from A to B, speed, no other transport available. All this still does not answer our Why-question, because there seem to be too many reasons for having cars, and not one of them relates to congested inner cities, polluted air, and injuries and deaths on the road. From the spaceship high up in the sky we might see it; down here on Earth we see it, we experience the strain and the frustrations of motoring, but this is all made up for by the satisfaction of all those other needs. After all, all those needs for status and speed, for comfort and individuality are much more directly personal than some 'high-flying' ideals about a clean and unpolluted environment. This is because we have managed to remove ourselves from our natural environment, and can only see the artificial one that we have created. The artificial environments are created, create, and are maintained and expanded by artificial needs and motives. The increasing complexity of our man-made environment blocks off more and more of the natural environment underneath and beyond it. As we shall explore later, according to the activity theory this has been an inevitable historical development, ultimately leading to the contradictions and conflicts, but also to the potential that we are facing now.

Reflect on the following statements which express both conflict and potential:

'It's difficult enough to keep the economy going, without having to worry about the state of the planet.'

'Producing more and buying more are important to earn the money to pay for health care and environmental protection.'

'Progress means having more, knowing more, producing more, needing more and now, producing faster, communicating more quickly.'

'The whole essence of industrialised society is anti-ecological. Industrial progress means nothing but to process nature bit by bit.'

'Humanity is in the process of turning the world into one huge production and consumption plant.'

The History of Sense and Meaning

Activity theory can explain how these contradictions, and their corresponding attitudes in our minds, have developed historically. Remember Rupert Sheldrake's example of the 'nine to five, Monday to Friday society' on page 7. It describes the conflict beautifully.

Leontyev distinguishes between the personal sense and the objective meaning that an activity and the associated object have. In primitive society without division of labour, both sense and meaning coincide.

> Psychologically this is as follows: the sense of the phenomenon that the individual is aware of and its sense for the group as a whole, fixed in meaningful language, still coincide. The undifferentiated character of senses and meanings in consciousness is possible because the range of the conscious still remains limited for a long time to those of men's relationships that are directly also the relationships of the collective, and also because the linguistic meanings are not sufficiently differentiated. . . .
>
> The first important change in the direction of an extension of the realm of the conscious was caused by the complication of work operations and of the tools themselves. Production more and more called for a whole system of co-ordinated actions from each participant in the work process, and consequently for a whole system of conscious aims, which at the same time were parts of a single process and of a single complex action. Psychologically this merging of separate partial actions into a single action was a conversion of partial actions into operations. The place in consciousness which was previously occupied by the conscious aims of partial activities, is now filled with the conditions for the execution of the complex overall activity.
>
> (Leontyev 1981: 234)

What we are looking at here is a paradoxical process of splitting and growing interdependence taking place at the same time. With the development of tools there came increasing division of labour, and the increasing development of systems of co-ordinated actions. To date the paradox, expressed in the earlier example of cars, seems to have reached its peak: society and the activities of groups and individuals within it are extremely separate and, at the same time, totally interdependent. What used to be subordinate operations have now taken on the properties of motivators and have thus created new needs. Personal sense and objective meaning of an activity are often light-years apart. People do different things and are often unaware of the connection that there is, say, between a coal-miner and a secretary in a computer software firm, between a psychotherapist and a gardener. Individuality has turned into separation and has become one of the main driving forces behind 'progress'.

What we are facing are different levels of alienation. This alienation is from the collective, and it has been necessary for 'progress'. The different levels of human alienation, or boundaries, are:

1 Division of labour and the development of tools create a situation where subordinate tasks and goals acquire the quality of being motivational and need satisfying in themselves. In a way, the objects of the activity create the need. For example, the production of stamps is only a small part of the overall postal services. However, someone might be extremely motivated to make stamps, while at the same time they are not interested in postal services at all. And someone else might collect stamps for their colourful images or because they are easier to store than, say, sports cars, or because there are so many of them available. However, at some level the communication potential between distant people and places comes into the production and the collecting of stamps – more or less consciously.

2 The development of language has led to the separation of the practical from the intellectual. Even though language has developed in close connection with practical activity, it has become, or seems to have become, quite independent as 'mental activity'. Jobs can be divided into the two groups of those who require mainly manual skills and those who require mainly intellectual skills. The fact that nowadays intellectual skills are rated more highly than manual skills is leading to divisions and separation between people and to economic illusions:

> This separation of men's mental activity also found refelection in their heads, so that they began to see in it not a historically arising form of the manifestation of the process of man's life, but a manifestation of a special, mental principle that formed a special world, the world of consciousness opposed to the world of matter, space and time.
>
> (Leontyev 1981: 247)

Again, the potential in this boundary is all that the human intellect as a separated activity has created – books, theories, models, philosophies. Intellectual activity has reached the potential to step outside the manual level of activities and to be an 'observer' of those levels. Leontyev's theory itself is the result of such mental activity.

3 The division between production and finance is what Marx saw as the ultimate capitalist perversion. With the development of money as a means of exchange, trade has become simpler, and human labour could be turned into a commodity with a money value attached to it. Money has become an equaliser between different products, different activities, different people and nations. Regardless of what someone does or has, the money value attached to each object and activity allows comparisons of everything with everything else. The snag is that, in order for it to work, everything needs to have such a value, even time. 'Time is money', hence it can become 'high quality time', 'valuable time', 'useless time', 'time wasted'. This is the basis on which money began to develop a life of its own: the money market, finance capital, interest rates, loans, profits, exchange rates, devaluations, etc. Today when we hear about 'the economy' we hear about share indexes, money supply rates, the money market. The interest we get on our deposit account bears for us no conscious relation to the production side of the economy, but rather to the activities of the 'money markets'. The positive aspect here is the potential for global interchange and comparisons.

4 Mass communication has created yet another level of alienation. It has produced means for communicating selectively and symbolically. The content of a message has become much less important than the way in which it is delivered. Björn Engholm uses the term 'symbolic politics' to describe the end result:

> Politics is changing; symbols and symbolic actions are increasingly taking the place of what we used to call politics. They are replacing disputes, public choices and political decisions. Symbolic politics always emerges where politics cannot change anything, or where it cannot meet the expectations it has created.
>
> (Engholm 1990: 38, my translation)

It is difficult to see the potential in this aspect of alienation, which is similar to the way in which advertising uses communication. Perhaps the potential lies in the possibility of reducing the increasing floods of information to shorthand elements – a kind of 'summarising' function.

5 Most individuals do not see themselves any more as parts of the whole. Greater interdependence has led to greater individualism, and individualism often means isolation and fragmentation. The alienation of the individual from the context of his activities and his life, as a result of the above stages of alienation, has led to enormous differentiation and

expertise. But it has also prepared the ground for rigid boundaries between individuals, between individuals and groups, between groups and nations. The effects of those boundaries as 'battle lines' are competition, domination, 'power over', mistrust, etc. However, underneath and beyond all this is a growing interdependence between individuals, groups and nations. I see the whole world as just having left the struggles of the BPM III state and, rather than moving towards the interdependence issues of BPM IV, it is trying to transfer the rules of 'struggle' from the previous state to the new one. The potential for union and partnership is there, and more and more voices are expressing it.

Not only have we created boundaries between those levels, but each level itself contains the creation of boundaries in our consciousness.

The alienation and separation that we face and have inside us nowadays cause a lot of grief, pain, depression, pollution and destruction. But behind or beneath it lies enormous collectivity – hardly a single one of our activities or motivations is possible or even thinkable without all the other activities and motives of other groups and people. This is true for individuals, groups and nations and it finds its final expression in the concept of Gaia, which sees our planet as one living organism.

Example One: Division of Labour Boundary

Recently, I visited the coal-mining town where I grew up. There, I met Achim who knows how to do things, i.e. decorating, etc. For him the practical activity is not yet separated from the mental (the coal-miner). I was envious, because I don't know how to do those things. I was brought up to be different from, 'better' than that. So I lost touch with this working-class quality. I was encouraged to form this split for myself, the split of mental activity from practical activity, and the practical side was given a very low value-rating: 'This is the kind of slave labour your father has to do; you must do better'. Now I am in a position where I put most of my energy into the mental activities of therapising, thinking, talking, and writing. When I need practical things done in the house 'I do not have the time'. This then means that I have to pay people who can do it. The less time I have – to make contact with people who can do things, to search for the best offer because my mental activities take so much time – the more I need to pay to get things done. So in order to value (rate, esteem) my mental activity appropriately, I need to take into account what I need to pay out to get a share of the practical side back.

But that's where the conflict arises. Psychotherapy is a 'caring' activity; it is a 'direct' dealing with people, and people need to pay for it directly. Usually in our society our different activities and operations are interlinked and separated in such a complex way that only very few people 'charge directly' for their services or products. The secretary of the sales director, the sales director, the coal-miner, the hospital doctor and psychologist are much further removed from this direct exchange of energies, i.e. money, than the greengrocer, hairdresser, and the psychotherapist in private practice. The conflict can arise between the necessary intimacy of the psychotherapeutic relationship and the directness of the money exchange.

Example Two: Objects and Part-objects Boundaries

Coming back to cars. The initial motive for building cars was as a means of transport, getting from A to B, increased mobility. Since then the simple concept of the car has been split up into lots of different cars – the flashy car, the fast car, the big car, the safe car, the environmentally friendly car (see Figure 6.1). Each one of those different cars (or aspects of car) has acquired its own set of motives and needs, and more needs have arisen out of this split. For example, mobility and speed have become needs in their own right, quite independent of needing to get from A to B for a particular reason. However, all these different needs are connected to a set of basic emotional needs which are often unconscious. The advertising industry has developed the skills and the methodology to link particular aspects of cars with the underlying, often unconscious, emotional needs, and to address them. It has thus become an aim in production and marketing to split up a product into as many different aspects as possible in order to speak to as many different emotional needs as possible. (Example: the need for 'newness' means that from time to time products are re-packaged.)

Internalisation/Assimilation (*Aneignung* = 'making it your own')

In the course of his ontogenetic development, man enters into special, specific relations with the world of objects and phenomena around him that have been created by preceding generations. Their specific character of those relationships is determined on one side by the nature of the objects and phenomena. On the other side their character is determined by the specific character of the conditions under which the relationships developed in the first place. The real environment, which most of all determines human life, is an environment that has been changed by human activity. This world is not, however, presented directly to the individual as a world of social objects, which embody human abilities that have developed in the course of social-historical practice. They are presented to each human being as a task. Even the simplest tools and objects of everyday life that the child encounters, have to be actively discovered (opened up) by him in their specific quality. In other words, the child has to perform practical or cognitive activities in relation to the objects that would be adequate

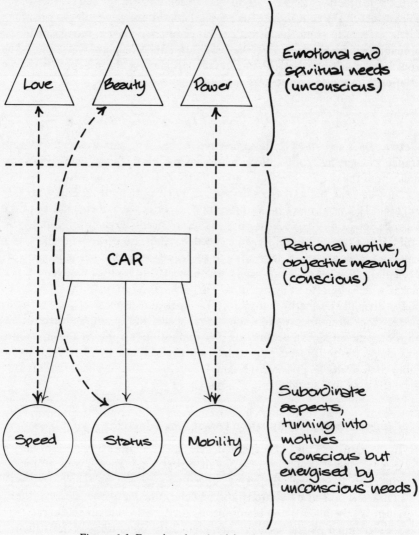

Figure 6.1 Emotional and spiritual aspects of 'car'.

(but not necessarily identical) to the human activity embodied in them.

(Leontyev 1981: 294)[3]

I think that the above passage by Leontyev analyses beautifully the dynamics of 'internalisation'. We can sense the complex dynamics that exist between the human individual and his environment, and the bridges that exist between the histories of the individuals and of the collective. Leontyev then moves on to quote Marx on the subject:

94

Only through the richness of human nature unfolded in objects, is the richness of subjective human sensitivity and sensuality (like a musical ear, an eye for beauty, in short, senses capable of human appreciation, senses which affirm themselves as essential human qualities) partly developed and partly created. For not only the five senses, but also the so-called spiritual senses, the practical senses (will, love etc.), in one word the human senses, the human nature of these senses, only come into being through the existence of its object, through humanised nature. The forming of the five senses is the work of world history to date.

(Leontyev 1981: 295)

(*The following passage is missing in the English-language version*):

Each one of his human relationships with the world, with seeing, hearing, tasting, feeling, thinking, watching, experiencing, willing, doing, loving, in short, all the organs of his individuality . . . are . . . in their behaviour towards the object the internalisation of the object – the internalisation of human reality.

(Leontjew 1971: 232, my translation)

Marx expresses clearly the creative and growth potential that is in the 'objects' of our human activities. This potential exists side by side with the alienation and divisiveness that is accumulating in our industrialised 'advanced' societies. Does this also mean that the creative and growth potentials are accumulating?

At this point, I should like to refer back to the CBT approaches presented earlier. It seems that behavioural analysis and cognitive therapy, by applying a sequential model, which includes practical and mental activity, come pretty close to encompassing the concepts of activity theory and 'internalisation' in their therapeutic practice. CBT takes automated human activities and divides them up into their mental and practical components, and then tries to put them together again in a different way. In this process the use of language is vital. The cognitive therapy method of 'self-instructional training' is a good example. It teaches people to talk to themselves, aloud first and then silently, while they carry out certain activities or are in certain feared situations. This is meant to interfere with the hitherto automatic process of action–thought–action–thought, because in this automatic process the thoughts are not necessarily verbal any more. Putting words to them again brings the process back to an earlier stage of internalisation (the stage where the child talks to itself aloud while carrying out certain tasks before moving on to silent talk and then to automatic and abstract thought processes in connection with the tasks). At this earlier (ontogenetically and phylogenetically) level, the whole activity (or experience) can then be re-internalised (or re-learned). Greenberg and Safran's 'emotional synthesis' model addresses a similar level of processing.

6.1 Reflection: The Objective World

This exercise aims at giving you a sense of the way in which the world of human objects and activities is connected with your personal history and with the history of humanity.

Pick a human-made object from your present environment. Explore the details of the object with your five senses. Be open also to the other human senses that you experience in the exploration of the object.

As you are exploring the object, you may experience thoughts, feelings, and flashes of memories in relation to the object or related (or unrelated) objects. Allow these sensations to be part of your exploration of the object.

Now bring to your conscious mind what you know about the history and the production of the object:
1 How is the object produced? What are the different stages of its production?
2 Imagine the people and their skills that go into the production of the object.
3 What is the history of the object, and of the people who are making it? What are the human emotions that you can sense in the history?
4 Now imagine all the people who are using the object. Where would it be used and who would use it? What emotions do you sense in the users of the object?

For most objects it is unlikely that we have sufficient knowledge to be able to trace its history accurately. However, this exercise aims at giving you a sense of the connectedness of knowledge, emotions, and of our individual and collective history.

7

THE GROWTH ILLUSION

In the previous chapter we looked at the psychology of human economic activity, and at the alienations and potentials that have developed in the process. Since Leontyev's days, and especially since the 1950s, the alienations (and unrealised potentials) have developed into a world-wide economic system that is so powerful that we are all caught up in it. The system is based on the division of labour, on capitalism, and on the increasingly powerful role of the international finance 'markets', and it has created a 'growth illusion' at all levels, from the intrapsychic to the economic. Richard Douthwaite is an economist and I should like to use material from his recent book *The Growth Illusion* (1992) to describe the system that we live in, and that is the context for the human-made environment that we have and are internalising. This chapter will therefore be economical and sociological. Thereafter this book will return to being psychological and spiritual.

In his book, Douthwaite shows that

> economic growth has made life considerably worse for people in Britain since 1955 and that, even if growth was beneficial at one stage in human history, it is now downright damaging. . . . Even the hope of further growth is harmful, because it lulls us into accepting changes like the continued rise in the world's population which, in a no-growth world, must be seen as disastrous. Equally importantly, the prospect of growth has enabled us to escape doing anything about the poor by telling them that things will get better for them if they just hang on. The promise of jam for all tomorrow has eased our consciences about the unequal division of bread today.
>
> (Douthwaite 1992: 3)

We seem to have accepted the need for economic growth as the most important principle of our society. The questions of 'why' and 'what for' are not being asked. Political parties, governments, EC, all aim at stimulating economic growth. Economic growth is seen as a good thing; everything else is bad. Party manifestos are judged, elections are won on the basis of who has the better plan to stimulate growth: inflation down, interest rates up,

GNP down. Hordes of economic commentators, presented as the 'wise men' in front of impressive computer screens, dominate the media, making it all sound very scientific and very complicated. Financial advisers tell us how to invest our pennies, how to get the best interest rates.

How has it happened that economic growth has come to dominate our personal, professional, political and cultural lives? Ultimately it all boils down to consuming more, regardless of what, and producing more, regardless of what. What is the driving force behind it, and why are we all accepting it so unquestioningly?

Douthwaite shows convincingly that the driving force behind it all is the borrowing of money and the interest rates on borrowed money. He also shows that the system that has developed is so complex that we are all caught up in it. The alternatives are 'grow or collapse' at personal and national levels. I should like to quote some of the examples he gives in his book, because I think they will enable us to begin to look at the system we are caught up in from the outside.

> It is easy – and valid – for one person to say that, as things stand, if he had a car he would be better off because it would be quicker and pleasanter than walking to the bus through wind and rain. But the process of giving a car to that person and to everyone else who wants one changes the situation so drastically that it is not possible to say whether, after the process has been completed, the community will be better off and the new car owners will get the benefits they thought they would. The increase in traffic might lengthen journey times to such an extent that the new car owners take longer to get to work than they did before. Other people's journey times will almost certainly go up as a result of congestion and the total time the community spends travelling to work could increase. Bus frequencies will probably be cut and fares raised for lack of demand. Thus, even though GNP will increase because of the extra spending on transport, it is possible – even probable – that the country as a whole will be worse off in welfare terms and that many people will be running their cars largely out of necessity because of the way things have developed and not because they like doing so.
>
> (Douthwaite 1992: 3)

It is obvious how this example could be applied to many other things, and how it leads to a situation where we have to buy certain goods out of necessity rather than choice. Douthwaite uses the example of double glazing that people near the airport runway might need. Other examples are water filters, sun-tan lotion, catalytic converters, air filters, etc. Douthwaite concludes:

> Because the world is so complex it is very difficult to say what

proportion of the purchases people make is truly voluntary, truly discretionary. If people have to buy a smart suit or drive a new car to maintain their position in the pecking order, rather than because they actually enjoy having them, these are involuntary purchases. The key word is 'maintain'. Any expenditure that has to be made in an attempt to keep things as they are, like the sound-reducing windows, is essentially involuntary and does not increase well-being. The spending on cleaning up after the Exxon Valdez oil spill in Alaska falls into this category: it has appeared in the US national income statistics as an increase in GNP, but no-one would claim it was done out of choice or that anyone got pleasure from it.

There is strong evidence that the proportion of involuntary expenditure consumers have to make out of the fraction of national income that trickles down to them rises sharply as income goes up. . . . it is certainly true that needs expand to fill the income available. How else can we explain the fact that, although per capita incomes in the Hamburg area are more than three times those in Ireland, people living there do not seem to be significantly better off in terms of the amount of discretionary spending they are able to undertake.

(Douthwaite 1992: 14)

A gloomy picture indeed. I have noticed that, as I have been copying these passages from Douthwaite's book, my mood has become increasingly gloomy. But I suppose we need to face it. I am beginning to wonder how much of my time I spend doing things out of choice rather than 'necessity'. My car is in the garage at the moment to have some bodywork repairs done, caused by a break-in and a collision within ten days of each other. Now the garage cannot complete the repair because they cannot get the right bumper. As a result I have to cancel certain long-distance trips, possibly a weekend in Suffolk, and I have to use taxis. I am also thinking how much time I spend, or 'should' spend, on doing tax returns, paying bills, considering pension plans, etc.

I should like to suggest an exercise here. I am sorry about the gloom and doom that it might create, but I do feel it is necessary that we face it.

7.1 Exercise: Objects and Activities

Divide a sheet of paper into three columns. In the left-hand column list your spare-time activities of the last three days. Call the middle column 'discretionary' and the right hand one 'involuntary'. Then give a percentage of discretionary and involuntary to each one of the listed activities. Note that the two percentages for each item should add up to 100.

Now list in the left-hand column all the non-regular purchases you have made in the previous month. Again, assign the percentage of discretionary and involuntary to each purchase.

Now add up all the percentages in the discretionary column and divide the sum by the number of activities and items. Do the same for the involuntary column. The result can give you some indication of how much of your spare time is spent and how many of your purchases are made out of choice rather than out of necessity. How do you feel about it?

Our economic system has now reached a stage where the need for growth and competition have created the polarity of 'expand or die'. Douthwaite uses the example of a village in India to illustrate the point:

When Hopper visited Senapur [in the mid-1950s], a field was irrigated by yoking two oxen to a rope tied to a big leather bucket down a well. During the past thirty years, however, electrical or diesel pumps have been introduced to the village. Although it required very much more capital to buy them in the first place and a regular input of energy from the outside world, the new pumps displaced the oxen and the men who drove them. The first farmers to go over to the new ways found that they were able to irrigate a larger area than in the past and that consequently they could either get higher yields of some of their existing crops or put a bigger area under water-demanding ones like rice, which tend to earn a higher return than the crops that can be grown almost anywhere.

So the pioneer farmers increased their production and altered the relative amounts of the crops they grew. For a while, prices remained unaffected and they enjoyed good profits [helping them to pay back the interest on the money they needed to borrow for the new pumps]. However, as more and more pumps were installed, output increased significantly and prices began to fall, reducing the income of those farmers who had failed to adopt the new irrigation method. This group suffered another setback too: the new power pumps meant that more water could be extracted from greater depths than previously possible, so the water table around the village dropped. Naturally, the old-style farmers deepened their wells and lengthened their ropes but because their oxen had further to haul, they were unable to raise as much water as they used to. In short, these farmers found themselves caught in a rather neat, but nasty, pincer movement: they could not produce as much as before because they had less irrigation water and the market price for their reduced output had fallen. Moreover if they tried to install pumps to catch up with their neighbours they would not get as much profit as the pioneers did, because of the price fall. Indeed the traditional farmers' situation might have deteriorated to such an

100

extent that they would be unable to service the loans on their pumps, even supposing they were able to arrange them.

Here is the growth imperative at work: once change begins to take place, no-one has the option of not adapting to it. Anyone who doggedly continues in the traditional way will be wiped out.

(Douthwate 1992: 22–3)

It is not difficult to see parallels between the irrigation in the Indian village and more recent economic collapses, like for example in the computer industry. Douthwaite's book has sixteen chapters and, being an economist, his analysis of growth is very detailed with lots of charts and figures; hence it is difficult to summarise. Fortunately he added to his chapter titles very brief provocative summary statements, and I should like to share the ones that seem important for our purpose.

Perhaps we can turn this into some kind of an exercise. I am not an economist, and I have certain difficulties with all the figures, statistics and probabilities, but I do know what feels right. I also trust that most people have a sense of rightness or wrongness with regard to the economy and the world around them. As an experiment, I should like to leave it to you to apply your feeling-sense to Douthwaite's statements. I suggest that you judge each of the following statements as either 'yes, feels right' or 'no, feels wrong' or 'maybe'. Let's try.

7.2 Exercise: The Growth Illusion

QUALITY OR QUANTITY

Politicians promise to raise the standard of living. What they do not say is that this will inescapably reduce the quality of our lives.

YES/MAYBE/NO

WHY CAPITALISM NEEDS GROWTH

Capitalism cannot survive without growth. Firms are compelled to expand to avoid collapse. In the world up to 1914, this compulsion built empires, destroyed indigenous cultures and, finally, led to world war.

YES/MAYBE/NO

THE BENEFITS OF WAR AND DEPRESSION

Major advances in the living conditions of the British people resulted from two world wars, the depression of the 1920s and 1930s and the fiercely redistributive policies of the 1945 Labour government. Whenever growth appeared, life for the majority got worse.

YES/MAYBE/NO

GROWTH AND THE NATIONAL HEALTH

It was not until 1955 that accelerating the growth rate became the major British economic obsession. Since then the methods used to generate higher levels of output have caused a large increase in chronic illness.

YES/MAYBE/NO

HOW GROWTH DAMAGED FAMILY AND COMMUNITY LIFE

All the indicators of the quality of life show that this deteriorated in Britain over the past three decades. Unemployment soared, crime increased eightfold and many more marriages ended in divorce.

YES/MAYBE/NO

WHAT HAS ALL THE GROWTH DONE?

Has growth kept its promises? An examination of the changes in Britain since the 1950s shows that the process brought very few benefits at all.

YES/MAYBE/NO

GROWTH MUST HAVE A STOP

Because their need for growth forces firms to adopt new technologies before their impact can be assessed, environmental disasters such as the large-scale release of CFCs and PCBs are inevitable. Innovation must only be permitted when it is clear that society and the environment will benefit.

YES/MAYBE/NO

THE MYTH OF SUSTAINABLE GROWTH

The only sustainable society is a stable society – there is no such thing as sustainable growth. What are the principles on which such a society can be built? In particular, how can we stabilise world population?

YES/MAYBE/NO

GUIDING THE INVISIBLE HAND

Morality lost almost all control over the direction of economic change after Adam Smith's concept of the 'invisible hand' gained acceptance. If the world is to have a bright future, it must govern our actions again.

YES/MAYBE/NO

102

What has been your reaction to Douthwaite's statements? Do you reject them, accept them, or are you indifferent? I do not think that we need to discuss the validity of his statements here. If you doubt his assertions or you just don't know, you can always study his detailed analysis for yourself. But what is it like for you if somehow, based on knowledge, experience and sensing, you agree with the above statements or if you just feel that they might be correct? What does this mean for you personally?

Douthwaite asserts that major changes in attitudes, lifestyles and politics are necessary if we want to save the planet for future generations of humankind:

> We are all the victims of an economic totalitarianism and have little freedom to determine what we do and think in the economic sphere. Our immediate goal must be to break out of the processes of thought that imprison us. The first and most important step is to reject the notion that the achievement of economic growth is a fit, proper or desirable goal for any nation.
>
> (Douthwaite 1992: 315)

What would that mean for each one of us personally – for the elements of our personal growth and achievement that are so closely linked to economic growth: career development, earning more, owning more, etc.? And what about our savings and the moneys that we have tucked away in private pension funds? Douthwaite says that capitalism's 'fundamental part is the payment of interest on borrowed money and it is this which has caused many of our problems, because it has created the system's need for growth' (1992: 320). Scary prospects and unsettling times may well be ahead, and that's why Douthwaite's final question is: 'Will the hardships we are about to face force us to carry on as we are, or will they compel us, out of desperation, to accept the risk of the new?' (1992: 322).

I do not quite agree with this last statement about 'risking the new out of desperation'. I think it misses the psychological and spiritual necessity of 'the new' emerging; and it also misses the fact that growth has given us the potential to move on to that new path. We could get into an argument here, where one side says that change is necessary and that it will happen out of desperation, and the other side says that we should not worry about all those 'doomsday predictions'. Let's just continue, the Earth will cope with it all as it has coped with life for billions of years. Ignoring the psychological perspective turns the whole issue into an intellectual argument about who is right and who is wrong. But this is not the point. To get to the point we need to look at the ingredients of people's suffering in a psychological and historical way. Once we look at it like this we see:

1 People are becoming increasingly afraid of each other and of their environment.
2 The economic system has created different levels of alienation.
3 There is a lot of confusion in people about their goals and objectives.

These statements are quite simple, and most therapists will agree with them. A lot of this we experience every day – we see it in ourselves and in each other, and we sense it in the world around us. Activity theory explains the historical dynamics and the inevitability of it. How relevant is it then whether we agree or disagree about the survival potential of planet Earth beyond the year 3,000 or 30,000? The question of whether we should leave a clean and tidy environment for future generations can become very academic indeed; the issue of our alienation and disconnectedness from ourselves, from each other and from our environment is a very real, 'here-and-now' concern.

It is surprising that very few people seem to be seeing the connections between increasing stress levels, the psychotherapy boom, earlier described as the 'search for sanctuary', and the economic system that determines the way we live. Behaviourism, despite its focus on observable stimuli and responses and its closeness to activity theory, does not go as far as questioning the determining character of the economic and political system. Psychoanalytic approaches do not seem to be able to make the connection between inner and outer worlds, and focus exclusively on the inner dynamics. Psychosynthesis and other psycho-spiritual approaches emphasise the determining character of the individual will, but do not appreciate that this 'inside-out' activity takes place within an economic framework, and that many of the intrapsychic structures are internalised external patterns in the first place.

Richard Douthwaite starts his book with the assertion that 'since no-one in advanced countries ever asked what society was trying to achieve, people were unaware that there was any need for choice about how resources were used' (1992: 3). This unawareness, lack of critical evaluation and goalless-ness in our societies is reflected in the blindness of psychotherapy towards the economic system. This unconsciousness, however, is a necessary ingredient of the system, a system which is characterised by its total belief in and devotion to growth. This leads to a rather disturbing question, a question which I as a psychotherapist would prefer not to ask: Is there a growth illusion in psychotherapy? Is psychotherapy caught up in the system just like everything else? Are we feeding people the illusion that things will get better if they have more therapy? Three issues with lots of provocative questions seem to emerge here:

1 Psychotherapy is part of the system. It is part of the service sector; fees are being paid and need to be earned; more sessions means more money. Those with more money can afford more therapy. Where does their 'more money' come from if not from economic growth?
2 People expect to 'feel better' as a result of therapy. They want their symptoms to be taken away. Are we sometimes helping people to cope

better with a rotten, ill-making system? Should we rather help people see the rotten ill-making system more clearly? But then they might feel worse rather than better. Do we have a choice in this?

3 Growth is not just a capitalist invention. It is an in-built human motive: growing up, growing knowledge, growing skills, etc. Has psychotherapy fallen into the trap of equating any kind of growth with economic growth? Can psychotherapy define the growth it strives for as something qualitatively different from economic growth?

I think we urgently need to ask questions about the objectives of psychotherapy. However much we can express our activities in fancy behavioural, psychoanalytic or psycho-spiritual models and terminology, we are ultimately dealing with the victims of systems which are dominated by economic growth, production and consumption. The systems may be parental, internal, groups, families, couples, subpersonalities – they are nevertheless internal and external structures that are ultimately determined by the way we are and have been leading our lives, and that is ultimately determined by our relationships across the planet, which are ultimately economic (whether we like it or not).

8

PSYCHOSYNTHESIS – THE
HIGHER PERSPECTIVE

INTRODUCTION

I should now like to use the basic models of psychosynthesis to develop a psycho-spiritual model of suffering, alienation, disconnectedness, boundaries and growth-illusion. For this we need to go back to Example 2 in the chapter on activity theory on page 93, and in particular to Figure 6.1, which shows how the object car gets divided up into different aspects and is connected with different emotional needs. The figure shows how easily the different aspects of the object (circles) can become connected with emotional needs (triangles). The ease of that connection is exploited by the advertising industry. The increasing variety of objects and part-objects created by humanity means that we become increasingly surrounded by 'things', and these things are often connected with deep inner needs. The satisfaction of those deep inner needs then turns into the need for possession of the objects best representing fulfilment of the emotional needs. We become caught up in the vicious circles of need–wanting–consuming objects, etc. Marx wrote that production not only creates the object for the need, but also the need for the object. All this happens with ever increasing numbers of objects competing for the satisfaction of limited numbers of emotional needs. We are caught up in the 'consumer society'.

> We feel that pleasure is something that is intrinsically lacking in the present situation, and that we must manufacture it by surrounding ourselves with sophisticated toys and gadgets. This reinforces the illusion that happiness and pleasure can be piped from the outside, an illusion which itself is responsible for blocking pleasure, so that we end up striving for that which prevents our own joy.
>
> (Wilber 1979: 117–18)

Production also gets pulled into this system: items are invented and produced solely in order to create more variety (e.g. fashion, electric razors). On the consumption side this system then brings out the shadow side of human nature. Extreme expressions of this are greed, theft, envy, eating disorders, addictions, shoplifting, etc.

However, this complex system ultimately leaves the emotional needs unsatisfied. From the system's point of view this is a good thing, because it leaves it with lots of 'hungry' consumers. At the same time it has turned people in the industrialised world into human beings who project the satisfaction of their emotional needs on to external objects. Emotional needs become 'objectified' to such an extent that people are not aware of their inner, emotional needs any more. The emotional needs are expressed in the need for consumption. Results are attitudes like 'I want more, greater, bigger things', 'I need to work harder, achieve more things', 'I need to be better than others', 'I need to work, produce more efficiently', 'I need to communicate more quickly' – in short, the 'rat race'. In the present times of world-wide economic recession and crisis, the needs expressed in these attitudes are becoming increasingly difficult to satisfy. As a result, competition is growing between individuals, groups, companies and nations, while at the same time there is now the opportunity to question and transform the addictive needs that the system has created.

Some big department stores in Germany have recently realised that 'just' shopping does not attract people into their shops any more, thus not increasing turnover and profits. They found that people really don't need anything any more. The question became 'How can we nevertheless seduce them to buy, to consume?' The solution is to create 'shopping experiences' – coffee bars, art exhibitions, music performances, and theme displays aimed at attracting overstimulated consumers into more shopping. Results indicate an increase in turnover in the stores that have introduced the new system.

THE PSYCHOLOGICAL GREENHOUSE

There we are, surrounded by objects on to which we have projected our emotional needs, our growth and our life journey. My image for this is one of the scenes that I put to you earlier:

I am sitting in my car, stuck in a huge traffic jam on the M25. It is one of those very hot and humid summer days that we have been getting lately. I am sweating. I'd love to open the car window, but I know that I would then breathe in even more directly the fumes of all those other cars around me. Even though there aren't any clouds around the air looks misty, with a yellow-reddish glow. Aeroplanes are flying low over my head, carrying vast numbers of fellow humans to their destinations. The weather-forecast man on the radio says the air quality in London would be very poor today. My eyes feel sore and my nose is running; my head is wondering how to make up for my delay in getting to my destination: I'll be running late, again. I feel imprisoned – in my car, in between appointments, in the air around me that I *have to* breathe, in the heat, the deadlines, the destinations, the cars and people around me and above me. Even the car radio, producing the most human sounds around me, feels inhuman, an intrusion.

In the above situation I am surrounded by a metal box, my feet are on a metal floor, the rubber tyres are in contact with the asphalt. I am not in contact with the earth. Above me, my contact with the sky is blocked by pollution, aeroplanes and noise. Even my most intimate interaction with my environment, through my breathing, is blocked by pollutants and by the smell of car exhaust fumes. And I am rushing between man-made objects, from A to B to C to D, disconnected from Earth and Heaven, disconnected from my inner Self.

In order to understand the alarming seriousness of this condition, we need to appreciate Assagioli's basic model of psychosynthesis. Whereas Freudian psychoanalysts would see consumerism as a substitute for the fulfilment of emotional needs, psychosynthesis would go one step further and see how it disconnects us from spirit, from our 'true self'.

Assagioli writes about the

> spiritual elements of our personality that come down like rays of sunlight into the human personality – into our personal consciousness – and form a link between our ordinary human personality and the spiritual 'I', the spiritual Reality. They are like rays of light pouring down, taking on various shades of colour and dispersing, depending on the permeability or the transparency of our personal consciousness. . . . Everything that exists externally, in concrete form and individually is the manifestation, effect and reflection of a higher, transcendent, spiritual Reality.
>
> (Assagioli 1991: 250)

He continues, 'This indeed is the secret: to recognise that external things have no true value, significance or reality of their own, that they only serve to highlight or represent inner realities and spiritual qualities' (p.253).

The Egg Diagram

The most important chart in psychosynthesis is the 'egg diagram'. A version of it is represented here (Figure 8.1), and I shall use it to develop some ideas about the spiritual damage of consumerism. The following descriptions of the areas of consciousness, as illustrated in the egg diagram, are taken from Assagioli's book *Psychosynthesis* (Assagioli 1965: 17–24):

1 The 'lower unconscious' contains 'the elementary psychological activities which direct the life of the body; the intelligent co-ordination of bodily functions; the fundamental drives and primitive urges; many complexes, charged with intense emotion; dreams and imaginations of an inferior kind; lower, uncontrolled parapsychological processes; various pathologi-

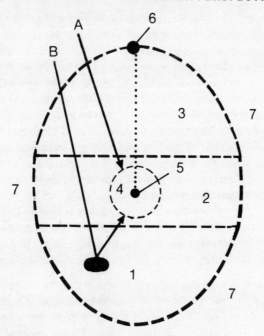

Figure 8.1 The psychosynthesis egg diagram.

cal manifestations, such as phobias, obsessions, compulsive urges and paranoid delusions'.

2 The middle unconscious 'is formed of psychological elements similar to those of our waking consciousness and easily accessible to it. In this inner region our various experiences are assimilated, our ordinary mental and imaginative activities are elaborated and developed in a sort of psychological gestation before their birth into the light of consciousness'.

3 The higher unconscious or superconscious: 'From this region we receive our higher intuitions and inspirations – artistic, philosophical or scientific, ethical "imperatives" and urges to humanitarian and heroic action. It is the source of the higher feelings, such as altruistic love; of genius and of the states of contemplation, illumination, and ecstasy. In this realm are latent the higher psychic functions and spiritual energies'.

4 The field of consciousness: 'the incessant flow of sensations, images, thoughts, feelings, desires, and impulses which we can observe, analyse, and judge'.

5 The conscious Self or 'I': this is the point of pure self-awareness, not to be confused with the personality. 'The changing contents of our consciousness (the sensations, thoughts, feelings etc.) are one thing, while the "I", the self, the centre of our consciousness is another.' The well-known 'disidentification exercise' (see page 134 for a version of the exercise) in psychosynthesis aims at creating awareness of this centre.

6 The Higher Self: The 'I' is a reflection of the Higher Self. 'The conscious self . . . seems to disappear altogether when we fall asleep, when we faint, when we are under the effect of an anesthetic or narcotic, or in a state of hypnosis. And when we awake the self mysteriously re-appears, we do not know how or whence. . . . This leads us to assume that the re-appearance of the conscious self or ego is due to the existence of a permanent centre, of a true Self situated beyond or "above" it.' Assagioli thus saw the aim of psychosynthesis: 'What has to be achieved is to expand the personal consciousness into that of the Self; to reach up, following the thread or ray to the star; to unite the lower with the higher Self'.

7 The Collective Unconscious: The egg diagram is always drawn with dotted lines as its perimeter. This is meant to indicate our interconnectedness at the levels of our psychological being. Each individual consciousness is influenced by, connected with, and influences the 'collective' surrounding it. The collective contains the evolutionary and historically grown, crystallised experiences of humanity and of life on this planet and beyond.

Earlier, on page 108, I quoted Assagioli's writing about the 'spiritual elements of our personality that come down like rays of sunlight into the human personality – into our personal consciousness – and form a link between our ordinary human personality and the spiritual "I", the spiritual Reality'. In the egg diagram (Figure 8.1) I have labelled those rays A and B. They are intuitive flashes, inspirations, 'callings' from the higher realms, in short, energies that help the reunification of the 'I' and the Self. Sometimes these rays, like ray B, may even be sufficient to transform a complex or a conflict in the lower unconscious. I believe that many of the Christian Church rituals such as confession, communion, and confirmation aim at this process.

The 'Greenhouse' – Objects as Protection

Let us now go back to consumerism. Essentially, human beings have to produce and consume in order to stay alive. Goods and objects protect the ego from the survival fears of the lower unconscious. Many of the childhood fears and depressions that lie dormant in the lower regions are related to the child's fear of abandonment, loss of emotional and physical nourishment, and ultimately death. Figure 8.2 places the objects as a protective barrier between the lower unconscious and the middle unconscious. The objects thus stabilise the ego, and 'hold it together'.

The objects in the diagram are rather simplified; apart from solid goods there are many 'potential objects'. The huge field of psychanalytic models and theories applies here, so that ultimately other people, the self-image, feelings and actions can serve as objects that make up the protective barrier. Eventually this barrier can turn into the 'neurotic space', which needs to be constantly filled up in order to offer protection from the underlying fears and

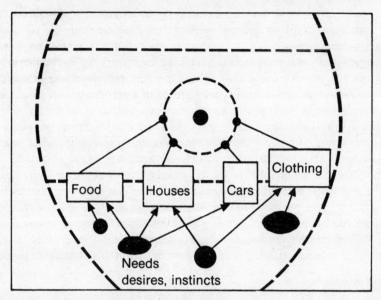

Figure 8.2 Objects as protection.

conflicts mainly rooted in childhood trauma. The objects then become interchangeable and, especially in eating disorders and addictions, the consumption of food and other substances serves this 'filling up' process.

At a different level, the ever increasing division of labour required to produce the ever more detailed parts and components of complex objects (e.g. the components needed to produce a car) turns activities into objects to fill the space. Thus we could have objects like career, mortgage, DIY, skills, etc. filling the space as well.

It is obvious how the growth obsession in our society feeds into this through the constant need for more objects. Even when the space is full more objects need to be squeezed into it, because 'grow or die' is the ultimate law. In the end the process requires the finding of new space in which to fit all the objects.

The 'Greenhouse' – Objects as Distraction

The continuous flow of objects into limited space requires the expansion of the available space. Money and finance have reduced the objects to a common denominator. Ten one-thousand pound notes require less space than a car, and thus the overriding consideration in society and, to a lesser extent, in our individual psyche has become to 'make money', to have insurances, pensions and profits. We cannot escape cheque-books, credit cards and 'budgeting' any more. Money has become the main driving force – it needs to be 'made', regardless of how. Money has created a market for itself

111

– the world's economies are run according to the rules of those markets. The most important rule is that money needs to grow; interest rates, investments, stocks, bonds, pension funds – they all assume that a certain amount of money 'grows' to a larger amount. It has become something like a natural law.

Money has become the main driving force, consumption and production are just subordinate elements; consumption and production are equalised and are measured with the yardstick 'money'. Money itself has become a commodity, and a quality that is attached to goods – the expensive car, the expensive house. Hence production and consumption have become means to make money, and the character, quality and quantity of the goods that are produced and consumed become increasingly irrelevant.

However, in order to produce more (to make more money), somewhere down the line people need to consume more. Hence growing populations mean growing markets, which mean growing consumption. The system has also devised numerous ways to stimulate consumption in the existing markets; advertising and re-packaging have become the motor of the process. The neurotic space becomes overcrowded with objects in colourful wrappings.

As the lower barrier became more solid, many people feeling well protected, the space needed to be widened, 'new motives' for producing and consuming had to be found. And they were found in the higher realms. Figure 6.1 on page 94 illustrates how subordinate aspects of the object 'car' are connected with unconscious emotional needs. We are now going one step further by saying that this applies to needs from the lower unconscious as well as the higher unconscious. The expansion of 'marketing' and advertising has meant that, increasingly, qualities from the higher realms have become associated with products. The shopping-experience example of German department stores (see page 107) shows how cultural and creative motives are being used to sell goods. As a result, the upper border of the middle unconscious with the higher unconscious is also becoming filled up with objects, or with aspects of objects. It is as if the higher qualities were pulled down from the higher realms, creating an objectified spiritual space, a reflection of the lower neurotic space.

An additional complication arises from the fact that some of the higher qualities carry in themselves the desire to 'own' them and are therefore particularly prone to this process. Assagioli writes about 'beauty':

> On the one hand we can say that among the attributes of God beauty is the most easily recognizable because it is the one first manifested in ancient times, the most tangible attribute, one that left its imprint in concrete, material forms, and the attribute that struck the senses and the imagination more directly than any other. On the other hand it is clearly the most dangerous attribute, one that more than any other ties man to matter and form, and one which more than any other produces in him

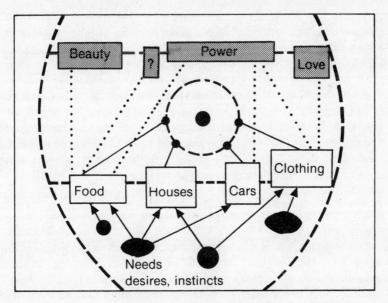

Figure 8.3 Objects as distraction.

the desire for sensory pleasure, the sense of selfish, separate ownership, an attribute that more than any other blinds and deceives man, enveloping him in the iridescent veils of maya – those of the Great Illusion – and thus the attribute which most distances him and keeps him separate from God, the deep Reality of Truth. . . . Because beauty is the divine quality that has assumed the most concrete expression, has been made tangible and manifested itself in matter, it is the one man can most readily abuse, without recognising its noble origin. The quality of beauty is no longer related to its source, rather it has come to be regarded as a quality that resides in matter itself and in its concrete forms.

(Assagioli 1991: 251–2)

The result is shown in Figure 8.3, where both the lower and the upper border of the middle unconscious are filled up with objects, aspects of objects, and reflections of objects. The space becomes rather crowded.

Ultimately, this situation turns into what I call the 'psychological greenhouse'. We are familiar with the global greenhouse effect, where the incoming heat from the sun gets trapped by greenhouse gases in the atmosphere, thus leading to rising temperatures and changes in climates on the Earth's surface. The psychological greenhouse effect is similar, in that energies from the higher and the lower realms get trapped in the middle unconscious and in the field of consciousness, thus leading to a 'heating up' of that area. The zig-zag line in the 'psychological greenhouse space' in Figure

113

8.4 represents the energies that get trapped in the areas of the 'middle unconscious' and the 'conscious'. Many of the stressful situations that govern our lives can be seen in those terms: the endless striving for more and more things and satisfaction; the increasing speed with which we need to do and have it all; the 'feeling trapped' and 'no way out'; the inability to step out.

The psychological problems connected with this effect of the psychological greenhouse are all the stress-related conditions that we see. (It is important to note here that these definitions of common stress-related problems do not intend to negate their origins in the dynamics of the lower unconscious, but rather intend to show how environmental conditions create a space where they are amplified rather than resolved, and to some extent caused.)

1 *Anxiety, panic, and stress symptoms*: Everything has become too much. Over a long period of over-stimulation and striving driven by fear, fear has finally overtaken and the striver is left behind. The gap becomes bigger and fear takes over more and more. Panic attacks triggered by certain stimuli are the body-mind trying to make sense of it all, thus attaching the fear to specific situations. The situations to which fear is attached usually have to do with too much or too many (people, objects in supermarkets, cars on the motorway), too little or too few (open spaces, loneliness) or the inevitability of death (striving leading nowhere).
2 *Obsessional rituals*: Children carry out rituals to structure, make sense, of a world that is too complex. People in the psychological greenhouse carry out rituals to create their own safe space, protected from the bombardment of objects. Cleaning and checking rituals, the battle against intrusive thoughts, can be seen as the individual's struggle against being taken over by the uncontrollable forces around him. Perfectionism, excessive worrying, inability to make decisions, are aspects of our disorientation in the face of a world crowded with people, objects and thoughts, and a lack of spiritual guidance.
3 *Sexual problems*: The one area of human interaction where intimacy and union are possible becomes dominated by performance and competition. The need to dominate over the partner turns people into objects and ultimately their own sexuality into an object as well. Thus 'objectified', sexuality becomes open to 'market forces': it can be split up, different aspects can be turned into objects, money can be made with it, and ultimately our fears of each other and of intimacy can be turned into something marketable rather than something that sexuality can help us overcome.

I have earlier defined the 'inner sanctuary' as an energetic experience of a connection between 'I' and Self. It happens when the 'I' is energised, infused, 'held' by the Self, rather than by the objects surrounding it. It is an experience of inner calm, stillness and solidity that is not dependent on external circumstances. If, however, the connection between 'I' and Self is blocked (see

114

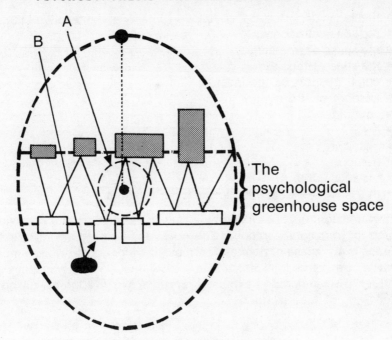

Figure 8.4 The psychological greenhouse.

Figure 8.4), then sanctuary will only be found in the withdrawal into the 'I'. The search for sanctuary can turn into separation, depression, alcoholism, addiction, autism, which are all ways of closing the 'I' off from the hectic activity, the heating-up that goes on around it.

8.1 Reflection: Your Psychological Greenhouse

In this reflection I should like you to imagine your own personal psychological greenhouse. Put a large sheet of paper in front of you and copy the egg diagram on to it. Put yourself right in the middle. At the border between the middle and the lower unconscious write down all the things that you have achieved and created in your life that make you feel safe. Put down also all your most important activities that create for you that feeling of safety and security. Be aware how important those things are for you. Be aware also how much energy and time you have been, and are, putting into creating this protective wall.

At the border between the middle and the higher unconscious write down those higher qualities that are connected for you with the objects and activities that you have put down below. You can choose from Maslow's 'values of the consciousness of being', which are:

• the sense of fullness, integration, totality;

115

- the sense of perfection, completion, vitality and intensity of life;
- the sense of richness;
- the sense of simplicity;
- the sense of beauty;
- consciousness of goodness;
- absence of effort;
- spontaneity;
- joy;
- cheerfulness;
- humour;
- the sense of truth;
- the sense of independence and inner freedom.

Also consider qualities like love, altruism, partnership and companionship in your considerations. The questions you are asking are: How much is my 'sense of richness' connected with my salary? How much is my 'sense of freedom' linked with the car I have and the holidays I can afford? How much do I express or receive love through the giving and receiving of material goods?

You may find that a lot of your higher qualities are firmly linked with just a few objects or activities. Obviously this could mean that there is great fear for you of losing those objects or activities, because it would mean losing the freedom, joy, love, cheerfulness and beauty in your life.

Spend a few moments reflecting upon your own personal psychological greenhouse. How do you feel right in the middle of it? And imagine what it would be like to have all those higher qualities independent of the objects and activities below. Can you imagine it? What would you really like to do and still have those higher qualities? What would you really like to own and still have those higher qualities? Make notes.

There is a second part to this exercise, which may be rather painful. You have now mapped your own psychological greenhouse. Don't worry about how well you have done it. The important part is that you are beginning to realise how important objects and activities have become to satisfy your higher needs, and how fear pushes you to do more and more, to own more and more in order to hold on to those higher qualities. Let's move on to the second part of this exercise.

I should like you to consider how much you feel you need to use the following qualities, characteristics and activities to keep your greenhouse going. Think of your daily life, work and private, and ask yourself how much you feel compelled, by circumstances or otherwise, to use, to experience or to have to put up with each of the following qualities. Rate each one of the qualities on a scale from 1 to 5 as to their relevance for you:

Anger	1	2	3	4	5
Boredom	1	2	3	4	5
Confusion	1	2	3	4	5
Control	1	2	3	4	5
Cruelty	1	2	3	4	5
Cynicism	1	2	3	4	5
Deceit	1	2	3	4	5
Destructiveness	1	2	3	4	5
Disappointment	1	2	3	4	5
Dishonesty	1	2	3	4	5
Fear	1	2	3	4	5
Force	1	2	3	4	5
Frustration	1	2	3	4	5
Futility	1	2	3	4	5
Greed	1	2	3	4	5
Guilt	1	2	3	4	5
Hostility	1	2	3	4	5
Hypocrisy	1	2	3	4	5

Ignorance	1	2	3	4	5

Ignorance 1 2 3 4 5

Intolerance 1 2 3 4 5

Isolation 1 2 3 4 5

Jealousy 1 2 3 4 5

Manipulation 1 2 3 4 5

Miserliness 1 2 3 4 5

Misery 1 2 3 4 5

Paranoia 1 2 3 4 5

Recklessness 1 2 3 4 5

Rejection 1 2 3 4 5

Revenge 1 2 3 4 5

Scarcity 1 2 3 4 5

Self-delusion 1 2 3 4 5

Self-importance 1 2 3 4 5

Self-indulgence 1 2 3 4 5

Selfishness 1 2 3 4 5

Spite 1 2 3 4 5

Stagnation 1 2 3 4 5

Stubbornness 1 2 3 4 5

Suspicion			1	2	3	4	5

Worry			1	2	3	4	5

Look at the drawing of your psychological greenhouse and look at those qualities that you have rated at 4 and 5. Then reflect on the following questions:

Is this how I want my life to be?
What do I really want in life?
What is really important to me in life?
What are my ideals and values?

With those questions in mind close your eyes and imagine yourself at the centre in your drawing. Imagine that you are asking those questions from deep down in your heart. Feel the energy that those questions have. Then imagine yourself standing in a meadow – feel the ground under your feet. You are looking up, and above you you can see a thick layer of grey clouds. Now focus all the energy of those questions, deep down from your heart, up to the clouds. Your feet are solidly standing on the ground. See how gradually an opening appears in the clouds. The sun shines through that opening down on you. Feel the warmth of the sun's rays as they reach you. There is also a symbol coming down to you with the sun's rays.

Draw the symbol on the sheet with your greenhouse map.

The Population Explosion

The 'psychological greenhouse space' is one of crowdedness and of increasing 'psychological heat'. The above reflection is meant to help you sense your own crowded 'greenhouse' space. The symbol at the end of the reflection may indicate how you can re-connect with the energies of Earth and Heaven. Later on in Chapter 12 I shall share with you my own, still very rudimentary, thoughts and ideas about freeing-up the crowded psychological greenhouse space. Perhaps you might like to take your symbol, if you got one in the exercise, to the last Chapter in order to develop your own vision of re-connection.

However, there is one additional aspect to the story, perhaps the most important one. It is the real overcrowding of our planet. It is also a problem that we do not like dealing with – little is reported about it, because the implications seem so inevitably disastrous. How aware are we that in the past 40 years the population of our planet has doubled from 2.6 billion to 5.5 billion? And the process is inevitably continuing – in the 1990s humanity will multiply at a record speed. There will be one billion more people on Earth by the turn of the century. The implications for the use of planetary resources are enormous, as are such consequences as refugees, migration, poverty, etc. The government of India, for example, will need to create 127,000 new schools per year, will need an additional 373,000 teachers per year, four million more jobs per year, and ten million more tons of food per year, just to maintain the present standard of living. By the year 2000 Tokyo will have a population of 28 million, São Paulo 22 million, Bombay 18 million (*Der Spiegel* 8 March 1993: 144–54). All the figures scream out that we are heading for disaster.

I have been thinking whether to include the above figures in my writing. They are so utterly depressing, that I am only now, at the revision stage, willing to put them in. But how can I see meaning in this 'population explosion'? How can I not be totally overwhelmed by the implications? It is easy to write about the psychological aspects of this and that. There is always the notion that change for the 'better' is possible. But if I include the very real overcrowding of the world in our considerations, I lose sight of hope, because there seem to be no solutions.

It seems apparent that we need to control the 'population explosion' – somehow. Certainly birth control, and equal rights for women, would slow down the process. Epidemics and wars would reduce our numbers. But the experts say that it is already too late to put a halt to the overcrowding. I am sorry that I am unable to come up with solutions, or even ideas about solutions, to this problem. However, I can ask myself what the 'meaning' of the population explosion might be.

It seems that the effects of increasing numbers of human beings on Earth are closely related to our considerations about boundaries and about the 'greenhouse'. Increasing populations mean that we are forced to be 'closer together'; our boundaries between each other and our 'individuality' are increasingly turning into relationship issues. The inner 'psychological greenhouse' seems to be paralleled by an outer 'interpersonal' one. The 'third world' is no longer two worlds away. The effects of overcrowdedness are increasing fear and violence, competition and envy. As the boundaries between us are collapsing, we are increasingly required to face our own shadow through being confronted with the shadow of humanity. Projections of the shadow on to other individuals and groups is becoming more difficult because of the closeness of the 'other'. Continuing our projections of the shadow in the 'greenhouse' will inevitably lead to more tension, heat, and destructiveness. The only solution seems to be for us to maturely deal with our relationships, and as a species to move from BPM III – separation – to BPM IV – interdependence.

A second aspect of meaning in the population explosion might be the growing awareness that the resources of our planet are limited and that we have to face our own personal 'growth illusion'. Smaller proportions of our populations will be able to afford all the goods, services and certainties that we have grown to want. A 'movement back to basics' may well be what is required of all of us, and this might include simpler lifestyles, simpler goals, and the focus on inner rather than outer growth.

The words 'all you need is love' are coming into my mind as I am writing this. Perhaps this is where the meaning of humanity moving closer together and of re-focusing on our inner world lies. Perhaps the message in the inner and the outer greenhouse is 'all you need is love' – the spiritual love that we can only discover when we go inside ourselves, and the interpersonal love that we can only give and receive once we have discovered it within. It's strange, but having written it like this has changed my initial feelings. Doom and gloom and inner blocks have given way to a warm feeling inside, a feeling of strength and connectedness.

The Potential in the Greenhouse

The danger is that the enormity of the economic, ecological, psychological and spiritual disasters overwhelm us once we begin to see them with open senses. As a result we may desperately want to repress our insights again, just to continue in our old sweet ways. Yes, it is nice to believe that there are niches in all the mess; that maybe we will get out of the recession and everything will be OK again; that maybe the Earth can cope with it all. I would love to believe that, but find it increasingly difficult not to see. I think it is more important to ask about the potential in the 'greenhouse'. Can we use technology, science, money and wealth in 'the right' way? What is the right way?

One obvious potential lies in the fact that spiritual qualities are brought down to Earth. They are often twisted and abused, but at the same time they are also very close. Michael Lindfield emphasises the potential in information technology:

> The new information technology is bringing about an even more fundamental change: it is the first technology to extend our mental capacity as a species and in effect is an expansion of our brain and nervous system. An increase in mental capacity and logical ability alone will not build the more caring future we so desire. We need a corresponding technology to expand the human heart and increase its capacity to love and care.
>
> (Lindfield 1986: 165)

In addition to information technology, the same would apply for transport, housing, the media and many of the other 'achievements' of humanity. Could this then be the solution? Could the power of the heart transform the overcrowded, claustrophobic psychological space into something else?

Assagioli (1991) addresses a similar issue. He probably wrote the following passages in 1937 and I should like to summarise the issue here, because I have

121

earlier shown how money and finance capital have increased and alienated the production and consumption of objects.

> More than anything else spirituality is concerned with considering life's problems from a higher, enlightened, synthetic point of view, testing everything on the basis of true values, endeavouring to reach the essence of every fact, neither allowing oneself to stop at external appearances nor to be taken in by traditionally accepted views, by the way the world at large looks at things, or by our own inclinations, emotions and preconceived ideas. . . . When spiritual light is focused on the most complex of individual and collective problems it produces solutions and reveals ways in which we can avoid many dangers and errors, sparing us much suffering and thus bestowing incalculable benefits on our lives.
>
> (Assagioli 1991: 213)

In his analysis Assagioli then moves on to use an approach that is quite similar to the one I have used in defining 'money'. He urges us to go back to seeing it as an instrument rather than a goal in itself:

> Thus the first spiritual act we need to perform is to free ourselves from this tendency to place too much value on the means, or on the instrument whereby worldly goods are acquired and exchanged: money. Let us be determined in our refusal to offer any further sacrifices on the altar of this false god, let us free ourselves from the fascination this idol has for us and, with an unclouded vision and calm indifference, reduce it to what it actually is: a mere instrument, a useful device, a practical convention. . . .
>
> The basis for correct individual use lies in the concept of possessions itself as a personal right. Legal ownership is purely a human invention, but one that is justified psychologically and practically in view of the limited level of moral development man has reached. The desire to possess is a primordial force that cannot be discounted: it cannot be killed or forcibly repressed. In spiritual terms, however, ownership has a very different aspect and significance. No longer is it a personal right, but a responsibility towards God and man. . . .
>
> From the spiritual point of view, then, man may only consider himself a trustee, guardian or administrator of the material goods for which he has obtained legal ownership. Those goods are for him a real test, a test he must submit to.
>
> (1991: 222–4)

We are trying to explore the potential in the psychological greenhouse, or how we can transform it so that it frees us rather than imprisons us. Assagioli and Lindfield offer two important strategies for this:

1 Assagioli advocates the more analytical approach of 'going back to basics'

and then applying spiritual principles to the basic components. We have done just that in the chapter on activity theory and its expansion using the psychosynthesis egg.

2 Lindfield suggests the 'seeing with the heart', the application of qualities like caring, compassion, service, altruism to the objects and the world around us, including ourselves. Other writers and thinkers describe this as the necessary shift in value systems from the masculine to the feminine. We shall go into this in more detail later.

How do these two strategies complement each other or differ from each other? Is one of them the masculine approach and the other one the feminine? How does each one need the other, and what would that look like in action? However, there can be no 'either/or'. To see it in terms of 'either/or' would create yet more boundaries. The psychological greenhouse is a model that is based on the creation of boundaries: boundaries between ourselves and the objects, boundaries between each other, and between our levels of consciousness.

Before we can develop practical ways of dealing with our own and each other's trappedness in the greenhouse, we need to consider how most people nowadays express their trappedness. Earlier we looked at the stories people wrote about their anxiety and panic attacks, and I have related anxiety problems, including obsessive-compulsive rituals and sexual problems to the greenhouse model. It has recently become popular to talk about stress.

9

STRESS

Stress has become a very popular topic. Is it just a new trendy thing to suffer from? Do people use it as an excuse, just to cover up their laziness? 'But we all need a certain amount of stress to function; without stress life would be boring'. We seem to be so caught up in the belief that life has to be a struggle, that it is common to be rather dismissive about the one shorthand term that describes our dilemma. I should like to see stress as the key term that brings together all our considerations so far about human suffering, fear, the search for sanctuary, alienation and the psychological greenhouse.

The following exercise aims at helping you explore the personal meaning that the word 'stress' has for you. In psychosynthesis and other psychotherapeutic approaches, the 'personal' is often used as a starting point for learning, rather than more 'general' theories. The danger in the scientific approach (objective rather than subjective) of starting off with a model, and then seeing how an individual fits the model, is that we might cut off important parts of the subjective experience. So, let us start off with the 'personal'.

9.1 Reflection: Stress

Close your eyes, make sure your feet are connected with the floor/ground. Sit upright, but don't overstretch your spine. Make sure your face and your stomach area are relaxed. Now relax your whole body by concentrating on the rhythm of your breathing. Check where in your body you still feel tension, and connect your breathing with those tense parts, breathing into those parts and letting tension flow out from them with each breath out. Also check what emotions are there for you at the moment, just checking and acknowledging. And have a look at the thoughts that are going through your mind at the moment. See if you can slow your thoughts down a bit, or distance yourself from them, so that you are making space in your mind to be able to imagine what I am going to ask you to imagine.

1 Now consider the word *stress*. What does it mean to you? Just allow thoughts, images and words to emerge.

Write down what emerged.

2 Close your eyes again. Look at your life and how it is at the moment; see yourself doing what you're doing in the different areas of your life. When and where and how do you most feel yourself? Imagine yourself doing the things you love doing.

Write down what you saw.

3 Close your eyes again. Look at yourself in the world around you.

Look at yourself at home.

Look at yourself at work.

Look at yourself in your community, village or town.

Look at yourself in your country.

Look at yourself in relation with the world.

What is your relationship with the world around you? When, how, and where do you feel connected to the world around you? When, how, and where do you feel disconnected from the world around you?

Make notes.

4 Read through all your notes and be aware of your physical sensations and of your emotions as you do so. Then close your eyes again. Calm down the signals you are receiving from your body, your feelings and from your thoughts. And then connect your feelings with the material that you have just written down. Allow a symbol, an image or a statement to emerge.

Make a drawing of the symbol or image that you saw or write down the statement that came to you.

After this exercise you could have some sense as to where you are in relation to stress and the world around you. Take your symbol, image or statement away with you into your everyday life and use it to become more aware of yourself, your stress and your relationship with the world around you and within you.

Earlier, we have defined the 'greenhouse' system as one that disconnects us from our selves, each other, from our spirit and from our environment.

Perhaps you would like to consider your experience of the above exercise in this context: do you feel less stressed when you feel connected, and do you feel more stressed when you feel disconnected?

When we say 'I am stressed' we are looking at the surface only. Underneath are all the internal and external boundary, alienation and greenhouse issues. When we are sitting in the car, driving along, we are disconnected from the ground by rubber tyres and asphalt. In a way the present craze for four-wheel drive jeeps might be expressing a need for more groundedness – at least we can then drive on proper non-asphalt ground. Mind you, there are still the rubber tyres, but at least they belong to the car. My image for the sadness that is in the disconnectedness is one of a small tree growing through a hole in the solid layer of asphalt.

The other general area of di(stress) is the inherent and increasing confusion between means and goals and goals and means. Mobility, for example, used to be the means to get from A to B. Now mobility has become a goal in itself and new means (holiday resorts, transport, roads, etc.) have been developed in order to satisfy the need for mobility. A similar confusion is true for food, clothes, houses, furniture, etc.

The disconnectedness from ground and heaven (see 'greenhouse' model) plus the rigid boundaries at all sorts of levels with the dissolution of boundaries happening at the same time, create the general 'greenhouse' conditions and the associated psychological distress. At the same time we are born into and developing in an increasingly complex and fragmented human world. Inevitably, the process of internalising the environment leaves many areas about which we know either nothing or very little. We internalise many things in extremely abbreviated and symbolic ways. There is always more 'not-knowing' than 'knowing'. Consequently we are all the time faced with the 'fear of the unknown', which causes a basic level of fear, and also causes us to block off the terror of the abyss that we are facing daily. On the positive side, somewhere along the line, at least some of us should by now have developed the ability to deal quite well with facing the 'unknown'.

The 'psychological greenhouse' means that 'sense-making' is becoming increasingly difficult. And if we cannot make sense of our environment, our relationships, our goals, our feelings and values, then that creates stress. So in order to find some structure in chaos and disorientation we often need to revert back to our basic biological survival mechanisms – the flight–fight response, which then shows itself as anxiety and stress.

Before moving on to exploring and including more traditional stress management procedures, I should like to invite you to reflect on a particularly powerful mind-set, the belief that life is a struggle. I think it is particularly powerful because it relates to the BPM II and III experiences, and it also relates to the archetypal concept of 'the warrior'.

LIFE IS A STRUGGLE

You have become caught in the illusion
that your identity
rests with your capacity to struggle.
It does not.

Your true identity
is awaiting you
beyond effort.

The key to remembering
is to remind the self
not to be afraid of anything
anywhere
anytime
ever.

Illusion cannot destroy reality.
Can a shadow on the wall
hurt you?

Death cannot kill you.
Pain cannot hurt you.
Disease cannot make you ill.
Years cannot age you.
Fear cannot touch you.
Welcome Home.

(Emmanuel 1989: 29)

9.2 Reflection: Life is a Struggle

What is your reaction to the quote from Emmanuel?

How much do you believe that life has to be a struggle?

How much has the belief that life is a struggle influenced you in your
life?
Scan your life story for this.
How is this belief serving you now?
How is this belief hindering you now?
What is your reality now?
How much do you struggle out of survival necessity and how much do
you struggle out of an old belief system?

Imagine what it would be like to find your identity without struggling.
Visualise, write, draw what it would be like.
What energy can you feel in that visualisation?

STRESS MANAGEMENT

It has become quite acceptable and trendy to talk about stress and its management, about 'coping with life', about having a rational approach to your problems, about thinking more positively. Earlier we have explored the deeper issues that are beneath it all. Let's now look at the more superficial approaches to stress management.

Stress management is being sold in 'packages', and the approaches are often very rational and structured. They often fit into your expensive time-manager and they teach you about structuring your life differently – from healthy eating, giving up smoking, more exercise, less drinking, to more relaxation, positive self-talk and even meditation. Two points need to be considered here:

1 Increasing numbers of people are going to their doctors and their psychologists to ask for help with their experience of stress. It seems to be becoming acceptable to do that. 'I am suffering from stress' seems to be developing into a symbolic expression of saying 'There is something wrong with me and with my world. I feel wrong and my relationship with my world, with my life feels wrong. My body is expressing it with stress symptoms'. The statement 'I am suffering from stress' seems to have become a shorthand way of saying those deeper things about our inner and outer world that we don't have words for.

2 In companies, it is still very difficult to offer people training in stress management. It is still seen as a 'dirty word'. If you suffer from stress symptoms, you are really saying, 'something is wrong, I don't like it'. Such a statement is not acceptable in our performance-orientated business world. Chances are that you, the sufferer, will be regarded as not being 'good value for money'. Your stress will most likely be seen as your personal failure to meet the demands that others seem to be able to meet without any problems. As a result people often struggle on, trying to get through their stress symptoms until it is too late. On the other hand, there are a number of companies which give their employees some training in stress management, offer counselling or refer people on for individual counselling. Obviously, in recessionary times, both tendencies will be very much evident: the reluctance to spend money on stress management; and the concern to keep the remaining workforce as sane and productive as possible.

It is unlikely that companies would be interested in exploring with their employees the deeper issues behind stress as I have defined them earlier. However, even very superficial stress management, like superficially applied behaviour therapy, can open the door to deeper issues. Let's look at what could be relatively safely used by companies without directly and immediately turning their employees into 'new age warriors'.

Standard stress management sees stress very much like a mechanistic term out of physics. It means that one object is exposed to the force of another object. The force of the second object is equal to or greater than the resistance of the first one. The strain put on the first object will eventually break it. It is a 'battle' between two objects – the stronger one will survive. Hence traditional stress management has focused on three issues:

1 The analysis of the strengths of both object A (the individual and his ability to withstand pressure) and of object B (the environment and its capacity to exert pressure). The 'general adaptation syndrome' considerations represent such an analysis.

2 How can we strengthen A to withstand more pressure from B?
Relaxation, meditation, healthy diet, exercising, all aim at physically strengthening A. In addition it has been found that A's perception of B, i.e. whether or not and how much A perceives B as a threat, determines the actual physical stress response. This is also related to the question why two different individuals would be stressed to different degrees by exactly the same situation. Cognitive therapy methods are employed here to analyse and modify an individual's perception of being threatened by B. What is being threatened and why? Is my interpretation of the situation realistic? What is the worst that could happen? It is easy to see how the asking of questions like this can lead to the asking of a more basic question: What do I really want out of life and does my work/home life still give me what I want and need? This is the 'cutting edge' of stress management, the point at which it can turn into deeper questions about goals, meanings and values. While companies are interested in having stronger, more stress-resistant employees, they are obviously not interested in having employees who put energy into working on their goals and values. This is because such work will quite inevitably also lead to a questioning of the meaning of work, the culture and the values of the company, and the type of relationships at work.

3 How can we make B less stressful?
This is a very delicate subject especially when it comes to the work environment. Obviously, a lot of things can be changed to make the work environment less stressful: changes in the physical work environment, improving communication, changing management styles, changing work allocation systems, giving employees the opportunity to express themselves. However, there is one boundary which these changes cannot cross, and this boundary is the competitiveness of the company. Hence employees' productivity, motivation and loyalty must not become impaired. But what happens to those employees who become more aware of themselves and their environment and who then might also become

aware of the 'growth terror', or of 'alienation' in the system? How could somebody like that still work in financial services or in marketing? The question then becomes: can consciousness remain limited in stress management; can we become more critical without beginning to question the system within and without?

STRESS MANAGEMENT WORKSHOP

Most of the available stress management techniques are based on behavioural and cognitive therapy and they try to establish a clear cause–effect relationship, whereupon programmes are designed to modify the identified causes, reactions and attitudes. Such programmes can be very useful in the same way that cognitive–behavioural methods can be very useful (see chapter 4). The fact that these programmes can open up deeper levels also applies. They may ultimately give participants glimpses into the issues around growth and alienation, and uncomfortable questions might be asked. I think that this is similar to the 'job-enrichment programmes' that were carried out in Detroit in the 1950s. Experiments were carried out in order to make the jobs of assembly-line workers in the car manufacturing industry more interesting. Work groups were formed which produced a whole car from beginning to end rather than each worker performing the same repetitive task day after day. It was found that the productivity of the work groups was higher than the productivity of the assembly-line workers. However, there was a side-effect. The work-group workers were also beginning to become more interested in overall company issues. Thus once their range of activities and therefore their range of consciousness was expanded to the car as a whole, they also wanted to become more involved in the running of the company as a whole. Obviously, this would be rather uncomfortable for a system that relies on control through hierarchies, division of labour and powerlessness of the work-force. Consequently the experiments were stopped because they were threatening the system.

I think the same must be true for any activity that tries to expand consciousness, whether it is behavioural, cognitive or stress management. The growth system relies on the maintenance and the heating up of the psychological greenhouse, and any degree of more awareness or consciousness is inclined to break through the layers of concrete below and the clouds above. As therapists, we must be aware of this, so that we can do our job in a responsible, careful and compassionate way.

I have used the following exercises in stress management training. I think they are good examples of how structured exercises can open up deeper psychological realms. The exercises are presented here as a resource, either for you to use with yourself, or to use in training courses that you might run.

130

9.3 Stress Management Exercises

1. FRED AND THE BANANA SKIN

After having developed the chart on anxiety and panic attacks for Over the Top *(see Figure 3.1, p. 42) friends told me that it was much too complicated and that no one would understand it. So, the cartoon story of* Fred and the Banana Skin *was born. It contains all the elements of the rather complicated flow chart in a story-telling way. Using it as an experiential exercise, it seems to address less intellectual and more emotional ways of processing. Why don't you read through Fred's story with an open mind and heart, and see what it does to you?*

This is the story of Fred. He is a bit of a perfectionist – he likes doing things well. Occasionally he gets nervous – but not too much. In the back of his mind he thinks to himself: 'I must be seen as coping well with life. I am just happy-go-lucky. Things could go on like this forever.

However, deep down Fred is quite soft and vulnerable, although he would not normally admit to this. Then, one day, as he is going about his businness, he feels a bit tired. Problems with the car, a few things at work, and the flu he's just had. He doesn't notice the banana skin right in front of his left foot.

Fred steps on to the banana skin, and he stumbles and falls. Suddenly the ground is taken from underneath him – he is upside down.

The fall really frightens Fred. His heart is beating extremely fast, he trembles and he is getting hot and cold. And being the sensitive person he is, he is very upset about his mishap. Suddenly the world seems all strange and not quite the same any more.

'Hope this won't happen again. Hope nobody saw me', Fred thinks to himself. But his heart is beating so fast, and the trembling – better go and see the doctor. Being more aware of his body than ever before, he stumbles into the surgery. The doctor checks him over: 'You're fine, nothing to worry about. It's just your nerves, a stress reaction'. Fred is reassured and he leaves the surgery feeling better. But he is still a bit worried, mainly about his heart and about banana skins.

Fred is now feeling quite reluctant to go anywhere near the area where he fell. In fact, even thinking about going there makes his heart beat faster. 'This is silly', he says to himself, 'I must pull myself together'. But just to make sure, he is beginning to watch his steps, carefully looking around corners. And one day it actually pays off – he is quite certain that there was this huge banana skin waiting for him just around the corner. Or did he just imagine it? Fred worries: 'Maybe I'm going mad. What will people think of me?'

Fred is now beginning to avoid more and more situations and places where he thinks there could possibly be a banana skin. He is imagining them everywhere – on buses, trains, in super-markets. He is thinking about banana skins a lot of the time; and a lot of the time he is slightly anxious – his heart beating fast and his hands trembling. Fred sighs: 'I wish things were the way they used to be; I was so strong and happy. Why has all this happened to me?'

 For fear of banana skins, Fred is now becoming quite reluctant to leave the house. But even indoors he feels anxious. He thinks: 'Maybe I'm ill. Maybe I should go to the doctor. After all, he helped me last time'. But just the thought of leaving the house makes his heart beat so fast, and he trembles all over. Fred imagines that there is this huge banana skin waiting for him right on his doorstep.

First of all check your emotional, physical and rational reaction to Fred's story.

Now make two lists of five of your own banana skins, both at work and outside work.

At work	Outside work
1.	1.
2.	2.
3.	3.
4.	4.
5.	5.

Consider how much those banana skins are influencing your feelings, your thinking and your behaviour. How far have you, like Fred, blown the dangers out of all proportion? There may be deeper reasons for this. On the other hand there may not, and all that has happened has been the operation of the vicious circles that we discussed earlier. You can now begin to question your anticipation of danger by asking how realistic your fears really are.

2. ANALYSE A STRESSFUL SITUATION

This exercise is based on the behaviour–analytic approach described earlier. It will help in the first stages of 'sense-making' and the benefits are: thinking about it, beginning to see connections, talking about it, accepting it, beginning to feel about it.

Think back to a recent stressful situation. Identify the day, time and place of the situation and imagine what happened as vividly as possible. Make notes:

a. How and when did the situation start?

b. *Who was saying/doing what?*
c. *What did you do and say?*
d. *What thoughts were going through your mind at the time?*
e. *What feelings were there at the time?*
f. *How did the situation stop being stressful?*

Look at the sequence of events and ask yourself: At what point(s) in the course of events could I have said, done, thought something different in order to make the situation less stressful?

3. BODY/FEELINGS/THOUGHTS

Sit in a relaxed position with both feet on the floor, upright, but not strained. Close your eyes and connect with your breathing. Then be aware of all the physical sensations you can feel. Do not change anything; just check all your physical sensations.

Then focus your attention on your emotions. What emotions are inside you at the moment? Again, try to be a detached observer of your emotions. Don't become over-involved with any of the emotions that are there. Just check them and acknowledge them.

Now move your attention to the thoughts that are going through your mind. Watch the thoughts and images that are going through your mind. Be aware that the thought 'I am not having a thought' is a thought as well.

Then ask yourself:

a. *How does my body usually experience stress?*
b. *What emotions do I experience when I am stressed?*
c. *What thoughts are going through my mind when I am stressed?*

Make notes about your observations, then talk about it in groups of three. Afterwards discuss it all within the whole group, including what it was like to 'go inside' and to focus on parts of the 'inner world', and what it was like to share the experiences in small groups.

Theoretical Consideration: Disidentification

The above exercise introduces the concept of 'disidentification', which was developed by Assagioli (1965) as one of the standard procedures in psychosynthesis. It assumes that experience can be divided into physical, emotional and mental. It also assumes that we can learn to go into an 'observer position' in order to just observe the body, the feelings, and the mind, rather than being completely caught up in one or two of those areas of our experience. It can be extremely useful to develop the ability to be able to look at experience from the observer position, because our whole identity often gets caught up in a physical sensation, a feeling or a thought. Examples of this are:

1 In panic attacks all the attention is focused on the physical sensations of panic. Vicious circles can develop between thoughts and physical sensations (see the cognitive-behavioural model of anxiety and panic that was developed in Chapter 3). Panic sensations trigger off panic thoughts – panic thoughts increase the panic sensations – more panic thoughts – more panic sensations. It is interesting to note here that most people with panic attacks are quite unaware of their emotions. One could say they have learnt to 'repress' their emotions. Usually the emotions concerned are ones that have become traumatised in childhood, like anger or excitement. It is as if the body was still expressing the emotions in a physical way, and the mind tries to make sense of it, but cannot access the repressed (hidden away) painful emotional content and context (this is also related to our earlier discussion of 'hidden triggers'). Disidentification offers a way of stepping out of those vicious circles by developing an attitude like 'My body and my mind are panicking again. I wonder what this is all about'. However, this may not be sufficient to access the repressed emotional content and context. But it will strengthen the awareness of a centre that is beyond our usual areas of experience (the observer, the self).
2 In depression the focus is on that one emotion only. Again, this exclusive focus can be a defence against other even more painful emotions. Disidentification can redress the balance by developing an attitude like 'This feeling of depression is there again. I wonder what other feelings are there or were there'.
3 With obsessive compulsive ruminations (worrying) the focus is on the thoughts, again possibly in defence of painful emotions. An observer-like attitude would be 'I know that my mind is worrying again. I wonder what emotions and physical sensations are or were there'.

Ken Wilber suggests the disidentification exercise as a way of developing and strengthening a 'sense of self'. Recently, Firman (1991) has criticised the whole concept as a dualistic one in psychosynthesis, which has led to many dualistic concepts and procedures, where holistic ones are needed. However, bearing in mind that the ultimate goal in therapy is obviously identification and unity, disidentification can be an important initial step to change established patterns of thinking and (not) feeling, and it can give people first experiences of a connection between the 'I' and the Self.

In stress management this connection with the Self can lead to the creation of the 'inner sanctuary' from which both the internal and external world can be approached differently. As we have discussed earlier, such a different approach can easily include the questioning not only of intra-psychic patterns, but also of the world around us. The question becomes whether companies, who are caught up in growth pressures and competition, can really afford employees who are critical and questioning. Yes, as long as stress management increases creativity and productivity. But what about the side-effects?

4. THE TYRANNY OF THE 'SHOULDS'

This exercise aims at changing 'mind-sets'. These are our attitudes, beliefs, assumptions, prejudices and stereotypes that help us to make sense of our experience. A brain without mind-sets would be like a computer without software. We need mind-sets to process all the incoming information. These cognitive structures can become very rigid because they have developed over a long period of time, often from early childhood. We then hang on to them as if it were a matter of life and death, even though the particular way of seeing things may not serve us any longer. The results are rigid boundaries that make it impossible for us to see things from a different perspective. Evans and Russell suggest two steps to approach the issue of mind-sets:

1 *We 'first need to become aware of which mindsets are operating in a particular situation. Then we have to ask ourselves, "How does this mindset serve me, and how does it limit me?" ' (Evans and Russell 1989: 104–5).*

2 *'To what extent am I the master of this mindset, and to what extent am I its victim?' (1989: 105).*

Important mind-sets are the 'shoulds' that we carry around with us. They are our rules for living. Without thinking about it for too long, see if you can make a list of your 'shoulds', by completing the statement 'I should . . .' ten times.

1 *I should* _____

2 *I should* _____

3 *I should* _____

4 *I should* _____

5 *I should* _____

6 *I should* _____

7 *I should* _____

8 *I should* _____

9 *I should* _____

10 *I should* _____

It does not matter if you wrote down fewer than ten 'shoulds'. It can help to rank the 'shoulds' in order of importance or strength.

Now take a large sheet of paper and some coloured pens to draw your map of 'shoulds'. Start off with the most important or strongest 'should' and draw a circle on the paper, its size and colour reflecting importance and strength. Write the should inside the circle. Then take the next 'should' and place it in relation to the first one in terms of distance, size and colour. In this way put all your 'shoulds' on the map. You can also connect the circles with lines – thick, thin or dotted – to indicate their connectedness or lack of it. Some of the circles may overlap; others may be totally disconnected.

Look at your map and visually take in the structure on paper. What does it look like? What does it feel like? What energy do you feel coming from the map? How does the energy relate to your experience of stress?

If you are doing this exercise in a group, get together with one other person and let that person be your counsellor. Show him/her your map and let the other person interpret your map for ten minutes. Just listen to how another person sees it. Then swap roles.

As a last step, go back to your original list of 'shoulds' and read them out aloud once – slowly and with an awareness of what each one feels like. Then go through the same list again, replacing 'should' with 'could'. What does that feel like?

Something else you can do with your map is to stand on it with your eyes closed. What does it feel like in your body? Feel the energy from the 'shoulds' in your body and let your body take on the posture of the map. Be aware of all the sensations and feelings in your body as you do this. Then step outside the map and stand on the floor/ground. What is it like? Take on the body posture. Be aware of feelings and sensations. Then step back on to the map and off it again. Become aware of the dance between the two positions.

Make notes about your experience with this exercise, and, if you are in a group, share your experiences.

5. MEDITATING WITH A TREE

I often use this exercise with people when I feel they have developed the habit of trying to make intellectual sense of physical sensations, thus bypassing the emotional part of the experience. This is particularly true of men who are referred to me with stress and anxiety symptoms.

137

In the grounds of the clinic where I do my therapy work there is an area of trees, including a willow tree. I usually have two chairs there and in the summer I use it as my 'consulting space'. For the meditation I ask people to sit facing the willow tree trunk at a distance of about two yards: 'Sit up straight in your chair; be aware of your feet on the ground and of the sky above your head, and be aware of your breathing. Breathe into your whole body. For ten minutes just observe the tree. As you do that, pay attention to what happens in your body and what emotions you experience. Also be aware of what goes through your mind, and allow your thinking to gradually slow down.'

Usually people get in touch with emotions and/or memories. It seems that the sitting outdoors, doing nothing while the attention is 'held' by the tree, has a very soothing effect. Some of my clients have taken up regular meditation practice with natural beings as a result.

BEYOND STRESS MANAGEMENT

Earlier, I defined the statement 'I am stressed' as an expression of deep distress in our inner and outer world. What does it then mean to uncover the deeper dissatisfaction and dis-ease that is underneath the top layer of 'stress'? What happens when we glimpse the growth tyranny, the confusion between means and goals, the alienation from our values and purpose? In short, what do we do once we want to clear the space surrounding us of all the objects – objects that have imprisoned us, but have also given us a sense of security?

I have no clear answer to the questions, but I would like to develop some guidelines for my and our journey. Perhaps 'guidelines' are too ambitious; it sounds a bit like aiming at a grand finale. Perhaps if I aim at enabling you to become a bit more aware of your journey in the 'greenhouse', you might be able to come up with your own individual guidelines. And perhaps you could send me a brief summary of your 'stepping out' process. I should love to compile a book of all your stories. We could call it *The Traveller's Guide to Stepping Out of the Greenhouse*. Let's look at a few stress stories.

1. The Therapist

Often nowadays, when I run groups and see individual patients, I can clearly see how their particular problems are related to 'greenhouse issues'. However, my training as a clinical psychologist and as a psychotherapist has not prepared me to deal with this. I can focus on the intrapsychic, and interpersonal dynamics, the transference and counter-transference. But what do I do when I can so clearly see them as rats in the Skinner-box of our systems – conditioned, trapped, limited, their human potential so crippled in terms of sensitivity, creativity and transcendence that it is hardly recognisable? What do I do with the pain and anger that I feel then? In the 1960s and 1970s when I could no longer bear to see my father's pain, pain that he drowned with alcohol, I discovered Marxism. I was then able to make sense of his trappedness, but unable to do anything for him with my knowledge. I became very angry with him, and with the system that was clearly responsible for his misery and mine.

Today I am the mature, responsible psychotherapist, but that part of me is not able to handle what I see. I can help people on their journey, I can bring them to the edge of seeing, but I cannot yet show them the safest way through the unknown territory beyond the 'greenhouse'. It is because I myself am standing on the edge of it, scanning and searching for a reasonably safe path. Maybe there is no 'reasonably safe' path? Do I now need to re-connect with the energy of the adolescent Marxist rebel, who knew that there was a better way and who shouted for it? It does feel as if action beyond being a psychotherapist is needed. This is what this book is all about – me writing my way into the unknown. It is frightening. But on the other hand it is more frightening not to act on what I see. Yes, maybe it was easy to be cynical, or to think that it is all people's own responsibility, or to think that at least with a psychiatric or psychological diagnosis and appropriate 'treatment' we can make them feel better. But how can I still live with that when I can hear my patients' screaming, echoed by the walls of the 'greenhouse'? Can I still be contented with the fact that I hear it but they don't? In a way I am again facing my father's pain and suffering.

2. Peter

Peter, aged 52, has just had major surgery and completed four months of chemotherapy for cancer. The scans are now clear, but it is a recurrence of twenty years ago. He is American and he has been living in England for four years. He is a sales manager for an American firm and he returned to the States for chemotherapy treatment. His placement in England ends in two months' time and he has to decide whether or not to stay on for another year. His industry has been badly hit by the recession. If he goes back to the States his job security will not be very good. He could take early retirement, but he could not live on his pension. If he stays in England he will miss the birth of his grandchildren (twins) in the States and he will still have to go back in a year's time. He does not like his job any more, he is unable to make up his mind, he cannot concentrate, he sleeps badly, he worries all the time, he is stressed. He has always been a worrier, but he thinks he should be happy. He gets panic attacks and he cannot relax, and he experiences a lot of guilt about things in his past. He worries so much that he often gets a tight feeling around his forehead and his temples.

I can see that Peter is very needy. He wants me to tell him what to do. I feel uncomfortable with taking the responsibility for his decisions, but at the same time I desperately want to help this 'poor man'. I am beginning to realise that Peter's present pressures are bringing up for him all the insecurities from his childhood – the fact that he never knew his father, who left when he was a baby, and that his whole childhood was cold and unsupportive. I am beginning to feel enormous pressure to help Peter, knowing that I probably have only one month to work with him. I know that the pressure I feel is similar to the pressure he feels. I am trying to do my best, knowing that I would need at least a year to get anywhere near the real issues. After four sessions Peter fails to turn up for any further sessions with me. I feel helpless and I am beginning to realise that Peter must be carrying a lot of anger in himself, and that he has probably proved to himself again that nobody can help him.

3. Michael

Michael used to be a top marketing manager in a financial services firm. He is now 43, married, has two adolescent children, a big house and a big mortgage. Four years ago Michael's wife became depressed and she received medication treatment and psychotherapy. Cracks in the marriage became more obvious, and his wife began to criticise Michael's behaviour – his excessive working hours, his constant exhaustion, his inability to express his feelings, and his often autocratic behaviour at home. Michael took his wife's complaints on board and went into therapy himself. He learned to be more aware of his feelings and to express them more. He also began to see how his extreme ambitiousness was still driven by 'little Michael' desperately trying to please his father. He was becoming increasingly dissatisfied with the coldness and falseness of communication and interaction at work. Michael's colleagues and superiors were noticing that Michael was 'different', he seemed 'softer', occasionally he would become tearful at work.

During a subsequent restructuring exercise at work, Michael was sidestepped and some of his responsibilities were taken away from him. His resilience and ability to deal with stress were being questioned. At the same time Michael was increasingly doubting his motivation for his work. Eventually Michael resigned from his very highly-paid job. He experienced an enormous sense of relief and freedom, but at the same time fear set in. He was feeling empty, worthless, useless, and he was desperately trying to make plans for the future, ranging from setting up his own horticultural business to doing private marketing consultancy work. His fears were interfering with the creative space he had made. Michael was bringing all this to my men's group, where others were dealing with similar issues around their newly-discovered craving for personal growth versus the performance pressures of career and mortgages.

Is this then the ultimate, inevitable result of stress management? People who can no longer conform with the 'normal' rules and demands, but who still have to pay their mortgages and car loans? What are the alternatives, the niches? Should all the more aware people work for 'green' businesses or charities? Should we all sternly refuse the demands and temptations of this seductive system and 'step out'? What do we step into? Are there alternatives out there?

Michael visited the Findhorn Community[1] for a week in order to experience different ways of working and living together. He did the 'experience week' and came back full of the spirit of Findhorn. He started telling me his story by saying how upset he had been that he'd forgotten to take his group photograph and address list when he left to come back home. 'I have never felt so close to a group of people in my life. When I got back I felt so empty.' He then proceeded to tell me about the last session of the week, called 'completion', where everybody just talks about their experience of the week. In accordance with an old Native American habit, a stone gets passed around from the person who speaks to the one who should speak next. At the end of the five-hour sharing, the question arose as to who should take the stone home. Four people said they wanted to take it. As the group went into trying to decide who should be given the stone, something in Michael suddenly told him that he wanted it. The reason was that he felt there was so much love in it, because everybody had been holding it as they spoke. In the end he got the stone and the experience that he had, for the first time in a long time, asked for something for himself. He had used his courage for a purpose reaching beyond greed.

4. Ormond Stores

While staying near Ballypatrick in County Tipperary, I drove to a small country shop/one-pump-petrol station to buy a few bits and pieces. In my usual 'civilised' manner I already had plans for the rest of the afternoon in my head: there was a leisurely pint to be had in the pub in Ballypatrick; there was Slievenamon, the mountain to be climbed before going back to England in two days' time; there was dinner to be prepared, etc. All in all, the shopping trip was a nuisance; there were other, more interesting, more important things to be done, to be achieved. Hence the plan was to spend as little time as possible in the shop. However, I got chatting to the woman owner behind the counter after having bought my items. We talked about England and Ireland, young people leaving Ireland to get hold of all the glossy things over there, but then wanting to come back because they couldn't find 'it' over there either. I was enjoying the natter, but there was also that little voice somewhere inside that said that I should be moving on now. And as I was talking and looking at her across the counter, my eyes were attracted to some red cardboard boxes behind the cash desk. They contained batteries. Suddenly I remembered. I had wanted to buy one 'AA' battery, but had forgotten about it. I bought it and told the woman the story of how I had almost forgotten it. Normally I would have rushed into the store, bought my things, my mind already dealing with things ahead and I would have probably noticed that I had forgotten to buy the battery in the car on the way back. I then would have turned the car around, driven back to the store, by then being in a terrible hurry, bought the battery, and rushed on again. Wasn't this a much more pleasant way of being reminded? And, efficiency-wise, the relatively relaxed chat probably required less energy, hustle and risk-taking than racing back and forth in the car would have taken.

The Stress Dilemma

The above four stories suggest ways of dealing with stress in a wider context. They range from the 'simple' solution of slowing down, to facing the need to 'step out'. I strongly believe that once we begin to work on our stress problems, we will sooner or later face those two issues: slowing down and stepping out of the 'greenhouse'. Many people will not face those dilemmas in this lifetime of theirs; others will be able to stretch the preliminaries like learning to relax more, learning to communicate better for long enough, so that they never come to the edge. Others will, like Peter, carry lots of repressed emotions through their lives without finding or accepting the opportunity to release them, but will instead develop physical illnesses. Many, however, will be standing there on the edge like the therapist and Michael in the above stories.

Lucien Sève (1972) wrote a book in which he tried to develop a Marxist personality theory. The book was extremely important to me at university in Berlin in the 1970s. Looking at it now, I think how can such a brilliant and thorough analysis be so heartless? Cold 'scientific' intellect dominated, as in most other Marxist publications in those years. However, I found one important statement that might take our considerations further. Sève writes that especially those individuals who 'love' their jobs will experience the limits of society as limits to their own personal development, and will therefore be the ones who will fight the limiting system.

Many of the people I see as patients seem to me to be struggling with their capacity to love. They are either searching for it or repressing it because their love was hurt, abused or rejected when they were children, or they are expressing too much of it out of guilt and anger, again dating back to childhood experiences. The emphasis here is on the fact that they *are* struggling with it, consciously or not. I often see them as vulnerable, sensitive children who are facing a cold, punitive, abusive internalised childhood world *and* a similarly frightening present external world. But even the internal childhood world is only an internalised external world.

142

Could it be that those vulnerable people who are coming to see me with their problems are the vulnerable, soft, potentially loving ones of this world? I often feel they are. What then is my task as a therapist? Do I guide them to hide their vulnerability and consequently their love better, so that they can 'function in the world'? Or do I guide them towards facing their vulnerability with all the fear and anger that that entails, so that they can ultimately express their love? I do not think that it is much of a question.

The second part of Sève's statement relates to people's relationship with their job. The stressed men in their 30s and 40s who come to me for therapy are often the ones who have spent ten to twenty years giving everything to their jobs. They may have neglected their emotional and interpersonal lives at the expense of work and career. And then, like Michael, they suddenly realise that they are expendable. The questions of 'why' and 'what for' are being asked, and they are beginning to sense that they have been used, exploited.

Sève's conclusion is that the people who love their jobs and who will therefore experience the limits of the system as limits to their own personal development will then become the 'fighters' who will change the system. But where and how can they fight today, at a time when socialism, as an alternative to fight for, is dead? The disintegration of socialism has also severely damaged socialist ideals as alternatives to capitalism. In a way, the capitalist system has regained credibility through the ending of socialism, a credibility that it hardly deserves. It is now more likely that people who come up against the limits and boundaries of the system will see it as their own personal failure rather than a failure of that system. This may be profitable for psychotherapists, because it is likely that those people with stress symptoms, low self-esteem, self-doubts and feelings of stuck-ness will be referred to us for therapy. But this is where the therapist's dilemma lies. How do we handle it? As in the therapist's story above, which obviously describes my own dilemma, I do feel that psychotherapy in all its different forms, and probably stress management in particular, are standing on the edge with our patients.

10

DOMINATION AND PARTNERSHIP

Our culture and society rely on domination for maintenance. Hierarchies, power over, control, fear, dominators and dominated are the features that are needed and reproduced in us from childhood onwards. I should like to quote Barry and Janae Weinhold from their book on co-dependency:

> We believe that approximately 98 per cent of all Americans suffer from some of the major effects of what is now called co-dependency. Estimates indicate that less than 1 per cent of these people are fully aware of the effects of co-dependency and even fewer of them are taking steps to correct these effects.
>
> Some of the major symptoms of co-dependency are:
>
> - feeling 'addicted' to people;
> - feeling trapped in abusive, controlling relationships;
> - having low self-esteem;
> - needing constant approval and support from others in order to feel good about yourself;
> - feeling powerless to change destructive relationships;
> - needing alcohol, food, work, sex or some other outside stimulation to distract you from your feelings;
> - having undefined psychological boundaries;
> - feeling like a martyr;
> - being a people-pleaser;
> - being unable to experience true intimacy and love.
>
> (Weinhold and Weinhold 1989: 3–4)

The authors define co-dependency as a cultural problem which is based on the dominator structure of our capitalist societies. They also see co-dependency in all our institutions: medicine, education, religion, politics. In their book, the Weinholds refer to Riane Eisler's *The Chalice and the Blade* (1988).

> 'Rational man' now spoke of how he would 'master' nature, 'subdue' the elements, and – in the great twentieth-century advance – 'conquer'

space. He spoke of how he had to fight wars to bring about peace, freedom, and equality, of how he had to murder children, women, and men in terrorist activities to bring dignity and liberation to oppressed people. As a member of the elites in both the capitalist and the communist worlds, he continued to amass property and/or privilege. To make more profits or to meet higher quotas, he also began to systematically poison his physical environment, thereby threatening other species with extinction and causing severe illness in human adults and deformities in human babies. And all the while he kept explaining that what he was doing was either patriotic or idealistic and – above all – rational.

Finally, after Auschwitz and Hiroshima, the promise of reason began to be questioned. What was one to make of the 'rational' and efficient use of human fat for soap? Or the highly efficient use of the hygienic shower for poison gas? How could one explain the carefully reasoned military experiments of the effects of atomic bombs and radiation on living and totally helpless human beings? Could all this superefficient mass destruction be called an advance for humanity?

(Eisler 1988: 157–8)

These are two paragraphs from Eisler's passionate book. There is a lot of material in her book that connects with my considerations about cognitive behaviourism, activity theory and stress. Eisler convincingly argues that only the re-emergence of the goddess will save us and our planet – feminine values need to be applied to technology which was developed under the reign of the 'war-gods'.

She puts an end to the widely held assumption that greed, competition and domination are part of human nature and therefore unchangeable by focusing on pre-historic times. Barry and Janae Weinhold summarise Eisler's findings:

When Eisler delved into prehistory, she found numerous legends and archaeological records that described an earlier form of civilization in which the culture was organized quite differently from what we know today. According to these records, there were large areas in Europe and the near East which enjoyed long periods of peace and prosperity. The social, technological and cultural development of the existent society followed a steady move upward. This civilization which she identifies as a 'partnership' society, was based on unity, cooperation and mutual need. The society valued the life-giving and nurturing qualities that we might consider to be 'feminine'. Burial of this era reveal a wealth of statues and artifacts devoted to the worship of a female Deity, The Great Mother. These artifacts, along with their ancient art, myth and historical writings, indicate a deep reverence for life, caring, compassion and nonviolence. The archaeological evidence also reveals that this early social structure was based on equality. Power, risk-taking and rewards were shared without regard to gender. This cooperative approach helped create unity and harmonious relationships among people and between the people and the planet. Eisler contends that at a point in prehistory, perhaps about 3500 BC, this 30–40,000 year era began to wane, and the qualities of the feminine were gradually replaced with more masculine values that structured a completely different kind of civilization that she identifies as a 'dominator' society.

(Weinhold and Weinhold 1989: 27–8)

For Eisler, the present emergence of feminine values is not some kind of idealistic utopian 'new age' dream, but a re-connection to our historical roots. This is the most important point of her argument: it can be different and we've been there before.

10.1 Reflection: Domination and Partnership

Consider the following dominator values and activities and how much you see them as part of our nature, part of human life:

Competition, greed, recklessness, spite, intolerance, dishonesty, cynicism, suspicion, manipulation, cruelty, destructiveness, deceit, self-importance, self-indulgence, jealousy, isolation, force, exploitation, violence, revenge, scarcity, futility, hostility, control, fear, selfishness.

Now consider the following partnership values and activities and how much you see them as nice but rather unrealistic and utopian (perhaps belonging to the world of art and family, rather than to 'real life'):

Grace, integrity, trust, compassion, love, tenderness, beauty, peace, responsibility, healing, openness, faith, delight, brother- (sister)hood, freedom, understanding, acceptance, patience, gratitude.

Then ask yourself which of those values are guiding your life and which ones you would like to be guiding your life. Why and why not?

It is interesting to note that psychoanalysis focuses very much on the first set of values. We could say that this is because in a dominator society it is those values that damage children very early on, and therefore psychoanalysis is about healing the damage that has been done by them. On the other hand, by focusing on the dominator qualities, psychoanalysis gives them a kind of biological and universal permanence.

Eisler's polarity 'domination versus partnership' seems vital for any analysis of what is happening within and without us. The boundary considerations have left us with the polarity of 'separation versus unification', where appropriate separation and boundary setting can then lead to a higher level of unification.

Riane Eisler and David Loye have developed the material from *The Chalice and the Blade* into an approach which they call *The Partnership Way*. In their practical guidebook they contrast dominator and partnership systems:

Dominator System	*Partnership System*
Rigid male dominance in all areas of life (as well as 'hard' or 'masculine' social priorities).	Equal partnership between women and men in all areas of life (as well as elevation of 'soft' or 'feminine' values in social governance).
'Strong man' rule, or a generally hierarchic and authoritarian family and social structure (where obedience to order is expected).	A more democratic and equalitarian family and social structure (where participatory decision making is expected).
A high degree of institutionalized social violence (i.e. rape, wife beating, child abuse, war), that is required to impose and maintain rigid economic, social, and political rankings.	More peaceful and mutually satisfying personal, community, and global relations based on interconnection (linking rather than ranking).
Emphasis on technologies of destruction and domination.	Emphasis on creative technologies that sustain and enhance life.
Conquest of nature.	Respect for nature.
Fear and scarcity as the primary motivators for work.	Stimulation of creativity, self-development, group or team responsibility, and concern for the larger community (from local to planetary) as primary motivators for work.

(Eisler and Loye 1990: 113–14)

The 'New' Man

I agree with Eisler's emphasis on the necessity of feminine values for the development of partnership structures within and between us. However, what I see regularly in my practice and in myself are the conflicts that this creates in and for men. At the same time I am fully aware of the conflicts that women have had to bear for centuries under dominator conditions. Many men, like Michael who went to Findhorn (see page 140), find themselves facing inner and outer contradictions once they have developed the previously repressed 'softer' side of themselves. Their work environment may require them to be obedient, ruthless, competitive, powerful, single-minded, etc., while they do not want to be like that any more. In addition, the 'soft man' may well come across women, for example as bosses, who have skilfully adopted male dominator qualities, thus perverting the potential for equality that feminism contains.

I have now been running men's groups for a few years, and I am touched by the struggles that those men are facing who want to be different. They often become confused between how they are exploited and oppressed in the work-place and how they are seen as exploiters and oppressors by women, while at the same time they are usually still expected to be the bread-winners. It is very confusing indeed to be an aware and conscious man these days, because the 'new male consciousness' has more or less developed as a by-product of the feminist movement. The danger is that new boundaries are being created between male and female qualities. As a result, several areas of confusion have arisen in the men I work with and in myself that need to be addressed in men's groups (I also think that they can *only* be addressed in men's groups):

1 The 'rational mind', typically seen as a masculine quality, is not very popular in therapy groups. Men are told to 'get in touch with their feelings', to which they often respond by producing more rational thoughts. While it is true that people often repress emotions and prefer to think them rather than feel them, I am more inclined to focus on people's whole experience along the lines of the emotional synthesis model (see Figure 4.3 on page 62). In my men's groups I do not tell people to get 'out of their heads', but rather encourage them to include emotional experiences in what they say. And yes, let's also talk about goals, achievements, plans.

2 I sometimes think that the emotional world of men is perhaps quite different from the emotional world of women. But when it comes to emotions, we seem to be so used to seeing 'mother' in women. And have we not learned to trust mother in what she says and does about feelings? As men, I think we need to reclaim 'father' in this. We need a male language for feelings, rather than trying to uncomfortably fit into the feminine one.

3 As 'conscious' men we are in the uncomfortable position of being confronted very directly with the nastiness of alienation and the greenhouse system: we suffer from it, often unconsciously; we represent it, operate it, have learned to live with it; and at the same time more and more women see us as oppressors and abusers of power, while we suffer from the system more and more. It is really confusing for us – we don't like what we are doing; we don't know what we are feeling (or don't want to know); we feel uncomfortable with what women tell us we should be feeling; and we desperately need women's (mother's) support and understanding.

4 It gets even more complicated because women are ambivalent as well. In terms of 'boundaries' they have probably projected their 'shadow' on to us, i.e. we are the 'baddies'. At the same time, when it comes to sex and protection, they often want the 'strong man'. So, while one side of our strength is wanted the other side is rejected. We feel pressured to do mental and emotional acrobatics to separate our 'really nasty strong bits' from our 'sometimes OK strong bits' – in short, to operate between being 'male chauvinistic' and 'soft man'.

Obviously there is a boundary issue here. I do think that Eisler's model could lead to confusion because it implies 'feminine rather than masculine'. It could reinforce rigid boundaries between the two, thus leading to projections and misunderstandings. What we need is to recover the nurturing, loving, protecting aspects of masculine qualities rather than replace masculine with feminine ones.

I am aware that I am writing here as a man. I am also writing as someone who believes that the process of 'breaking walls and building bridges' needs to take place in a way that does not mean that one side takes over the other, because this ultimately leads to the erection of new walls. This process requires the acknowledgement of the pain of separateness, of the projections both ways, and ultimately of the value on both sides.

I recently carried out an experiment which I should like to share with you, because I think it says something about the wall that exists between men and women. I asked a group of fifteen female psychiatric nurses to complete the statement 'men are . . .' several times. I also asked the ten men in my men's group to do the same with the statement 'women are . . .'. The following words were used by the groups:

Men are . . .	Women are . . .
(have) same needs as women	tender
aggressive	caring
ambitious	exciting
arrogant	loyal
blinkered	disloyal
boastful	mysterious

149

caring
childish and demanding
courageous
cuddly
depressing
frustrating
generous
handy
impossible
insensitive
interesting
lazy
liars
little boys wanting 'caring'
manipulative
not showing emotions
often wrong
out of touch with feelings
a pain in the neck
pathetic
physical
practical
privileged
promiscuous
selfish
strong and helpful
unfaithful
useless
vulnerable

misunderstood
clamish
supportive
important
frustrated
powerful
possessive
nice
good friends
single-minded
birth-giving
devious
painful
playmates
frightening
my life
tantalising
too much
a problem
great
pleasing

It appears that the men had many more positive things to say about women than the other way around. Does this still reflect a situation where women feel oppressed by men and are therefore angry with them? How can we get to 'partnership' from these positions?

On the other side of the 'battle line' some men are going to extremes to emphasise their maleness, in a way which most of us do not dare express. A book by Joachim Bürger, entitled *Mann, Bist Du Gut*! ('Man, you're great!') was published in Germany in 1991 and became a bestseller. The author appeared on television chat shows and several similar books have followed since. The book with the subtitle 'What men have always wanted to say to women' wants to provoke, and it is written as a 'counter-attack': 'On the following pages you will be confronted with a man's world in a placative, self-righteous and chauvinistic way. May it contribute to the compromises that are needed between the sexes' (Bürger, 1991: 10). According to Bürger, men are biologically and psychologically different from women. He sees the main conflict between men's sexual needs and women's security needs. He states that 'progress' has left women with an unbalanced 'energy potential':

> While it has taken men a century to reduce the 12-hour working day by one third to achieve the eight-hour working day, women have managed to reduce their working time by about two thirds to four hours' intensive work per day. . . . This accumulated energy potential is now directed against men . . . and is supposed to hit men . . . below the belt.
>
> (1991: 8, my translation)

I found Bürger's book difficult to read, because it is written in a 'talking style' (it was probably dictated on to a tape recorder), it is repetitive, and it is so full of cynicism and anger, without the author disclosing where his anger with women comes from. He does not own up to his anger, and that is a risky thing to do. Nevertheless, he does have a message, otherwise his book would not have been so popular. I do feel that we somehow need to include the extremes of male chauvinism if we want to build bridges between the sexes, and if we want to get to partnership. It is about including the shadow on both sides. I should like to give you a paragraph from Bürger's book as a 'taster':

> A man will probably never be able to find his way into the female way of thinking. Every woman thinks differently, behaves differently and expresses herself differently. The only common characteristics seem to be: a lack of logic and unpredictability. It is not even possible to complain to women about this. Their response would be: 'But that's exactly what you love about me', – and that would immediately get us back to the starting point of the discussion.
>
> The real man has to slow the woman down in her uncontrollable urge to act. Because everything she does, ultimately has to be paid by him. Now, a woman will never put too much thought into the question who it is that brings in all that money. It appears like a miracle and can be disposed of. Her attitude towards money is disturbed: Either she hordes it and tortures the whole family with her miserliness, or she wastes it. Balanced budgeting, determined by needs, investment, necessities, is extremely difficult for the female brain.
>
> (Bürger 1991: 81, my translation)

Very provocative indeed. How dare I write these things, even if I am quoting someone else? But yes, I have had thoughts like this, and I know that other men have struggled with similar views. The danger is that the necessary global shift towards feminine values, as propagated by Eisler, turns into a boundary elimination process, where one side is 'better than' the other. This could then stimulate the kind of anger that we find in Bürger's book,

151

and the boundary turns from a potential meeting point into a battle line. My vision would be to go through the painful process, in pairs and in groups, of consciously strengthening the wall (blocks, boundaries) between men and women by including all the prejudices and projections that are aimed at the other side. At the same time each side needs to own up to their 'nasty bits' (their shadow). Only then can the wall be gradually taken down, and the projections be taken back. The question is not whether domination or partnership is the goal, but rather how can we engage in the process of moving from domination to partnership. I feel strongly that such a move needs the 'positive male qualities', and that, as men, we need to connect with those qualities, so that conflict can be constructive rather than destructive. It is this process of owning and accepting, of trying to get from 'win–lose' to 'win–win', that ultimately allows the spirit to enter the 'space-in-between', the space that was previously filled with battleaxes. This is similar to the process that often takes place in individual and group therapy, where the open struggles between people, subpersonalities, therapist and client allow 'something bigger' (spirit) to enter the space.

Bürger's provocations indicate that battle lines between men and women have already been drawn. Men need to include 'father' in their masculinity, and this can be done in men's groups. I am often surprised and sad about how some men and women react when I say that I run men's groups. From men I have heard (humorous?) remarks like, 'Are you all transvestites?' or I have received condescending smiles and grins. Women often giggle, wink and say, 'I wonder what they are up to'. I have never heard any remarks like this when women's groups are mentioned. There is a lot of work that needs doing. Fortunately more and more men are trying to do this work, and the American men's movement is finding its way across the Atlantic.

The American poet Robert Bly is running workshops for men on both sides of the Atlantic. David Findlay has been running his 'Brothers' programme in this country for a few years now. Both are trying to help men explore their (hi)stories as men.[1] David Findlay includes a quote from Robert Bly on his leaflet: 'The wild man leaned toward the boy and whispered through the bars of the cage, "The key is under your mother's pillow" '. I should like to end this section on the 'new man' by quoting from Robert Bly's latest book *Iron John*, where he explores the issue of 'father':

Jung said something disturbing about this complication. He said that when the son is introduced primarily by the mother to feeling, he will learn the female attitude toward masculinity and take a female view of his own father and of his own masculinity. He will see his father through his mother's eyes. Since the father and the mother are in competition for the affection of the son, you're not going to get a

152

straight picture of your father out of your mother, nor will you get a straight picture of the mother out of the father.

Some mothers send out messages that civilization and culture and feelings and relationships are things which the mother and the daughter, or the mother and the sensitive son, share in common, whereas the father stands for and embodies what is stiff, maybe brutal, what is unfeeling, obsessed, rationalistic: money-mad, un-compassion-ate. 'Your father can't help it.' So the son often grows up with a wounded image of his father – not brought about necessarily by the father's actions, or words, but based on the mother's observations of these words or actions. . . .

It takes a while for the son to overcome these early negative views of father. The psyche holds on tenaciously to these early perceptions. Idealization of the mother or obsession with her, liking her or hating her, may last until the son is thirty, or thirty-five, forty. Somewhere around forty or forty-five a movement toward the father takes place naturally – a desire to see him more clearly and to draw closer to him. This happens unexplainably, almost as if on a biological timetable. . . .

If the son learns feeling primarily from the mother, then he will probably see his own masculinity from the feminine point of view as well. He may be fascinated with it, but he will stay afraid of it. He may pity it and want to reform it, or he may be suspicious of it and want to kill it. He may admire it, but he will never feel at home with it.

(Bly 1991: 24)

The Quality Cards

These cards, 'a guide to self acceptance', were designed by Harley and Cally Miller. I should like to use them here as an example, because the cards are a wonderful example for bridgebuilding. The bridges are built between the poles of each quality. Thus:

You are not going to be asked to change your ANGER into PASSIVENESS, or your DISSATISFACTION into CONTENTMENT, or even your FEAR into COURAGE. Of course society is always cajoling us to change – If I am an INTROVERTED and QUIET person then I am encouraged to become OUTWARD-GOING and JOLLY; if I am an ENERGETIC and NOISY person then I am told that I should learn to be RELAXED and CONSIDERATE.

(Miller and Miller 1989: 6)

Hence to be a chauvinistic and aggressive man may not mean that you have to turn into the opposite, but rather that you can aspire to reach a higher, or 'the highest' level of those qualities.

There are 23 quality cards in the set. Each card contains a quality at its

153

different levels from 10 (top) to 1 (bottom). I have chosen six cards out of the set, because they are most likely to be relevant for the 'masculine qualities'. At the bottom level they are the following: vicious, tyrannical, despising, interrogating, arrogant, terrified. Here are the ten levels of each one of those qualities:

10. Passionate	10. Celebrating	10. Compassionate
9. Spirited	9. Loving	9. Comforting
8. Animated	8. Affectionate	8. Benevolent
7. Excited	7. Responding	7. Sympathetic
6. Stimulated	6. Insisting	6. Commiserating
5. Irritated	5. Demanding	5. Patronising
4. Cross	4. Overbearing	4. Condescending
3. Angry	3. Domineering	3. Resentful
2. Furious	2. Oppressive	2. Scornful
1. **Vicious**	1. **Tyrannical**	1. **Despising**
10. Discovering	10. Excellent	10. Aware
9. Uncovering	9. Perfect	9. Sensitive
8. Exploring	8. Pure	8. Prudent
7. Seeking	7. Refined	7. Careful
6. Curious	6. Dignified	6. Cautious
5. Questioning	5. Proud	5. Apprehensive
4. Nosey	4. Superior	4. Nervous
3. Inquisitive	3. Pretentious	3. Fearful
2. Examining	2. Ostentatious	2. Frightened
1. **Interrogating**	1. **Arrogant**	1. **Terrified**

Work with the quality cards consists of locating yourself at the appropriate level, and accepting that that's how you are. Through acceptance you will release some of the stress connected with the level of the quality. You can then gradually move upward towards the highest level of expression of that quality. The authors maintain that when one quality moves up, the same energetic shift takes place for all the other qualities.

I think that the quality cards describe the most essential energy shift that takes place in the psychotherapeutic process. People often say, 'Nobody really ever changes. So why all this therapeutic effort?'. They are right, because by 'changing' we usually mean dropping one quality and taking on the opposite one. But the only change that can and must occur is the energetic shift of qualities to their own higher levels.

Many of the therapeutic methods described earlier, like subpersonalities, and the acceptance aspect of CBT, can be seen in terms of the conceptual framework that the quality cards suggest.

THE STORY OF WRITING

I already know what you will be reading on the following pages. Computers and word processors make writing both easier and more complex. I wonder what it does to reading it all. Well, let me explain. The parts about German unification, which you have not read yet, were actually written first. It probably had to do with me being in Germany at the time and with what I was dealing with within and without myself at the time. As I was exploring the issue further, new ideas were coming up. At the same time, all around me changes were happening at an increasing speed, and it felt like many of the rapid changes needed to be included in my writing. Now, as I am writing this, Germany is drifting to the right. Very worrying developments are taking place. They cannot all be included here. However, the developments seem to confirm that there is a 'heating up' process going on.

The word processor allowed me to go into different parts of the document and expand them rather than needing to stay mainly sequential, i.e. adding things on at the end. Thus different bits of the story were growing at different times, while the surrounding bits were remaining the same and being pushed further out. Hence the character of the story changes in more ways all the time than if I were to just add things on and occasionally 'cut and paste'. I am not sure yet what effect this will have on the finished product. The image is one of lots of small circles within one large circle, and when one of the smaller circles is expanded the relationship of the small circles towards each other changes and it might even expand the bigger surrounding circle. Technology makes this kind of writing possible. The difficulty is in 'holding' the constantly changing overall structure.

The same is true for our 'high tech' society in general. The potential and the possibilities are enormous. But what happens to our need for containment, structure and simplicity? It is this need that constantly tempts us to use power, control and rigid structures to cover up the risks and uncertainties of our inner and outer relationships, while we are at the same time faced with the means to break boundaries, to transform the straight line into a circle and perhaps even into a spiral.

Chapter 11 describes an example of unification and separation on a very large scale – German unification. We will discover all the elements that we have so far explored in that process, and we will see how this national process contains issues of our inner and outer attempts at breaking boundaries and bridgebuilding. The context for the following part is the wholeness and connectedness of the personal and the impersonal, the individual and the national, the inner and outer.

11

UNIFICATION PROCESS – GERMAN EXAMPLE

What is now emerging as difficulties in Germany, will determine the future in Europe and in the world more strongly than we would like. This 'social market economy' has already reached its limits. Indeed, money has won over a political bureaucracy, but this will not be enough in order to pacify the whole world, especially qualitatively. If the power of money is not in relation to the power of human relationships, then the collapse of socialist utopias will be followed by the chaos of a ruthless distribution-battle and by the final ruin of an already shifted ecological balance. . . . Today in Germany we are the puppet stage where the big world stage is having a rehearsal.

(Maaz 1991: 55–6, my translation)

The unification of Germany can serve as an example that shows the need for inclusion and partnership in the process of removing boundaries. Unfortunately this is not how the process is taking place. As I am writing this I have just come back from a visit to East and West Germany. I was shocked and disturbed by the expressions and feelings of mistrust, depression and anger that I met in the East, and the fear and arrogance that I met in the West. For a number of weeks now we have been able to witness the extreme expressions of this on our television screens – the violent attacks by young people on the homes of foreign refugees in Germany. At the same time the political system seems helpless; the old methods of party politics offer no solutions and the economic system, the market economy, is feeding into this frightening process of escalating despair and violence.

I shall try to use my own personal involvement in this process, to put across personal learning in that process which some would see as 'political only'. But as much as the political includes the personal, so does the personal include the political. The question is not which one is primary, the political or the personal, but rather how they reflect each other (see Leontyev's theory). This reflection, or reflectivity, is most obvious when a person is, or persons are, directly involved in political happenings. My personal involvement in the process of German unification is through my being German, having gone to university in Berlin, and having had a close relationship with East Germany. At the same time I have been an observer of Germany from England for fifteen years now.

The process of German unification and the difficulties that have arisen since can be seen as the difficulties with the psychological process of the unification of polarities (opposites). In Ken Wilber's terms it would be the process of the elimination of boundaries, boundaries that we had erected in order to protect us.

As I am writing this book it is also becoming increasingly obvious what kind of qualities have emerged out of the unification process. A recent *Spiegel* article is entitled 'The new division – Germans against Germans' (*Der Spiegel* 17 August 1992b). I have collected the qualitative words that are used in the article to describe the situation (my translation):

> Depression, indifference, helplessness, frustration, confrontation, impatience, ignorance, dependence, lies, tension, survival fears, battle, prejudice, coldness, insensitivity, hatred, misunderstandings, enemies.

These words are very similar to the ones I have used earlier to characterise the dominator system, and the qualities that are listed in the 'greenhouse' reflection on pages 117–18.

What has happened to a process that was so emotional when it started? How and why has it all turned so sour? What went wrong in the process of walls breaking down, and how is this related to the process of our own inner walls, our defences breaking down in the process of psychotherapy? Can we look at the story of German unification and learn from it for our intrapersonal and interpersonal walls? And can we, by personalising it, become aware of the relationship between the personal and the wider context so that we can work on both levels? It is this 'working on both levels' that is becoming increasingly necessary: psychotherapy needs to include political and economical boundary issues while economics and politics need to include what psychotherapy has to say about boundaries.

UNIFICATION – THE POTENTIAL

The point is that all of the lines we find in nature, or even construct ourselves, do not merely distinguish different opposites, but also bind the two together in inseparable unity. A line, in other words, is not a boundary. For a line, whether mental, natural or logical doesn't just divide and separate, it also joins and unites. Boundaries, on the other hand, are pure illusions – they pretend to separate what is not in fact separable. In this sense, the actual world contains lines but no real boundaries. A real line becomes an illusory boundary when we imagine its two sides to be separated and unrelated; that is when we acknowledge the outer difference of the two opposites but ignore their inner unity. A line becomes a boundary when we forget that the inside co-exists with the outside. A line becomes a boundary when we imagine that it just separates but doesn't unite at the same time. It is fine to draw lines, provided we do not mistake them for boundaries. It is fine to distinguish pleasure from pain; it is impossible to separate pleasure from pain.

(Wilber 1979: 25–6)

The effect of unifying the two parts of Germany, like the effect of unifying other separations between and within ourselves is very powerful. This is especially true when each side carries the projected shadow of the other side. We experience ourselves and the world around us full of conflicts and contradictions. The external and internal boundaries seem to protect us and help us orientate ourselves. The experience that a dividing line can be a meeting point, that the two sides of a conflict are not mutually exclusive, can be very powerful. It is an inner 'freeing'; a block in our consciousness is removed; we feel joy and unity at a deeper (higher) level. But the process can also create fear and disorientation – the part of us that relies on rigid boundaries (clear maps) for our orientation is again facing the 'unknown', a white area on the previously well-divided map of reality.

The process of German unification shows all those aspects. It is a particularly powerful example because the dividing line was reinforced by barbed wire, the wall, and the mines. The first moment in the process was when the boundary became a meeting point.

Meeting Across the Wall

In the unification process of two separated sides the 'space-in-between' the two parts needs to be seen, accepted, often negotiated like a stormy sea, and the potential that is in that space needs to be released, because it contains the creative energy between the polarities. This release is one of emotional energies, and 'working through' those emotions is what the process is all about – in psychotherapy as well as in the process of the unification of countries.

In Germany the emotional release was particularly obvious when the Berlin Wall started to crumble. This is similar to what we experience when a wall within us begins to crumble: The protection of the wall is still there, but we can see through to the other side; we can even cross over to the other side, but still retreat back to 'our side'.

The joy of 'meeting at the border' took place in Berlin at the 'Brandenburger Tor' on New Year's Eve 1990: suddenly there were holes in the wall, the emotions were overwhelming, people were overwhelmed.

After my return from Berlin, full of the emotions of this experience, I wrote the following poem.

The Gate across the Wall
1990 at 'Brandenburger Tor'

Sitting in an English pub waiting for the muse to
guide my writing hand;
listening to two nurses nearby, talking about New
Year:
'New Year's Day – what a dreary day it is . . .'.
And I am sitting in England, writing this in English.
Two days earlier I was in Berlin.

The Wall is down?
Not down, but it has big holes.
It's being opened – crumbling away,
under the hammering of old and young,
of individuals and states.
The rhythms of hammers and chisels,
splitting concrete and quartz,
the sound to welcome the 1990s.
Saubermachen – cleaning up the mess of 28 years.

Impressions from Eastern Middle Europe,
starting 1990 at the Brandenburger Tor,
Prost Neujahr Deutschland,
Prost Neujahr Europe,
Prost Neujahr World,
Prost Neujahr Humanity.

Half a million people united in joy and tears,
at the Gate,
sitting on the Wall,
shaking hands,
hugging bodies.

Eruptions of fireworks,
the floodlit Tor,
and people flowing from East to West to East to West,
to each other and themselves.

The border guard takes off his black leather glove,
to shake hands,
Eastern and Western skins touching – Happy New Year.

Stepping through the Wall!,
no, flowing through the Wall with masses of others,
under lit skies.
The feeling: this is it, this is new,
this is really new,

this is Forever captured in a moment,
the fear of crowds replaced by the honouring,
of IT, of US.

The lady with the aristocratic face smiles,
in the middle of the crowds,
not at anyone,
not for anyone,
just at IT,
just because of IT.

The lecturer from Cambridge – drunk and elated.
The graphic artist from Hamburg,
desperate to catch the moment and reproduce it later.
The fat woman in a red coat – walking slowly and
crying quiet tears.

Smiles and shivers everywhere,
a crowd controlled by joy,
a crowd celebrating themselves, each other, the
moment.
The everlasting, never returning moment
of New Year 1990 at the Gate.

Reinhard Kowalski, January 1990

That joy was real, very real. That joy had something very un-German about
it. It felt as if something had been released. This sudden get-together after
decades of solid and irreversible barbed wire, mined borders, the wall; two
opposing ideologies manifested in two very serious, very solid states –
suddenly the separation was no more. People who, like me, had grown up to
accept, and had even learned to appreciate[1] the division of Germany into
two states, unexpectedly found themselves in tears. This was very dis-
concerting. It was as if an inner wall had been torn down. And we had not
even known that that inner wall had existed. The tears were of painful joy –
the sudden realisation of the wall at the moment of its disappearance, like
the moment when an inner wall collapses.

THE DIALOGUE

The ever changing kaleidoscope of the dialectic relationship between the
personal and the political has been at the heart of the quest of many thinkers
and writers. Hans Joachim Maaz's books on German unification are
contemporary examples. In *Gefühlsstau* (1990) ('Emotional Constipation')
the East German psychotherapist analyses the psychodynamics of East
German society and draws conclusions as to why the system was doomed to
fail. In *Das Gestürzte Volk. Die Verunglückte Einheit* (1991) ('The Fallen

People. Unity Gone Wrong') he applies his psychodynamic analysis to both East and West and to the process of unification.

In an exciting project, Hans-Joachim Maaz and Michael Lukas Moeller apply the methodology of partnership therapy to the situation between the unified parts of Germany. Moeller, a West German psychoanalyst, has developed *das Zwiegespräch* (the dialogue) in his work with couples. In their book *Die Einheit beginnt zu zweit. Ein deutsch-deutsches Zwiegespräch* (Maaz and Moeller 1991) ('Unity Starts With Two. A German–German dialogue') the two psychotherapists talk and listen to each other at a personal and political level about Germany. They introduce their book as follows:

> Their disturbed relationship reminds us of a disrupted couple-relationship – outwardly unified, the Germans in East and West are developing growing hatred towards one another. The 'Ossis' are playing the traditional part of the woman – they are seen to be depressed, shy and want to be taken care of. The 'Wessis' are more like the typical man – they are dynamic, dominant, and often arrogant.
>
> (Maaz and Moeller 1991: text from jacket, my translation)

The two psychotherapists then talk about themselves and their experience of the other and his country. Throughout, there is the search for unity without negating difference. Here are some of the topics: the barren sadness of the East and the terror of fullness in the West; the 'cuddly toy complex' of GDR mothers (towards their children) and the blinkered shopping behaviour in the West; the low self-esteem of Easterners and the superiority climax of the Westerners.

In their dialogue the two therapists do all the things that human beings do when they attempt dialogue – they compete and they show interest; they join up in agreement and they disagree, and they also talk about their feelings towards each other. Unfortunately the verbal exchange of emotional experience could be more, and the exchange of information and facts perhaps a little less. As I am writing this I notice that I am getting out of touch with what I am writing. *Das Zwiegespräch* is an important book and I want to do it justice. I want to summarise the important facts and at the same time present a critical review. It would then probably read something like this:

> *Das Zwiegespräch* (Maaz and Moeller 1991) is an important book. The two psychotherapists, one from what used to be the GDR and the other from the now dominant West, engage in what they call 'dialogue'. This dialogue was developed as a form of therapy for couples by West German psychotherapist Moeller. Maaz and Moeller see similarities between a disrupted couple relationship and what goes on between East and West Germans at the moment. Their book is

trying to suggest a model of how the two sides can begin to understand each other as a prerequisite for living together. Like in so many marriages, however, the dialogue is starting after the vows have been made. Too late or at last?

That's where my struggle is. I do not want to write like this any more. Words arranged in sentences leading to an ultimate climax of meaning? Is the written word so limited in describing and creating experience? Apparently not when it comes to novels, but has anyone ever 'lived' in a book on psychotherapy? Maaz and Moeller do try, but factual intellectualism dominates nevertheless. Perhaps it shows how elementary our attempts at 'communicating' and 'getting on' with each other often are. How can we include our feelings of vulnerability, hurt and anger in the process of getting together? All we can do is try, and be aware of why we try it. Be aware of why we try it?

Having included my own struggle in writing this, I have now become aware of what I want to write: what is missing in the dialogue between Maaz and Moeller is that they do not talk about why they are talking. What are their goals and values, what is their context for talking? And that's exactly where psychoanalysis differs from psychosynthesis. It also says something about the lack of context for German unification. Such lack of 'higher' context reinforces the lower-level fears that any breakdown of boundaries brings with it. The higher context is needed to contain the fear. The deeper (higher) motivation that strives for unity needs to be realised as the driving force so that it can govern the process. This process of containing and including (learning from) the fear is not easy. It is often approached by trying to compromise between the two sides in order to reach a consensus. However, the starting point for relationship is to not ignore separateness and mistrust, because that brings us in touch with our own inner separateness and mistrust (betrayal) and from there we can meet. At the same time, compromise and consensus are essential when 'breathing space' is needed. (Sanctuary allows the 'space-in-between' to be there.)

What might be the wisdom in the process in Germany? It seems that the politicians are caught up in what they see as their 'job' – trying to reach endless compromises in a situation where compromises are not possible. As a result they appear to be out of touch and impotent. At the same time the populations in both East and West act out all the mistrust and separateness that has been there, and that has, for forty years, been projected on to the other side. Unfortunately this acting out is happening according to the old established, defensive patterns on both sides, thus leading to new rigid boundaries, separations, scapegoating, oppression and power-over principles. Mistrust and separateness need to be included in the process; people's own inner divisions and boundaries need to be included and worked through. In his writings Maaz makes passionate pleas for such a process. Will he be heard?

> A true German–German reconciliation will only take place if 'work' becomes a central theme, and if a wide discussion starts as to which level of work and what level of wealth is necessary and bearable for us, for the next generation, for the planet and for nature. This wide discussion of the theme 'work and wealth – basic needs and substitute needs' would be the first 'therapeutic' step.
>
> (Maaz, 1991: 129, my translation)

Here we seem to have come full circle. Activity theory defines work as the central human activity, which in its historical development has created divisions and alienations, peaking in the capitalist system where the worker himself is turned into a commodity. Douthwaite shows how human activity is turned into the means for maintaining the economic 'growth illusion'. Our human relationships are thus dominated by exploitation and competition. Sadly, but in tune with our times, the unification of Germany has been mainly left to 'market forces' to sort out. The whole process started with the 'economic union' between the two parts, which was mainly about the West introducing its currency and goods into the East.

I remember the day of economic union between East and West Germany on 3 June 1990. I was in Berlin at the time and in the morning I took the train to a small GDR town north of Berlin. I stood there and watched people using the new money and looking at the shop windows, which were now full of colourful goods from the West.

Daydream

I see people in the east of the uniting country going about their business. It all looks quite normal, perhaps their movements are a bit slow and careful. They seem to be spending a lot of time looking out, at shop windows, at the money in their hands. Yes, they look a bit like robots, or like people in a dream. And then I suddenly discover why. Inside, in their stomach area there is this huge dark hole, as if something had been ripped out with great force. The walls of the hole still look red and sore. And the people don't want to feel that hole and the soreness. So they need to look outside, at all the new colourful things in the shop windows, at the new cars, at all the new things from the West. But the holes in their stomachs are trying to say something. I can hear a chorus like a deep rumbling: *H-o-o-o-o-m-e*.

They want a home? Why? And what are they doing about it? I am puzzled by the contrast between their outwardly calm, serene, robot-like movements and the deep inner pain and the cry for home. What are they doing and how are they experiencing it? All they seem to be doing is eating; they are eating with their eyes, their mouths and their ears: the little boy taking the colourful wrapping off an ice-cream bar; the group of young men gathered at the sleepy town's market place, opening aluminium tins of beer from the West; and the women drinking in the colours and shapes of the new dresses in the shop windows. I feel an emptiness in my own stomach area and sadness in my heart. They all look like lost children, guided by the pretty colours of tins, boxes and wrappings.

Then the image of the small town market place fades, and another image comes. It's deep under the ground and high up in the skies, still the same country in the East. I know that I am now seeing the country as a whole, but at a deeper and higher level. And what I see increases the sadness in my heart, pushing tears up to my eyes. I see a huge dark hole, similar to the ones I saw in individuals; the same sore, ragged edges, as if something had been ripped out with great force. The walls of the hole are moving, contracting and expanding, slowly and heavily, as if trying to digest something. And then I see what this hole is trying to digest: through an opening high up in the cave come the wrappings and the tins that people are throwing away, falling down into the moving cave. Some of the colourful rubbish gets stuck in caverns and folds of the pink, sore-looking walls, being crushed but not digested, while at the same time the tins are cutting into the wounded walls of the hole. At the bottom of the cave small piles of rubbish are beginning to build up. And then the image fades again.

BEING GERMAN

For as long as I can remember, I have found it rather difficult to be German. Born in 1948 I never felt I belonged in my environment, the working-class, coal-mining environment that I was growing up in, and the nation that I was supposed to be a part of. I started school in 1954, and thinking back now I realise that all my teachers then, even the youngest ones, had lived through the war and through the collapse of Germany as it was. My awareness of my country's past started around the age of 10. A German teacher with strong humanistic values introduced us to the horrors of Nazi Germany. Even though history lessons never went beyond 1914, we were made aware of the Holocaust. Other older teachers were clearly sadistic and, thinking back now, probably had a fascist past. The question 'what did my father do during the Hitler years?' came up more and more. Lots of grown-ups were still expressing fascist ideas. We were beginning to hate the 'older generation', the establishment.

In my teens I began to travel in Europe and when I was 17 I spent a year in the United States. I envied the people of other nations for their national pride, but at the same time national pride was something 'reactionary' and very uncomfortable. I wished I did not have a German passport. I felt guilty about being German. I did not like the language, the culture, the people. We were a 'lost generation' haunted by the sins of our fathers.

The following exercise asks you to include your feelings about your national identity, and how you can, with an awareness of your characteristics, meet people from other nations with their different characteristics. Such meeting without ignoring difference is becoming increasingly vital in our world.

11.1 Reflection: Your National Identity

See yourself in the country where you have grown up – be aware of your language, your traditions, institutions, educational system and how you have internalised them as your own or how you have been opposing them. Be aware of your inner experience as you connect with your national identity. Also be aware of the voices of your upbringing – parents, teachers, friends, colleagues.

Allow an image or a symbol to emerge for your national identity.

Hold that symbol or image for a while, and then imagine all the people in the other nations of this world with their own national identities and symbols.

Now imagine meeting one person from another nation – you holding your symbol and the other person holding his/her symbol.

Be aware of the difference between you and the other person. What are your assumptions and your prejudices about the other? What do you imagine the other's assumptions and prejudices about you are?

Then imagine representatives from all the other nations with their symbols and form a circle. Imagine that all the mutual assumptions and prejudices are there in the circle, but nobody is leaving that circle. Imagine that you are all joining hands, thus making the circle very solid. Feel how gradually the circle and the contact become stronger than the assumptions and prejudices in the circle. Feel how gradually the energy in the circle is being transformed.

Capitalism, Socialism and Me

Socialism is now dead. The Lenin statue has been removed from what used to be East Berlin. The German Democratic Republic, the 'first socialist state on German soil', does not exist any more. Sixteen million people, now citizens of the Federal Republic of Germany, are having to bury forty years of their history, their past. Gleeful 'we-have-always-known-better-anyway' attitudes are now freely being acted out by westerners, whose fragile identity has suddenly been injected with a hitherto unknown strength. 'If it is now clear that *they* have always been wrong, then *we* must have always been right, even though we didn't know it.' What a relief! One belief system is being confirmed by the death of its counterpart. It is as if the plants and trees were rejoicing in the confirmation of their 'superior' life form after the extinction of the dinosaurs.

I am thinking of Karl Marx and all the hours, days, months, years he spent researching and writing in the British Library. I am thinking of German communists and socialists suffering, dying and surviving for their beliefs in concentration camps. I remember the place in Buchenwald where Ernst Thälmann was shot. Was all this in vain?

When I was 19, Marx and Engels' theories helped me to make sense of my working-class environment. The concepts of 'exploitation' and 'alienation' helped me to understand my father's suffering. I began to understand Josef the coal-miner, his dissatisfaction and his drinking. It was an understanding that I desperately needed. My childhood world was beginning to make sense. It was this understanding that Marxism gave me, that I was then able to take to university in Berlin, where we started learning about psychology from Marx's *Capital*, Volume 1. The concepts of 'character-masks' and of 'the labourer as a commodity' were deeply meaningful. I had experienced it all in Josef and in myself and others during my apprenticeship in the steel mill. Marx and his scientific analysis of capitalism provided me and my generation of students at university with an understanding of our society and gave us the motivation to fight for something better. Capitalism was not 'God-given' and the only way in which we could organise our lives. Capitalism was only one way, but there were others. In West Berlin one of these other ways was right next door – the German Democratic Republic. Based on Marx's analysis of capitalism they were trying to organise a different society, a society that was not based on the private ownership of the means of production, a society with equal opportunities for everybody, a society with humanistic and humanitarian values.

I remember when I first met and developed friendships with people in 'the other Germany', how impressed I was with their different attitudes, their supportiveness, their lack of greed, their human-ness. There I was able to see how Josef could have been. How he could have been a coal-miner without feeling degraded. How he could have done his work, and still have had the opportunities to use his artistic and creative skills. How he would not have just been treated as a commodity, but as a whole person. It made some sort of deep emotional sense, despite the fact that this socialist state eventually shut me out when I developed an intimate relationship with Kerstin, one of its citizens.

POST-UNIFICATION: WARRIORS AND CONFORMISTS

However, it all went wrong. In his book *Der Gefühlsstau* Maaz analyses why it went wrong. He convincingly uses psychoanalytical concepts in his analysis:

In the language of analytical psychotherapy the development of the GDR was arrested at an oral and anal level. . . . The GDR never reached the 'genital phase': autonomy, sense of self worth, responsibility, openness and forthrightness were very rare characteristics which were not encouraged. Instead, the whole GDR was always characterised by low self esteem and an addictive need for recognition.

(Maaz, 1990: 86 and 89, my translation)

But, at the same time, Hans-Joachim Maaz now travels and lectures in a 'united' Germany, criticising the 'consumption-terrorism', the excessive performance pressure, and the aggressive competition in the West. Does this imply that we in the West have reached the 'genital phase'? If this is so, which it probably is, then I am beginning to wonder about the relationship between autonomy, sense of self-worth, responsibility, openness and forthrightness on one side and consumerism, performance pressure and aggressive competition on the other. Are they all members of the same family? This is a possibility that I do not like at all, because it throws all those 'higher' human qualities in with all those 'nasty bits'. But maybe that's the way it is: the light and the shadow and the creative energy between them is what makes life 'interesting'. If light and dark are indeed existing around us, then their reflection is also within (or vice versa). The creative tension between polarities creates electricity, creates energy. This energy can both destroy and create new qualities.

Kerstin, the friend from the East, now a citizen of the extended Germany, writes:

I would have never thought that this society, that we have been dumped into, can be so shitty, inhuman, and so terribly interesting. The inhumanity I experience every day when I see what is being done to people, how quickly they move from a socially safe situation into poverty and despair. And it gets interesting when you know how the system works and how you try to use that knowledge and your physical and psychological strength in order to achieve the best for yourself. We in the East have one big disadvantage – we have been brought up to be much too humane, therefore we are not yet able to fully utilise the existing 'cut-throat' rules. But we are able to learn. . . . I have now become a 'business woman' and have no time for intellectual things; being human has to take second place. But we are struggling for survival. I hope that in a few years I will have time again for the really important things in life, if by then I will not have changed too much.

Kerstin, what do you mean by 'interesting'? What can possibly be 'interesting' about that struggle that you describe? Perhaps it is the uncertainty, having to face the unknown, that now energises you. Do you remember our holiday in Poland twelve years ago?

We met at the railway station just across the border in Poland. Armed guards were everywhere. I had driven the 50 miles from West Berlin with a visa for Poland. You had taken the train from your home in East Germany. At the time you were able to enter Poland without a visa, so Poland was a safe country for us. You were standing at this run-down railway station in the middle of nowhere, and the guards were watching as you got into my car. Then we drove off towards Posnan. It was a grey and rainy day and you were very quiet. I could feel the uncomfortable atmosphere in the car. When I asked you, you described your fear, because never before had you just driven off, not knowing where you would end up that evening. It took you a few days to get used to it, and then you began to really enjoy it. Was that the unknown, the fear of the unknown, and facing it?

Is this it then? Does capitalism tap into the human need for uncertainty, variety and the unknown? In the GDR everything was structured, organised, completely safe. Education, work, holidays, prices, sense of belonging, sense of good and bad were all clearly organised and planned – uncertainty was removed from life. There was no fear of survival, and at the same time there was no opportunity for growth, no opportunity for developing autonomy, sense of self-worth, responsibility, openness and forthrightness.

The German word for 'division' is *teilen*. *Teilen* also means sharing. The necessary sharing of values, material and ideological, is difficult. Strikes in West Germany, voices saying 'We do not want to give up our wealth, our standard of living. We do not want to share, we'd rather be divided'. The voices in the East expressing envy and dislike of the arrogance of the Westerners. New boundaries are emerging. They are partly geographical – entering the east of Germany still feels like entering a different country. But boundaries are also emerging in the minds and hearts of people and between all sorts of different groups.

Model – Warrior and Conformist

There seems to be a new model, the possibility of another bridge, emerging from the analysis of the German unification process. The model tries to look at the archetypes that have probably developed in the East (socialism) and West (capitalism) in terms of 'who makes it' (see Figure 11.1).

Conformists and Warriors in the two systems mean different things, because of the different external conditions that shape them.

In the capitalist system most of us need to fight for our survival. The struggle to get our basic needs met is the norm. In the socialist system such fighting for survival was unknown, because everything was organised, planned and very secure. Conformity and obedience were the required

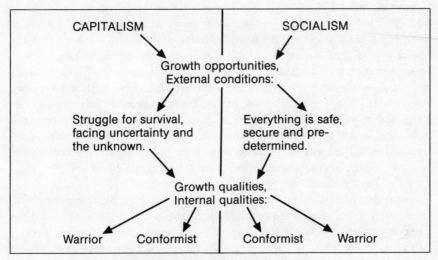

Figure 11.1 Conformist and warrior.

characteristics, while 'fighting' was used as an abstract term to describe social activities in favour of socialist goals, e.g. the fulfilment of the goals of the five-year plan, the support of freedom fighters in the Third World. The activities mostly consisted of meetings, demonstrations, etc. The fight for survival within the capitalist system seems much closer to the struggle of the famous mythical heroes, and thus closer to our traditional archetypes. Some people in our capitalist society are able to take their warrior spirit beyond the 'struggle for survival'. They fight for a cause, an idea, a business. The Thatcherite 'entrepreneur' is one of those warriors. Conforming is alien to him. However, most people in our capitalist society are, like Josef, completely caught up in the struggle for survival and never get beyond it. They also need to conform in order to at least have some peace and quiet in their struggle. Nevertheless, the ideology, the potential of the non-conformist warrior who faces the unknown is there, somewhere in our consciousness.

In the socialist system of the GDR the conformist was the ideal. Fighting was turned into an abstract unreality, or it was expressed in 'illegal' rebelliousness. Kerstin now needs to fight the capitalist way. She has to face the unknown; she has to struggle for survival. And she senses the excitement, the potential that is in that struggle. However, the energy of her struggle may well all get used up for survival. But then it may not. Kerstin may have the opportunity to combine her idealistic and abstract GDR fighting spirit with the capitalist, down-to-earth skill of struggling. Such a combination could be very powerful indeed. I would like to assume that the success of German unification as a model for the synthesis of socialism and capitalism lies in that emergence of the 'new warrior', the fight for survival combined with the struggle for ideals. Unfortunately this potential is blocked off by bitterness, mistrust, guilt and hatred.

At the day-to-day level, conformity in the GDR had a lot to do with the 'collective'. Even though our evaluation of the system now focuses very much on the fearful conformity to rules and regulations that were enforced by police, army, and secret service, there was also nevertheless a sense of responsibility of the individual towards the collective (work team, or neighbourhood group) and vice versa. Altruism, co-operation and empathy were the norm in relationships between people, often strengthened in opposition to the all powerful state. Again, the discipline and the connection with the collective that were in that conformity could be extremely useful qualities for the tasks that lie ahead of us.

Conformity in capitalist West Germany was/is quite different. The state prides herself on being a *Rechtsstaat* (justice or law state), meaning that the judiciary or law-enforcing system is independent of all the other institutions of the state. Obviously this has great advantages, not least that a citizen can take the state to court. However, those rules of law are very much based on the 'bourgeois' tradition. Their main aims are to protect the individual, his constitutional rights and, most importantly, his belongings. And protection is what the individuals in a capitalist society need – protection from the state, from each other, protection from the worst excesses of competition. The law then protects the free competition of individuals, and also tries to protect them from the most abusive practices of such competition. This conflict is the reflection of a basic conflict in bourgeois capitalist society – the values of individuality and freedom (based on the French Revolution) on one side and their capitalist usage as freedom of choice (consumerism), individual responsibility (everybody for himself), and competition (for work, markets, against each other, etc.) on the other.

Conformity to the rules in the West therefore also means competition, separation and isolation, whereas the emphasis in the East used to be on co-operation and the collective – excessive individuality was discouraged. It is obvious that Western conformity is much more closely related to 'fighting for survival' than Eastern adherence to the rules.

A synthesis between the two conformities could be possible between the Western qualities of lawfulness, protection of the individual and the Eastern qualities of co-operation and the collective.

I should now like to invite you to look at the qualities of conforming and fighting in your life. The following reflection is meant to help you discover how you have been leading your life in relation to the rules within you and those of the world around you.

11.2 Reflection: Fighting and Conforming

Think back through your life and remember a time when you

1 HAD TO FIGHT FOR YOUR SURVIVAL
Remember yourself clearly in that situation.
Connect with your feelings at the time, and allow an image or a symbol
to emerge for that experience.
Draw the image or symbol.

2 WERE FIGHTING FOR WHAT YOU BELIEVED IN
Remember yourself clearly in that situation.
Connect with your feelings at the time, and allow an image or a symbol
to emerge for that experience.
Draw the image or symbol.

3 HAD TO CONFORM OUT OF FEAR
Remember yourself clearly in that situation.
Connect with your feelings at the time, and allow an image or a symbol
to emerge for that experience.
Draw the image or symbol.

4 WERE CONFORMING BECAUSE YOU BELIEVED IT WAS RIGHT
Remember yourself clearly in that situation.
Connect with your feelings at the time, and allow an image or a symbol
to emerge for that experience.
Draw the image or symbol.

*Spread the four symbols or images out in front of you and look at them
individually:*

How do you now feel towards each one of them?

What are the different energy qualities in each?

How has each one served you and hindered you?

Can you see or feel connections between the four?

With this and other reflections, your personal experience counts. Be aware
of your emotions, physical sensations and thoughts, even if they do not seem
to be related to the questions. Try to make sense of your experience as best
as you can. Please do not worry; there is no right or wrong way of doing this
exercise. You are in the process of discovering yourself in relation to the
questions.

UNIFICATION – THE PAIN IN THE PROCESS

Now, two years after economic union, I am again visiting East Germany, walking around the centre of a small town. Nothing looks right, nothing feels right. A lot of it still looks the way it used to look – the cobbled streets, the road designs and layouts not particularly made for traffic. But there are new things that do not seem to fit into the environment: the bright, colourful signs of new shops and petrol stations from the West, the bright, 'happy' advertising posters.

It is as if a special kind of 'neutron-bomb' has fallen on the land – a bomb that has eradicated all the structures and rules of society, all the existing societal boundaries, and the new rules and boundaries are symbolised by a few new blobs of bright western advertising colour. People look disorientated and lost. When I entered a pub in a small village, clearly recognisable as a 'Westerner', the hostility in people's eyes felt frightening. Talking to people I notice their cynicism and bitterness, and their tendency to withdraw into their families and into themselves. It is sad, that while in the west of Europe and in America there is a growing movement towards alternative ways of being, in East Germany there is disillusionment with both capitalism and socialism. The transforming qualities that were there in people in East Germany, despite the pressures of a Stalinist system, are at present not available for the global transformation process. What can I, what can we in the West do about it? Even asking the question feels arrogant, because the people in East Germany are receiving instructions and lectures from Western management consultants and politicians – they do not want Western psychotherapists lecturing them as well.

Maaz describes the 'loss syndrome' in East Germany:

> The outer structures that have determined our lives have collapsed, and we have lost stability and orientation. This is a massive threat for people, who had to give up any kind of feeling and inner orientation in the bitter struggle with a repressive system.
>
> Now even our inner compromises are questioned, thus increasing our confusion. Principal questions of meaning are coming up again, leading to depressive and obsessional worrying: What will happen? Who am I now? How shall I choose? What is right now? And convincing answers with clear orientations are not forthcoming. The loss of the GDR is provoking a questioning of our own identity, and the de-valued life leads to questions about the value of life in general. It is not surprising that there is resistance, denial and acting out. We would have plenty to do just to work through all this. But in addition we also have to come to terms with the Western way of life, a way of life that we had longed for, but which now cannot keep the promises that were made. And we had put all our unfulfilled longings into that basket. . . .

172

We are now carrying a double burden: In addition to our own problematic history we now have a questionable new one, and the psychosocial problems are exacerbated. . . . We used to live in a petit-bourgeois family: sufficiently taken care of materialistically, with narrow intellectual boundaries and rigid prejudices and attitudes, prudish, full of lies, under the rules of obedience, discipline and order – but all that we could count on. The rules were clear. The space was known. Even the nastiness was predictable. Those who submitted lived quite well, those who did not could survive, only those who rebelled loudly and openly were punished.

(Maaz 1991: 35–7, my translation)

Maaz then moves on to describe how this situation is reflected in his psychotherapy practice:

The breaking open of the experiences of existential loneliness and responsibility is at present the main cause of deep disturbance and fearfulness. In the groups that I have run recently with so-called patients, with colleagues, and with 'normal' citizens in the East, this has always been a central theme of threatening powefulness. The loss of the GDR has in many people activated the separation and loss traumata of early childhood. . . . Now, with some encouragement, the bitter memories of nurseries, children's homes, and even the suspicions of being an unwanted child or having never been loved, are breaking through frequently.

(1991: 38–9, my translation)

This sounds very similar to what I see happening in our 'greenhouse' environment with the growing numbers of stress-related complaints. I would guess that the full range of psychological distress, like anxiety, panic attacks, depression, is increasing dramatically in East Germany, probably with particularly strong experiences of 'abandonment depression'. The difference between what has happened in East Germany and what is happening in our 'greenhouse' seems to be the sudden 'neutron-bomb effect' there, while the disintegration of our structures feels more like a slow-growing virus.

So not only is what is happening between East and West Germany an issue of the boundary between East and West and a 'puppet performance' of global issues, but it is also an amplified example of what is happening within our system. This interdependence of the different levels of boundary issues feels overwhelmingly complex, but it also means that work at each of the levels will have an effect on all the other levels. I think that, as psychotherapists, we need to be very aware of the fact that the boundaries between the different levels of boundary issues are rapidly disappearing. It is at this meta-level, where all our previously comfortable scientific, professional, and expert niches are being questioned, that we have to face the interconnected-ness of everything. And I think that it is at this level that spirit enters the equation.

PSYCHOSYNTHESIS AND THE 'SPACE-IN-BETWEEN'

Synthesis is the unification of opposites, the unification of different aspects at a higher level: thesis–antithesis–synthesis. Hegel developed the philo-sophy of dialectics to express this and Marx based his theory of the development of human society on Hegel's dialectics.

Psychosynthesis is a psychology that tries to see meaning in all the different aspects of human life. Life and any human being is full of opposites, of contradictions, of different parts. Psychosynthesis wants to see meaning and purpose in and between those contradictions, it wants to 'synthesise' the opposing forces. The opposite poles can become rigid; the dynamic happens in the space between the poles – the 'space-in-between'. Our human tendency is to harmonise conflict and reduce the effects of difference by choosing one side instead of the other. German unification is a perfect example – one side is taken over by the other, rather than the acknowledgement and inclusion of the qualities of both sides and ultimately risking the emergence of the new which is neither this nor that. We are so used to approaching difference from the 'dominator principle' that even bridges are often built before the space in between is looked at or appreciated. 'Dangerous' voids are covered up; the bridge becomes the focus of attention, while the energy of the roaring river underneath gets lost, and becomes invisible.

Embracing Difference

The space in between us separates us, or so it seems,
So we want to build bridges,
Made of experience and demand,
of compromise and rejection,
of projection and pressure,
of winning and losing,
To create the oneness we know best:
You are mine and I am yours.
And while we are busy building bridges,
We don't have time to look and see,
To look at the space between us,
To see the space between us,
Because doing feels better than looking and seeing.

What if we did look and see what is in the space between us?

174

What might we find that is already there for us,
Has always been there for us,
And must be there, because it is part of us and everything.

But looking and seeing is scary, you might say;
Looking and seeing is passive,
Only doing counts, you might say;
My eyes can only see bricks and bridges, you might say;
And the new frontier is turned into an illusion,
Invisible under bricks and bridges.

Then, some day, some time, we might allow ourselves to just look,
and see the space between us.
And, reluctantly, we see – see what?
We may see beauty and love,
Pain, longing and be-longing,
Flowers and trees.
And sometimes I can see it best,
from the bridge that I am trying to build.

Reinhard Kowalski, July 1987

The parallel to psychotherapy and in particular to psychosynthesis is obvious. Clients often come to us because they want to make the past 'unhappen'; they want to be the way they used to be. We, as therapists, then engage them in a process that is called 'working through'. It consists of bringing past experiences into consciousness so that they can be accepted and included in the client's psyche. The neurosis is not the conscious inclusion of a traumatic past experience but the desperate attempt of keeping the pain, hurt and anger connected with it out of consciousness.

DOMINATION AND PARTNERSHIP – WARRIOR AND CONFORMIST

The process of negotiating the 'space-in-between' is what is happening in Germany at the moment. However, it is happening from the 'dominator principle' – the West has annexed, conquered the East. Opposites are being unified in the traditional way of one side winning over the other – fighting for dominance, winning, opportunism and oppression are the prevailing qualities. In all our conflicts between different parts, and across boundaries, the tendency will be to apply the well-established dominator principles to the process. Many of the changes that are presently taking place in Europe, in the NHS and in Social Services, in the management structures of companies, often revert back to more rigid hierarchies and control where the opposite approach would be needed.

I should now like to bring together the qualities of the 'warrior' and 'conformist' with the ones of 'domination' and 'partnership'. This gives us four different combinations:

1 Warrior within a dominator framework,
2 Warrior within a partnership framework,
3 Conformist within a dominator framework,
4 Conformist within a partnership framework.

	WARRIOR	CONFORMIST
Domination	oppressor, ruler, control, power, rebel.	subordinate, victim, opportunist, helpless, cynic, bitterness.
Partnership	authority, leader, protector, motivator.	co-operation, trust, responsibility, inner leader, part of the whole.

The above shows that what we need is a synthesis of the masculine and capitalist warrior qualities and the feminine partnership context, and of the feminine conforming and socialist qualities within a true partnership framework. Bridges need to be built between the different elements rather than creating new walls through the application of the 'either–or' principle. The danger of 'either–or', of splitting and of new walls is clearly visible in Germany. I think that many people are aware of the inappropriateness of the 'domination' led processes that are taking place. Some of those people are also fed up with just conforming. But at the same time the process has unleashed repressed anger and violence. The terror of that violence combined with a deeply ingrained fear of authority is creating helplessness and lethargy. When a patient in psychotherapy reaches such a deep level of terror of his own violent impulses, a very deep depression could be the result. I see such a depression in Germany, and as a German I am extremely worried about it. Conformity and fighting within a dominator framework can turn into the extremes of paralysis and destructiveness, which is exactly what Germany acted out 50 years ago.

12

STEPPING OUT

I am finding it very difficult to write this last chapter. I have set myself a deadline; I have spent the last few weeks using every free minute for writing; my head is full and empty; I don't want to let go of this. I am worried about how my writing will be received; I feel vulnerable in this. And, I really cannot offer any solutions for the conflicts that I have written about. All I have is a few ideas as to how I would like to be engaged in the process. This is quite different from the manner in which 'new' therapeutic approaches are usually 'sold'. They are usually worked out in detail, they are exciting, and they hold the promise of 'new solutions'. In short, they have a 'growth potential'.

But it is this 'growth illusion' that I have been questioning. It is the need for honestly facing 'the unknown' with all the pain that that entails (BPM IV) that I have been emphasising. Yes, I think I have tried to map the territory, and the new territory will emerge as a result of all our activities. What each individual does about it depends very much on that individual's inner and outer conditions. I can only write about what I am doing and maybe into what areas I think psychotherapy needs to expand. A lot of this ground has already been covered earlier in this book; hence I should like to end by presenting two projects that have grown in me recently. This last part is very much in note form, and hopefully it will stimulate your own feeling and thinking.

STEPPING BACK

You will have noticed that there is an Irish connection in my writing. Parts were written in Ireland. When I first visited Ireland seven years ago, to run a training workshop with nurses, a shiver went up and down my spine when the aeroplane touched down in Dublin. I had not expected that; Ireland had no particular meaning for me at the time. Now I am beginning to appreciate the healing energies in the Irish environment: the people, the land, the mysticism, the groundedness and the madness. At a rational level Ireland is still underpopulated and relatively unpolluted. In scene four on page 6 I describe the transition over Christmas from the gloss of Germany to the natural beauty of Ireland. I should like to discuss this transition a bit further.

How could I possibly experience safety and structure in the man-made world of cities, consumer goods, motorways and multi-storey car-parks? Isn't this odd, because that man-made world is packed with things that I cannot control, cannot create, and for most of it I cannot even comprehend how it works. How come I can feel safe in it then, safer than in the natural environment of trees and mountains and rivers? Where does the illusion of safety that civilisation carries for me come from?

It must be that the 'civilisation things' are man-made. I sense my fellow human beings, their skills and activities in all those things. Even though I cannot comprehend most of them, I know that somebody can make this or that thing. The feeling of safety and security comes out of the trust I have for my fellow human beings and out of the sense that I am part of it all as much as everybody else is. There is a sense of collectiveness in this.

But this is the point where the illusion starts. My senses are betraying me, because many of the man-made things around me are *not* there to protect me and to comfort me. They are there to *do business with*, for profits and competition, in short for goals that have absolutely nothing to do with collectivity, safety or security. However bad, however destructive, however useless many of the objects are, my deeper sense of collective connectedness still makes me feel safe in an environment where I am surrounded by cars, aeroplanes flying over my head, news of crashes and disasters coming from the television. I call those mishaps 'accidents', the unwanted side-effects of a generally workable system. What happens to me when I realise that the mishaps are not unwanted, but part of it all? What happens when I cannot any longer project my 'collective trust' (trust of the collective) on to the man-made environment? What happens when I realise that I am part of a collective destructiveness that gives me the illusion of safety and security?

These thoughts have stimulated the development of a 'Stepping Out' programme in Ireland. It is a way of trying to go back to basics, to re-discover the healing potential in nature, and to be able to look at the 'greenhouse' from a different position. This step reminds me of the conflict that Llywelyn (1991) describes in her epic novel of the Gallic Wars. On the one side are the Celts and their Druids with their aim to remain in balance with the natural forces, and on the other side the Romans and their new brand of civilisation, consisting of rational structures, trade, roads, deceit and manipulation, in short, disconnectedness from the natural forces. 'Stepping out' is about re-connecting with the wisdom of the Druids. This is how we have planned and worded the programme.

Stepping Out

> In every human being,
> there is a special heaven,
> whole and unbroken.

Stepping Out is a one-week programme of retreat and self-discovery. We will consciously leave the pressures and worries of work, home, overcrowding and environmental chaos behind in order to have the space and freedom to come to our senses and to experience again our connectedness with inner and outer resources. We will go through the following stages:

Stepping In: We will face the fear and the inner emptiness that can emerge when we let go of all our distractions and worries. Surrounded by natural beauty we will then rediscover our inner strength and creativity while gradually letting go of the fear of ourselves and each other. We will also glimpse the freedom and power that being in the present can give us.

Stepping Back: By re-connecting with our inner sense of self we can let ourselves remember what is really important to us, our vision and purpose. With the will to choose again, we will step back to allow us to form an overview of the shapes our lives have taken, to see if the reality we have chosen is still in keeping with our 'purpose'.

Stepping Forward: Led by our inner resources and wisdom we will affirm our past choices and set goals for the future. We will prepare for re-entry into the rat-race with the knowledge that we can face it with inner strength.

BREAKING WALLS

This is a game that I first thought of at Findhorn two years ago, when the German unification process had just started. Throughout my writing this book the game has come back again and again, and I have thought of new elements. The game is for groups that want to work on their boundaries between them. It could be one group of men and one of women, one of East Germans and one of West Germans, one of bosses and one of employees. The game aims at helping participants to connect to inner and outer boundary issues as a group process and inter-group process.

The game consists of the two groups actually and physically building a cardboard wall between them and then going through the process of taking it down. In the process the projections on to the other side are pinned to the wall, and the individual fears are worked through by each group and connected to values. In the process of taking the wall down, each side has to deal with projections that are pinned to the wall by the other side.

LETTING GO

I need to let go of this now. The book is finished, yet at the same time it feels so unfinished. This is now in the final stages of BPM III, and I am looking back to all the painful stuck-ness, BPM II, that was there at times – some call it 'writer's block'.

But it is also a 'letting go' of something that has now been my companion for over a year. It has been part of me and my processes, at work, at home, in Ireland and in Germany. Now this complex, frustrating, exciting process called writing is manifested in a material form – written words on paper. You, the reader, will read these words, and they will become part of your process. The book itself is a bridge between my process and your process, and it is an example of 'breaking walls and building bridges'.

I am a bit concerned that I have not given you any firm answers, but rather expressed my questions and partial answers. The 'perfectionist' and the 'scientist' in me are still pushing for clear-cut solutions. But I am beginning to accept that we need to go beyond this old way of solving problems. We need to explore boundaries, lots of them, and build bridges. However, there are practical steps arising from my writing that, I feel, need to be taken:

1 It is becoming increasingly impossible to separate our inner and outer worlds. The process of 'breaking walls' is happening inside and outside. We need to be working with our fears and other feelings about ourselves and each other in this process. Psychotherapeutic methods and practice have a lot to offer, and as psychotherapists we need to see our work and our clients' suffering in a wider context.

2 As psychotherapists we are 'bridgebuilders'. We need to become more aware of the bridges we have built and still need to build between all our different approaches. Especially with the professionalisation, certification, accreditation of psychotherapists on the agenda, the danger is for boundaries between the different schools to turn into battle lines rather than meeting points.

3 The psychological greenhouse requires us all to re-examine our attitudes, goals and motives. In this process we need to be receptive to the 'rays' of spirituality. In particular, as Maaz points out, it is our attitude towards work that needs re-evaluating. Work is where the contrast between growing fragmentation and growing interdependence can be most directly experienced by all of us. Communities like the Findhorn Foundation are practising a work structure that includes 'the personal' and 'the emotional'. In a way, the concept of the socialist collective attempted to bring co-operation and caring into the work environment. We need to ask ourselves: What am I doing, and why and how does this connect me to what other people and nations are doing?

4 In order to approach our problems and the planet's problems we need to find our inner sanctuary. The psychotherapeutic relationship can provide a 'safe space'. In addition meditation, dreamwork and bodywork help us to open up to spiritual energies. I also feel that we need to go back to basics and to nature in order to free ourselves from the trappedness of the

psychological greenhouse. The 'stepping out' programme is one way of getting in touch again with Earth and Heaven.

The Choice for Love

What does the voice of fear
whisper to you?

Fear speaks to you
in logic and reason.
It assumes the language
of love itself.

Fear tells you,
'I want to make you safe.'
Love says,
'You are safe.'

Fear says,
'Give me symbols.
Give me frozen images.
Give me something
I can rely on.'

Loving truth says,
'Only give me
this moment.'

Fear would walk you
on a narrow path
promising to take you
where you want to go.

Love says,
'Open your arms
and fly with me.'

Every moment of your life
you are offered the opportunity
to choose –
love or fear,
to tread the earth
or to soar the heavens.

(Emmanuel, 1989: 3–4).

NOTES

1 SETTING THE SCENE

1 In psychotherapy this refers to those approaches that advocate a neglect of rationality in favour of emotionality, spirituality, or 'the body'. However, a temporary emphasis of parts of the human experience other than rationality is probably inevitable in order to redress the balance. Ultimately we are searching for intergration and a 'holistic approach'.

2 PSYCHOTHERAPY AND PERSONAL CONFLICT

1 I did my training with the Institute of Psychosynthesis, The Barn, Nan Clark's Lane, London NW7 4HH. Please contact them if you would like to find out more about their training.

3 COGNITIVE AND BEHAVIOUR THERAPY

1 See especially the *Strategies for Mental Health* series, published by Routledge, series editor Reinhard Kowalski.
2 In psychoanalysis this process is called counter-transference, but it is limited to the therapeutic process. 'Activity theory' looks at the wider issue of mutual reflectivity between organisms and their environment. The latter theory will be presented in more detail later.
3 In psychotherapeutic terms we are dealing here with the complex issue of 'counter-transference'. In order for the therapist to use his own feelings within the therapeutic process for the benefit of the client, it is essential that the therapist is able to separate his own issues from the client's issues. This obviously requires the therapist to know about his own agenda. Otherwise the therapeutic process can become very muddled indeed.
4 A discussion about the benefits and limitations of the behavioural approach can be found later in this section.
5 I have made a tape with this exercise on one side and a muscular relaxation one on the other side. The tape is called 'Re-Lax', and is available from Winslow Press, Telford Road, Bicester, Oxon OX6 0TS.

6 ACTIVITY THEORY

1 Psychosynthesis refers to this as 'the space in-between', a concept that will be discussed later.

2 I believe it is this 'eternal growth' illusion that ultimately led to the collapse of Eastern European socialism. it ment that on a planetary level socialism had to compete with capitalism, whose economic laws have governed the world markets. In a sense socialism had to, or thought it had to, sacrifice its immanent humanitarian values to the principles of economic growth and productivity, thus creating contradictions which ultimately the system was unable to hold.

3 When I compared the English and the German translations of Leontyev's writings I discovered that there were important differences. For example, the German word 'gegenständlich' appears in the English version as 'objective', but it should be 'object-related'. I have therefore amended the English translation by comparing it with the German one. In the references, however, I refer to the English version. The bibliography gives both versions.

9 STRESS

1 The Findhorn Community in Scotland is the 'mother' of spiritual communities, formed by Eileen and Peter Caddy in 1962. Today there are nearly 500 people living and working there, in a way that is based on the values of co-operation and partnership. The Findhorn Foundation offers a wide range of courses, including the 'experience week' that Michael attended. For further details write to: The Findhorn Foundation, Cluny Hill College, Forres IV36 0RD, Scotland.

10 DOMINATION AND PARTNERSHIP

1 If you would like to find out more about the Brothers programme please write to Brothers, 207 Waller Road, London SE14 5LX.

11 UNIFICATION PROCESS — GERMAN EXAMPLE

1 For many of us post-war Germans a united Germany was too much like the 'Third Reich'. We were seeing aspects of a 'new Germany' in the GDR rather than in the capitalist West. The call for reunification had become the battle cry of right wing, conservative, and fascist politics.

BIBLIOGRAPHY

Assagioli, R. *Psychosynthesis*. Turnstone Press, Wellingborough, 1965.
Assagioli, R. *Transpersonal Development*. Crucible, London, 1991.
Beattie, M. *Co-dependent No More*. Harper & Row, New York, 1987.
Bly, R. *Iron John*. Element Books Ltd, Shaftesbury, Dorset, 1991.
Brady, K. and Considine, M. *Holistic London*. Brainwave, London, 1990.
Bürger, J.H. *Mann, Bist Du Gut*! Verlag Peter Erd, München, 1991.
Capra, F. *The Turning Point*. Collins, Glasgow, 1982.
Der Spiegel, 10 February 1992.
Der Spiegel, 17 August 1992.
Der Spiegel, 8 March 1993.
Douthwaite, R. *The Growth Illusion*. Green Books, Devon, 1992.
Eisler, R. *The Chalice and the Blade*. Harper & Row, San Francisco, 1988.
Eisler, R. and Loye, D. *The Partnership Way*. Harper & Row, San Francisco, 1990.
Elton, B. *Gridlock*. Sphere Books, London, 1992.
Emmanuel's Book, *A Manual for Living Comfortably in the Cosmos*. Bantam Books, New York, 1987.
Emmanuel's Book II, *The Choice for Love*. Bantam Books, New York, 1989.
Engholm, B. *Vom Öffentlichen Gebrauch der Vernunft*. Claassen, Düsseldorf, 1990.
Evans, R. and Russell, P. *The Creative Manager*. Unwin, London, 1989.
Ferrucci, P. *What We May Be*. Turnstone Press, Wellingborough, 1982.
Firman, J. *'I' and Self*. John Firman, 459 Hawthorne Avenue, Palo Alto, CA 94301, USA, 1991.
Galperin, P.J. 'Die Entwicklung der Untersuchungen über die Bildung geistiger Operationen', in Hiebsch, H. (ed.), *Ergebnisse der Sowjetischen Psychologie*. Klett Verlag, Stuttgart, 1969.
Gray, J.A. *The Psychology of Fear and Stress*. Weidenfeld and Nicolson, London, 1971.
Greenberg, L.S. and Safran, J.D. Integrating affect and cognition: A perspective on the process of therapeutic change. *Cognitive Therapy and Research*, **8**(6), 559–78, 1984.
Grof, S. *Realms of the Human Unconscious*. Souvenir Press, London, 1979.
Grof, S. *The Holotropic Mind*. Harper & Row, San Francisco, 1992.
Hayward, S. *Begin It Now*. In-Tune Books, Crows Nest, NSW, Australia, 1987.
IPLTM (Institute of Psychosynthesis Training Materials). Unpublished Manuscript, June 1989.
Jung, C.G. *Von Mensch und Gott*. Walter-Verlag, Olten und Freiburg im Breisgau, 1989.

BIBLIOGRAPHY

Klein, R. 'Introduction to the disorders of the self', in Masterson, J.F. and Klein, R. (eds) *Psychotherapy of the Disorders of the Self*. Brunner/Mazel, New York, 1989.

Kowalski, R. Behavioral psychotherapy in primary health care. *Child and Family Behavior Therapy*, **8**(1), 1–20, 1986.

Kowalski, R. *Over the Top*. Winslow Press, Bicester, 1987.

Laing, R.D. *The Facts of Life*. Penguin, London, 1976.

Leontjew, A.N. *Probleme der Entwicklung des Psychischen*. Volk und Wissen Volkseigener Verlag, Berlin, 1971.

Leontyev, A.N. *Problems of the Development of the Mind*. Progress Publishers, Moscow, 1981.

Lindfield, M. *The Dance of Change*. Arkana, London and New York, 1986.

Llywelyn, M. *Druids*. Mandarin paperbacks, London, 1991.

Maaz, H. J. *Der Gefühlsstau*. Argon Verlag, Berlin, 1990.

Maaz, H. J. *Das gestürzte Volk, Die Verunglückte Einheit*. Argon Verlag, Berlin, 1991.

Maaz, H.J. and Moeller, M.L. *Die Einheit Beginnt zu Zweit. Ein deutsch-deutsches Zwiegespräch*. Rowolth, Berlin, 1991.

Mair, M. *Between Psychology and Psychotherapy*. Routledge, London, 1989.

Masterson, J.F. and Klein, R. (eds) *Psychotherapy of the Disorders of the Self*. Brunner/Mazel, New York, 1989.

Meyer, V. and Turkat, I. Behavioral analysis of clinical cases. *Journal of Behavioral Assessment*, **1**, 159–270, 1979.

Miller, H. and Miller, C. *The Quality Cards*. College of Roseisle, Morayshire IV30 2YD, 1989.

Rayner, E. *The Independent Mind in British Psychoanalysis*. Free Association Books, London, 1991.

Rowan, J. *Subpersonalities*. Routledge, London, 1990.

Ryle, A. Object relations theory and activity theory: A proposed link by way of the procedural sequence model. *British Journal of Medical Psychology*, **64**, 307–16, 1991.

Sève, L. *Marxismus und Theorie der Persönlichkeit*. Verlag Marxistische Blätter, Frankfurt am Main, 1972.

Sheldrake, R. The rebirth of nature. *Kindred Spirit*, **2**(3), 16, 1991.

Totton, N. Therapists on the couch. *I to I*, **11**, 26–7, July–Sept. 1992.

Watson, J.B. and Rayner, B. Conditioned emotional reactions. *Journal of Experimental Psychology*, **3**, 1–14, 1920.

Weinhold, B.K. and Weinhold, J.B. *Breaking Free of the Co-dependency Trap*. Stillpoint Publishing, Walpole, 1989.

Wilber, K. *No Boundary*. Shambhala, Boston, 1979.

INDEX

abandonment 3; depression 69–70, 75–6; fear of 110; in Germany 173

acceptance 17, 19, 28, 43–4, 58; self acceptance 153

activity 16; activity theory 83–96, 163; activity theory and cars 106; and behaviourism 104; and internalisation 53; mental 90; and object relations 83; practical 92; Wilber 79

Adam 67, 79

advertising 91, 93, 106, 112, 172

affirmations 55–6

agoraphobia 25, 28

alienation 77, 85, 95, 97, 103, 138; and men 149; and stress 124, 130; in Marxism 166; levels of 90–2

altruism 116, 123, 170

anger 3, 19, 32, 117, 135, 139, 140, 142, 143, 151, 153, 156, 162, 175, 176

anxiety 19, 20, 25–42; anticipatory 60; and avoidance 49; and behaviourism 33; and boundaries 82; Elaine 35–6; flight–fight 126; Fred 131–3; in Germany 173; and meditation 137; model of 41–4; and panic, stress 114; and self-statements 54; and stress management 25, 128–34

anxiety and stress management 25, 128–34; see also anxiety

Assagioli, R. 108, 110, 112, 121, 123, 134

assessment, behaviour-analytic 37–40

attributions 41, 62

Auschwitz 145

avoidance 10, 43–4, 49–50, 58, 60, 72

Ballypatrick 141

basic perinatal matrices 70–8; death–rebirth 73–4, 76

Beattie, M. 82

behaviour-analytic approach 25, 27, 34, 35, 37, 39–41, 133

behaviour therapy, 25–8, 32, 44, 56, 128, 130; beyond 58; case study 35–8; and cognitive therapy 39; and Leontyev 85; and me 17–18; and psychotherapy 34; see also behaviour-analytic approach; cognitive therapy

behavioural analysis see assessment; behaviour-analytic approach

behavioural medicine 26

Berlin 17, 157, 163, 166, 168; Brandenburger Tor 158–9; critical psychology 84; East Berlin 165; Wall 65, 80, 158

Berlin Wall see Berlin

birth see basic perinatal matrices

Bly, R. 152

body: awareness 80; body-feelings-mind 134; and emotions 64, 135; lower unconscious 108; and mind 79, 114; panic 29, 41; posture 3, 63; relaxation and meditation 45–6, 50–2, 55, 63, 124–5, 138; sanctuary 14; and 'shoulds' 137; and stress 128, 132, 134

boredom 19, 77, 117

boundaries 21, 45, 58–62, 65–6, 67–82, 83, 144; and activity theory 85, 90–2; and basic perinatal matrices 70–6; breaking walls 128; and cars 93; and co-dependency 82; and division of labour 92; domination and partnership 147, 175; and German

unification 155–8, 162, 168, 172–3; men and women 148, 151, 152; no boundaries 76–82; and object relations 68–70; and psychological greenhouse 123, 126; in psychotherapy 180; and shadow 149; and 'shoulds' 136
BPM *see* basic perinatal matrices
Brady, K. 11
Brandenburger Tor *see* Berlin
bridgebuilding 5, 17, 18, 25, 39, 58, 65, 80, 83, 85, 94, 149, 151, 153, 155, 168, 174, 175, 176, 180
Buchenwald 166
Bürger, J.H. 150, 151, 152
burn-out 17

capitalism 65, 85, 87, 91, 97, 101, 103, 105, 143, 144, 145, 163, 165, 166, 168, 169, 170, 172, 176
car 6, 7, 28, 29, 30, 31, 42, 44, 47, 49, 56, 87, 88, 90, 93, 98, 99, 106, 107, 108, 111, 112, 114, 116, 126, 130, 142, 168, 172, 178
Celts 178
child, children: abuse 147; and basic perinatal matrices 72, 75; inner child 3; internalisation 53, 93, 95; and mindsets 136; and object constancy 68
childhood 14, 61, 173; childhod fears 110, 111, 114
clinical psychology 17, 25, 26, 41, 138
co-dependency 82, 144
COEX 70–2, 75
cognitive therapy 25–8, 34, 39, 44, 53–55, 63, 95, 129, 130; *see also* behaviour therapy
collective 16, 86, 89, 90, 94, 96, 121, 170, 178, 180; unconscious 15, 70, 110
common sense 18, 25, 32
communication 1, 90, 91, 129, 140
conforming, conformist 2, 13, 141, 166, 168, 169–71, 175–6
consciousness 53, 56, 58, 67, 71, 76, 81, 83–7, 89, 90, 92, 104, 108, 109, 110, 113, 115, 123, 130, 148, 158, 169, 175
Considine, M. 11
consumer society *see* consumerism
consumerism, consuming 78, 82, 89, 98, 105–8, 110–12, 167, 170, 178

defences 21, 68, 75, 135, 157, 162

depression 3, 19, 25, 26, 27, 35, 43, 44, 45, 46, 69, 70, 75, 76, 92, 110, 115, 135, 140, 156, 157, 161, 172, 173, 176
disidentification 1, 109, 134–5
division of labour 89, 90, 92, 97, 111, 130
domination 13, 92, 144, 145–8, 152, 157, 174, 176–7
Douthwaite, R. 97, 98, 99, 100, 101, 103, 104, 163
druids 178

economic growth 97, 98, 103, 104, 105
egg diagram 108–15
ego 68, 73, 74, 76, 77, 81, 82, 110
Eisler, R. 78, 145, 146, 147, 151
Elton, B. 87
Emmanuel 10, 14, 60, 127, 181
emotional schemata 63
emotions 3, 4, 8, 11, 19, 47, 122, 125, 134, 149, 179; and affirmations 56; and basic perinatal matrices 70, 71, 74; and behaviour therapy 18, 27, 45, 58, 61; and depression 135; emotional blocks 79–80; emotional needs 93; 106, 108, 112; emotional synthesis 61–5, 96; fear of 28; and Germany 157, 158, 160; and meditation 138; and obsessions 135; and physical symptoms 33, 135, 142; and psychotherapy 31; rational and emotional 28; and relaxation 52; and stress 132, 133, 134
Engholm, B. 91
environment 7, 17, 73, 76, 81, 83, 85, 88, 93, 94, 97, 102, 103, 104, 108, 125, 126, 129, 145, 172, 178, 179
envy 20, 107, 168
Evans, R. 10, 136
externalisation 39, 40, 53, 55

false self 69
father 92, 139, 140, 148, 152–3, 164, 166
fear 3, 7, 19–22, 28, 32, 34, 36, 41–4, 48, 50, 58, 61, 76, 84, 110, 114, 116, 124, 126, 127, 133, 140, 143, 144, 146, 147, 153, 156, 158, 162, 168, 170, 171, 176, 179, 180, 181; of fear 44, 58–60; *see also* anxiety
feminine 123, 145–9, 151, 153, 176; *see also* masculine
Ferrucci, P. 1, 23

Findhorn 141, 148, 179, 180
Firman, J. 135
Fishguard 6
flexibility 9–11
flooding 44, 49, 50
fragmentation 5, 15, 23, 24, 91, 126, 180
Fred and the banana skin 131–3
frigidity *see* impotence

Gaia 15
Galperin, P.J. 17, 39
German Democratic Republic 161, 163, 165–7, 169, 170, 172, 173
Germany, German 2, 5, 6, 65, 76, 80, 84, 85, 107, 112, 150, 155, 156–74
gestalt therapy 17
goddess 145
Gray, J.A. 34
Greenberg, L.S. 61, 62, 64, 95
Grof, S. 70, 71, 72, 74
group therapy 26, 152
guilt 20, 37, 82, 139, 142, 164, 170

hand-washing rituals 34
Hastings 30
hatred 20, 157, 161, 170
Hayward, S. 19
heart 5, 8, 13, 15, 16, 29, 60, 119, 121, 123, 131, 142, 164, 168
hidden triggers 47, 63, 135
Hiroshima 145
historical materialism 84
humanistic therapies 17, 56
humour 116, 152
hypothesis 26, 39, 56

image, imagery, images 8, 9, 14, 16, 21, 22, 28, 47, 50, 55, 56, 71, 74, 107, 109, 114, 125, 126, 134, 153, 155, 164, 165, 171, 181
impotence 20, 73
in-vivo exposure 44, 49
independence 61, 73, 75, 76, 116
inflation 97
information processing theory 61
inner child *see* child
integration 5, 33, 115; emotions and cognition 64; in psychotherapy 66
interdependence 41, 90, 92, 173
interest rates 91, 97, 98, 112
internalisation 53, 93, 95
Ireland 6, 7, 99, 141, 177, 178, 180

joy 8, 21, 61, 82, 106, 116, 158, 159, 160
Jung, C.G. 16, 19, 86, 152

Kapra, F. 13, 16
Kerstin 166, 167, 169
Klein, R. 68
Kowalski, R. 18, 37; poems 159–60, 174–5

Laing, R.D. 15
language 78, 87, 89, 90, 95, 148, 165
Leontyev [Leontjew], A.N. 84, 85, 86, 87, 89, 90, 91, 94, 95, 97, 156
Lindfield, M. 121, 123
Llywelyn, M. 178
love 68, 71, 73, 74, 95, 109, 116, 121, 141, 142, 143, 144, 146, 175, 181
Loye, D. 147

M25 6, 107, 114
Maaz, H.J. 156, 161, 162, 163, 166, 172, 173, 180
Mair, M. 17
Marx 84, 91, 94, 95, 106, 166, 174
Marxism, Marxist 85, 139, 142
masculine 58, 123, 146, 148, 149, 154, 176; *see also* feminine
Masterson, J.F. 68, 69
memory 48, 62
mental handicap 26
Meyer, V. 17, 27, 35, 37, 39
Middlesex Hospital 17, 27, 39
Milky Way 57
mindsets 126, 136
money 89, 91, 93, 98, 100, 103, 104, 111, 112, 114, 121, 122, 128, 151, 153, 156, 163
mother 68, 71, 72, 73, 74, 145, 148, 149, 152, 153, 161

narcissistic and borderline personality disorders 68–70, 175
National Health Service 26, 175
neurosis 13, 19, 175

object constancy 68
object relations theory 68–70, 76, 83
objective meaning 87–90; *see also* personal sense
obsessive compulsive 19, 26, 27, 34, 123, 135

panic 3, 19, 25, 27, 28–32, 33, 36, 39–44, 47, 48, 49, 53, 54, 59–61, 82, 114,

123, 131, 135, 138, 173; *see also* anxiety

partnership 11, 13, 65, 76, 92, 116, 150; and domination 143–7, 175–6; and Germany 156, 161; men and women 151, 152; society 78, 145; values 146

perfectionism 44, 82, 114, 131, 180

perinatal *see* basic perinatal matrices

personal sense 87–90; *see also* objective meaning

phobias *see* anxiety; behaviour therapy

physical *see* body

Poland 168

polarities 3, 19, 21, 100, 146, 157, 167

population explosion 119–21

pre-attentive 61, 63; *see also* emotional synthesis

primary health care 26, 40

primitive society 87, 89

problem analysis *see* assessment; behaviour-analytic approach

production 78, 89, 91, 93, 96, 100, 105, 106, 112, 121, 166

psychiatry 15, 26, 27

psychodrama 17

psychological greenhouse 12, 81, 85, 107–23, 126, 130, 180, 181

psychosynthesis 1, 3, 13, 17, 18, 21–4, 27, 28, 41, 45, 56, 65, 70, 71, 72, 73, 85, 86, 104, 106–23, 174, 175

psychotherapy 4, 25, 26, 31, 53, 65, 66, 68, 78, 81, 83, 92, 104, 140, 143, 157, 158, 162, 177; and behaviour therapy 34; boom 11–14; and conflict 19–21; and Germany 167, 173, 175, 176; and growth 105; and me 15–18; professionalisation 12–14

quality cards 153–4

Rayner, E. 11, 12

real self 1, 44, 69, 75

rebel 2, 73, 75, 139, 173, 176

recession 107, 121, 128, 139

rejection 20, 70, 82, 174

relationship 2, 4, 11, 82, 89, 105, 125, 144, 155; and basic perinatal matrices 73; with body 50, 52; and boundaries 65, 69; Germany 161; between inner and outer 86; internalisation 95; and men 153; and money 156; and partnership 146, 170; between personal and political 160; and power 84; and psychological greenhouse 81; and stress 128, 129, 130; between subject and object 85; therapeutic 21, 40, 69, 93, 137, 180; between thoughts and feelings 25, 27, 58; with work 143

relaxation *see* body, and emotions

religion 16, 71, 77, 78, 144

Romans 178

Rowan, J. 1, 2

Russell, P. 10, 136

Ryle, A. 83

Safran, J.D. 61, 62, 64, 95

sanctuary 9–11, 14, 23, 104, 114, 115, 124, 135, 162, 180

schizophrenia 15, 31

scientific 2, 15, 16, 17, 25, 26, 40, 56, 77, 84, 85, 86, 98, 109, 124, 142, 166, 173

self 1, 78, 108, 109, 114, 127, 134, 179; acceptance 153; -blame 43, 53, 54, 75; consciousness 20; -discovery 16, 82, 179; disorders of the 68; -evaluation 53, 55; false 69; help 25, 82; higher 110; -image 40; -observation 40, 41, 44, 45; -statements 33, 44; -talk 53, 54, 128; -worth 167

self-observation *see* self

self-statements *see* self

Senapur 100

separation 64, 68, 69, 72, 73, 74, 75, 76, 90, 92, 115, 146, 147, 155, 160, 162, 170, 173

Sève, L. 86, 142

shadow 20, 60, 106, 127, 149, 151, 152, 158, 167

'shoulds' 136–7

sitar 23

socialism 65, 85, 86, 143, 165, 168, 169, 172

soul 1, 22

Soviet Union 5, 65, 84

stability 9, 10, 172

stimulus 32, 37, 45, 62, 63

subpersonalities 1–4, 21, 65, 71–3, 75, 105, 152, 154

systematic desensitisation 44, 50

tension 19, 29, 34, 44, 50–3, 73, 79, 80, 89, 124, 157, 167; *see also* anxiety; body, and emotions

therapeutic relationship 21, 40, 65, 69, 93, 137, 180
Tipperary 141
Tony O'Malley 7
transpersonal 17, 56, 70, 74, 81
trees 5, 6, 7, 8, 10, 126, 137–8, 166, 175, 178
trigger 32, 33, 46, 47–8, 63, 135

unconscious 15, 19, 20, 25, 27, 33, 53, 56, 58, 61, 67, 70, 93; higher 109, 112, 115; lower 108, 110, 112, 114, 115; middle 109, 110, 112, 113
unemployment 102
unknown 22, 84, 126, 139, 158, 168, 169, 177

Valium 29, 30, 33
vicious circle 36, 43, 44, 48, 49, 57, 58, 59, 106, 133, 135

warrior 76, 126, 129, 168–71, 175–6
Web of Wyrd 15
Weinhold, B.K. 82, 144, 145
Weinhold, J.B. 82, 144, 145
Wilber, K. 13, 19, 20, 21, 32, 41, 52, 58, 66, 67, 69, 76, 78, 79, 81, 85, 106, 135, 157
womb 71, 72, 75

Yugoslavia 5, 65